Help Me! Guide to Android Lollipop

By Charles Hughes

I0411440

Table of Contents

What's New in Android Lollipop?

Table of Contents

1. Transferring Data to a New Device

Android Lollipop introduced a new feature, called Tap and Go, which allows you to use Near Field Communication (NFC) to transfer your settings, applications, contacts, and other data from your old phone or device to your new one. To transfer data from your old device to a new one, touch the two devices back to back when NFC is turned on. If your old phone does not have Android Lollipop, this feature will not work. Refer to *"Transferring Contacts and Applications to a New Device"* on page 23 and *"Wirelessly Transferring Data to Another Device"* on page 254 to learn more.

2. Searching Using Your Voice

The Google Voice assistant can now perform searches right from the lock screen, as well as from Standby mode, or without the need to turn on the screen. Standby mode voice searches are only available on newer Lollipop devices. When the voice assistant is turned on, say "OK Google" to start a search. Refer to *"Using Voice Search"* on page 316 and *"Customizing Voice Search Settings"* on page 303 to learn more.

3. Waking Up Your Android Device

The way that you wake up your device from the lock screen have been completely redesigned in Lollipop. There are now several ways in which you can interact with the lock screen. Refer to *"Waking Up Your Android Device"* on page 9 to learn more about the new lock screen.

Some devices, such as the Nexus 6 and Nexus 9 can even be woken up by touching the lock screen twice quickly. This only works on newer Lollipop devices.

4. Battery-Saving Lock Screen Notifications (Nexus 6 and Later Only)

Some Lollipop devices let you to view notifications on the lock screen without turning on the entire screen. You will still see the rest of the lock screen when a notification comes in, but it will be in black and white to save battery life.

5. Interactive Lock Screen Notifications

Interactive notifications now appear on the lock screen. For example, you can touch a notification twice to navigate to the application that sent it. If an email notification comes in, you can touch Reply right from the lock screen. Refer to *"Working with Notifications"* on page 24 for an overview of notifications in Lollipop.

6. Customizing Priorities for Application Notifications

The new Priority Mode feature in Lollipop lets you choose which application notifications appear on the lock screen and in the notification bar. You can even set a range of time during which only certain notifications are allowed. When outside the set range of time, normal notification activity resumes. Refer to *"Customizing Notification Priorities"* on page 277 to learn more about this feature.

7. Guest Mode

While the ability to use multiple user accounts on a single device already exists, a new feature in Lollipop is the ability for an unregistered user, or Guest, to use the device. A guest receives a clean slate, as if he or she just started using the device. They do not have access to the main user's applications, contacts, or any other personal data. In addition, a guest's progress is saved, and the option to continue from where the guest last left off is given when logging back in as a guest. Refer to *"Using the Device as a Guest"* on page 93 to learn more about this feature.

8. Using Application Locking as Parental Controls

Lollipop devices let you pin, or lock, a single application, which prevents the user from leaving that application. This is especially useful for allowing your children to use the device without worrying about their surfing the web or checking your email. Refer to *"Using Application Pinning for Children"* on page 93 to learn more about this feature.

9. Adjusting Quick Settings

The quick settings window has been redesigned. This window was always accessible by touching the top of the screen and sliding your finger down. To access the quick settings window in Lollipop, touch the top of the screen with two fingers and slide down. From the quick settings, you can adjust the brightness, turn Wi-Fi, Bluetooth, and Airplane mode on or off, and control other settings, such as location and automatic rotation.

10. Improved Multitasking

Multitasking in Lollipop is called "Overview." Overview lets you view many more recent applications than before. Overview also creates multiple cards for a single application, if necessary. For example, when you compose a new email, both your inbox and the new email appear in Overview, and you can switch freely between the two. Recently used applications are even remembered after you restart the device. Refer to *"Viewing Recently Opened Applications"* on page 116 to learn more about this feature.

11. 15 New Languages

The following 15 new languages can now be used to enter text when using your device:

- Basque
- Bengali
- Burmese
- Chinese (Hong Kong)
- Galician
- Icelandic
- Kannada
- Kyrgyz
- Macedonian
- Malayalam
- Marathi
- Nepali
- Sinhala
- Tamil
- Telugu

12. Using the Flashlight Application

Some compatible Lollipop devices now have a built-in flashlight application, which uses the

device's LED camera flash as a flashlight. To use the flashlight, touch the icon, and then touch **Flashlight**.

13. Searching the System Settings

You can now search system settings to find particular settings, such as notification customization, much more quickly. Refer to *"Searching the System Settings"* on page 317 to learn how to use this feature.

Getting Started

Table of Contents

1. Button Layout

Most Lollipop devices have two buttons and two jacks. The touchscreen is used to control all functions on these devices, with the exception of turning the device on and off and adjusting the volume. Lollipop devices have the following buttons and jacks:

Note: Buttons and their locations vary based on the device. The Nexus 6 is used as an example below, and is one of many devices that runs Android Lollipop.

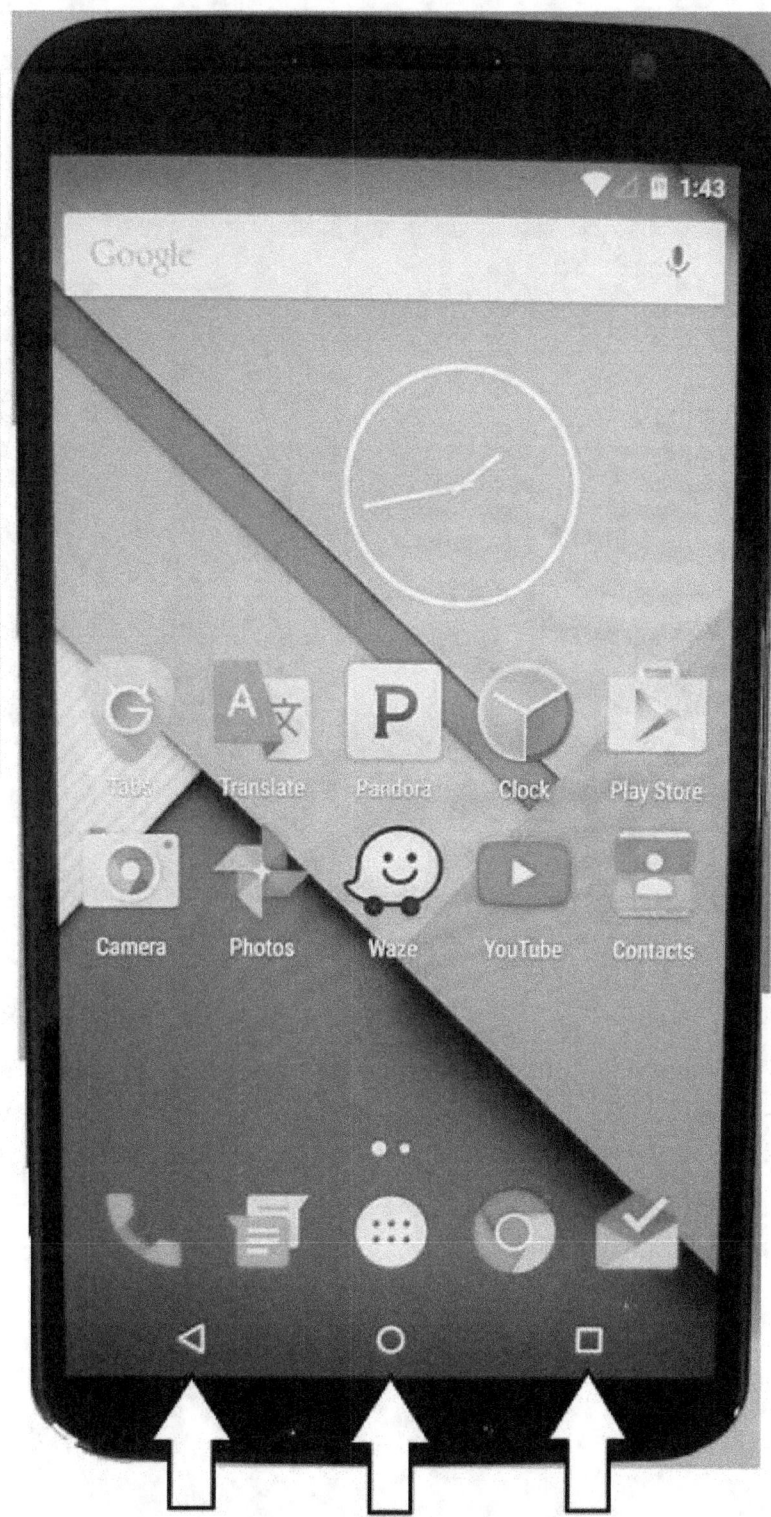

Back Key   Home Key   Overview Key

Figure 1: Front View

On-Screen Navigation Keys - The navigation keys described below respond to your touch. Touch each key on the screen to perform the corresponding action, as follows:

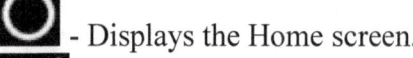 - Displays the Home screen.

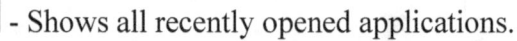 - Returns to the previous screen.

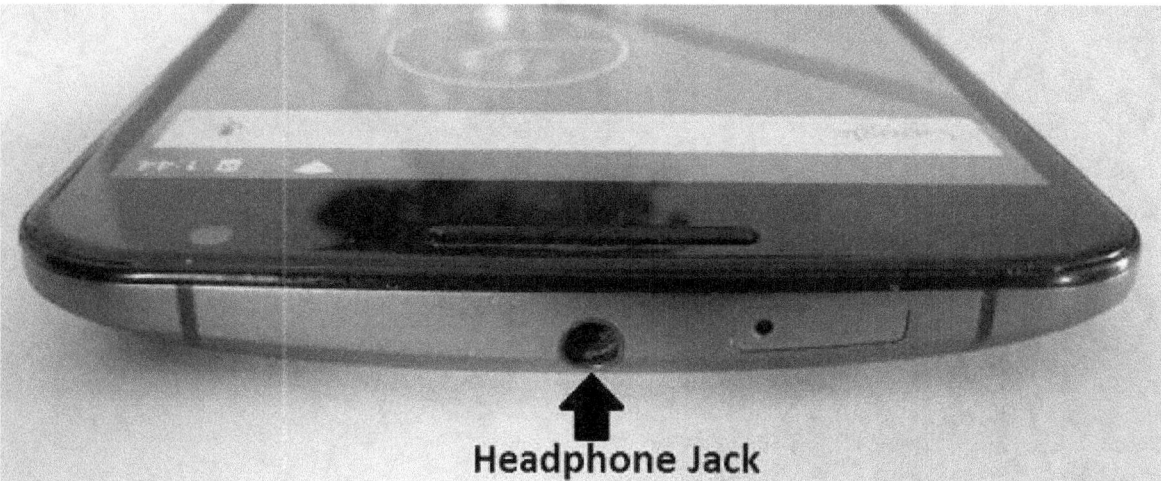 - Shows all recently opened applications.

![Headphone Jack]

Figure 2: Top View

Headphone Jack - Allows headphones to be connected to the device.

Figure 3: Bottom View

MicroUSB Port - Connects the device to a computer in order to transfer data.

Figure 4: Right Side View

Power/Sleep Button - Turns the device on and off. Pressing it also puts the device to sleep.
Volume Controls - Increases and decreases the media volume

2. Charging the Device

To charge the device, use the included charging adapter to plug the device in to a power outlet. Do not use a USB port on a computer, as it may not charge the device fully. When the device is done charging, the charge percentage is 100%. To charge the device while it is turned off, simply plug it in. The device will not turn itself on when it is plugged in to a power source.

Note: Some Lollipop devices, such as the Nexus 6 smartphone, are compatible with Turbo chargers. These new chargers can fully charge the battery of a Turbo-compatible device from 20% to 100% within one hour.

3. Turning the Device On and Off

To turn the device on, press and hold the **Power** button for three seconds or until 'Google' appears. The device takes several moments to start up.
To turn the device off, press and hold the **Power** button until 'Power Off' appears. Touch **Power off**. The device turns off.

4. Waking Up Your Device

There are several ways in which you can interact with the lock screen. Refer to the following tips when controlling your device from the lock screen:

- Touch the screen and move your finger up to unlock the device.
- Touch the screen and move your finger to the left to turn on the camera.

- Touch the screen and move your finger to the right to open the Phone application (smartphones only).
- Touch the screen and move your finger down to view notifications and the current weather.

5. Navigating the Screens

There are many ways to navigate the device. These are a few of the methods:

- Use the ⬤ key to return to the Home screen at any time. Any application that is currently in use continues to run in the background, and is in the same state when it is re-opened.

- Touch the ⬛ key to view all recently opened applications. Touch an application in the list to switch to it. Refer to *"Viewing Recently Opened Applications"* on page 116 to learn more.

- While viewing a Home screen, slide your finger to the left or right to access additional Home screens. The device allows you to customize up to five Home screens.

- Touch the ◀ key at any time to return to the previous screen or menu.

- Touch the ▼ key when using the keyboard to hide it.

6. Types of Home Screen Objects

Each Home screen on the device is fully customizable. Refer to *"Organizing Home Screen Objects"* on page 19 to learn how to customize the Home screens. Each screen can hold the following items:

- **Widget** - A tool that can be used directly on the Home screen without opening it like an application. Widgets usually take up a fraction or all of the screen, while applications are added as icons. The Books widget is shown in **Figure 5**.
- **Application** - A program that opens in a new window, such as Gmail or a game. Applications are added to the Home screen as icons.
- **Folder** - A folder of application icons or shortcuts.

Note: A folder cannot store widgets.

Figure 5: Books Widget

7. Organizing Home Screen Objects

Customize the Home screens by adding, deleting, or moving objects. Refer to *"Types of Home Screen Objects"* on page 17 to learn more about them. To add an object to a Home screen:

1. Touch the ![icon] icon at the bottom of any Home screen. A list of all installed applications appears, as shown in **Figure 6**.
2. Touch and hold an application icon. The Home screen that you were previously viewing appears.
3. Release the screen. The object is placed in the selected location on the Home screen.

To add a widget, touch and hold an empty space on a home screen, and then touch **Widgets**.

Follow steps 2-3 above to learn how to add the widget to the selected Home screen.

Note: If you are returned to the home screen, then you have tried to place the object on a Home screen that does not have sufficient space. The message "No more room on this Home screen" will also appear at the bottom of the screen. Refer to the following hints to learn how to create space on a Home screen.

There are multiple ways to clean up the Home screens. Use the following tips to create space on Home screens:

- To remove objects from the Home screen, touch and hold the object until **Remove** appears at the top of the screen. Move the object over **Remove** and release the screen. The object is removed from the Home screen. It is still installed on the device, and will continue to appear in the list of installed applications. Refer to *"Uninstalling an Application"* on page 110 to learn how to remove the application from your device.
- To move an object, touch and hold it until **Remove** appears at the top of the screen. Move the object to the desired location and release the screen to place it. Move the object to the edge of the screen to move it to another Home screen.
- To create a folder, touch and hold an application icon, and drag it on top of another. To add more icons to an existing folder, drag the icons on top of the existing folder. To remove an icon from a folder, touch and hold it, drag it anywhere outside the folder, and release the screen.

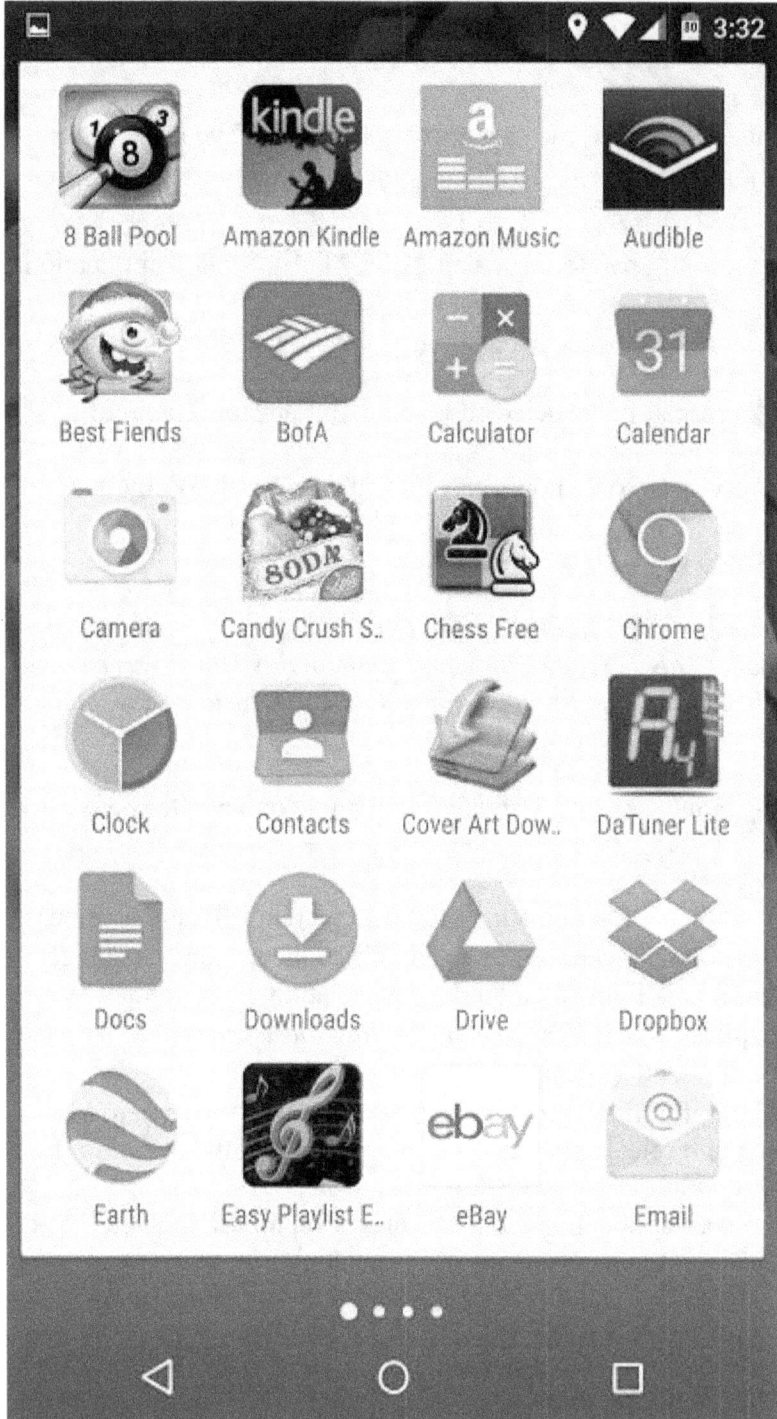

Figure 6: List of All Installed Applications and Widgets

8. Exporting and Importing Files Using a PC or Mac

You can import files, such as images and documents, to the device from a computer. You can also export files from the device to a computer. To export and import files using a PC or Mac:

1. Connect the device to your PC or Mac using the provided USB cable. "Connected as a media device" appears at the top of the device's screen. If you are using a Mac, download the Android File Transfer application at **www.android.com/filetransfer/** before proceeding.

2. Double-click the ⬚ icon in the Computer folder, as outlined in **Figure 7**, if using a PC. On a Mac, open the Android File Transfer program. The device folder opens. To access the

   Computer folder on a PC, click the ⬚ button and then click **Computer** in Windows Vista or later. Double-click **My Computer** on the desktop in Windows 95 or later.

3. Double-click **Internal storage**. The Internal Storage folder opens on a PC, as shown in **Figure 8**, or on a Mac, as shown in **Figure 9**.

4. Double-click a folder inside the Internal Storage folder to view its contents. The folder opens.

5. Click and drag a file into the folder from your computer, or drag one to your computer from the device folder. The file is transferred.

Note: Operating systems prior to Windows Vista may not be able to recognize the device when it is connected. The image below is for a Nexus 7, and will vary based on the device that you use.

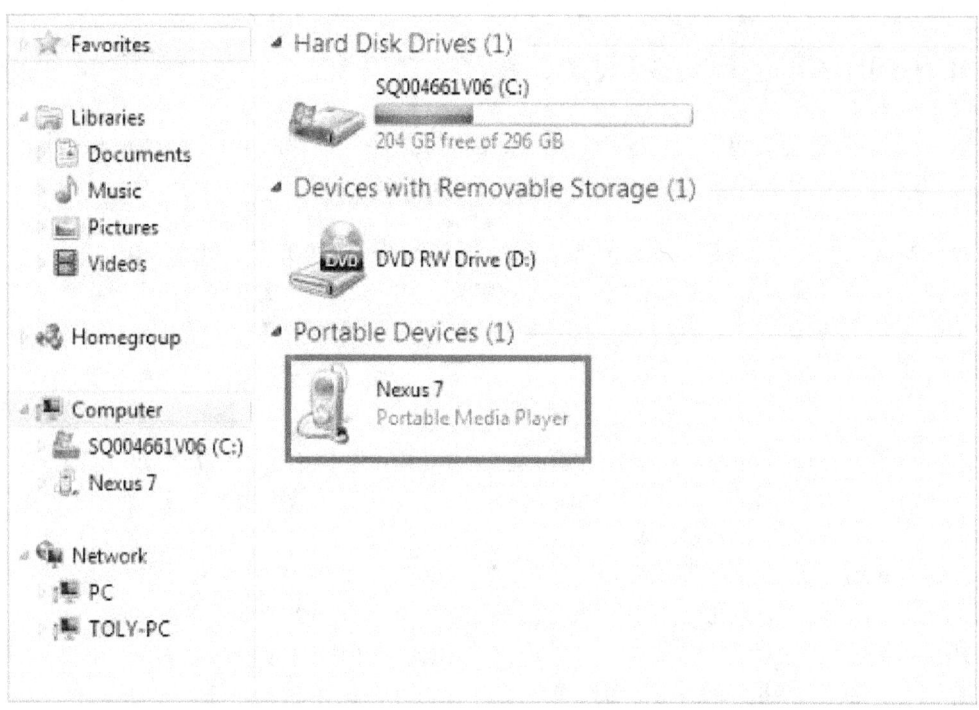

Figure 7: Device Icon on a PC

Figure 8: Internal Storage Folder on a PC

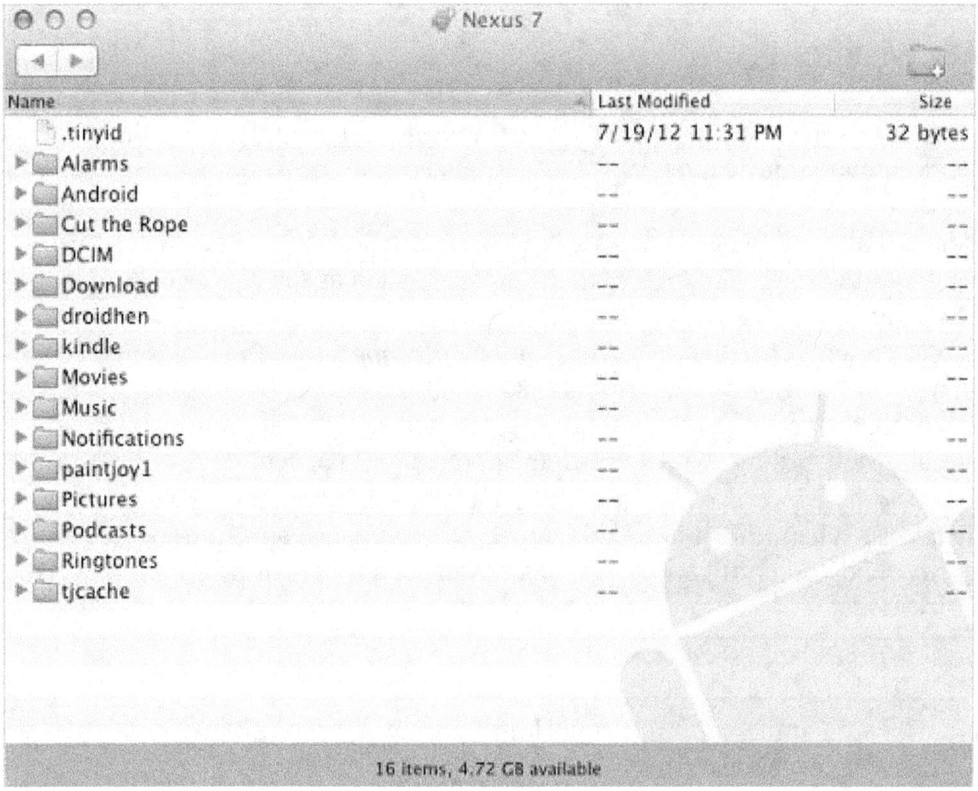

Figure 9: Internal Storage Folder on a Mac

9. Transferring Contacts and Applications to a New Device (Smartphones Only)

Lollipop introduced a new feature called "Tap and Go", which allows you to transfer your contacts, applications, and other data from your old smartphone to your new Lollipop smartphone. To use Tap and Go, make sure that NFC is turned on. Refer to *"Wirelessly Transferring Data to Another Device"* on page 254 to learn how to turn on NFC. Refer to the instruction manual for your old phone to learn how to run on NFC (it is usually located in Wireless or Network settings). When setting up your phone for the first time, touch the phones back to back to begin transferring data.

Note: Tap and Go only works for transferring data from an old Android phone. If your old phone is an iPhone, Tap and Go will not work.

10. Working with Notifications

There are several new features surrounding notifications in Android Lollipop. Refer to the following tips when working with notifications:

- **Ambient Display** - This new feature allows you to view notifications on the lock screen without turning on your screen. On devices that support it, such as the Nexus 6, Ambient display is automatically turned on.
- **Interactive Lock Screen Notifications** - Notifications that appear on the lock screen can now be used in new ways. For example, if you touch a notification and slide your finger down, you are sometimes presented with options, such as to reply to or archive an email. You can also touch a notification twice to open the application that sent it.
- **Priority Mode** - Priority Mode is a new feature that lets you customize which applications can send notifications. When Priority Mode is turned on, only those applications that you have given priority send you notifications. You can even set a timer for priority mode. To customize priority mode:

1. Touch the ⊞ icon at the bottom of any Home screen. A list of all installed applications and widgets appears.
2. Touch **Settings**. The Settings screen appears, as shown in **Figure 10**.
3. Touch **Sound & notification**. The Sound & notification screen appears, as shown in **Figure 11**.
4. Touch **App notifications**. The App notifications screen appears, as shown in **Figure 12**.
5. Touch an application that you want to allow to send notifications when your device is in Priority mode. The Application Notification Settings appear, as shown in **Figure 13**.
6. Touch **Priority**. The application is now allowed to send you notifications when in Priority mode.

To turn on and customize Priority mode:

1. Press the **Volume Up** or **Volume Down** button. The Volume bar appears, as shown in **Figure 14**.
2. Touch **Priority**. Priority mode is turned on.
3. Touch **For 1 Hour** to set a timer for Priority mode. When the time is up, Priority mode is turned off, and all notifications are allowed.

To turn off Priority mode, press the **Volume Up** or **Volume Down** button, and then touch **ALL** or **NONE**. Touching **ALL** allows all notifications to come through, while touching **NONE** disables all notifications.

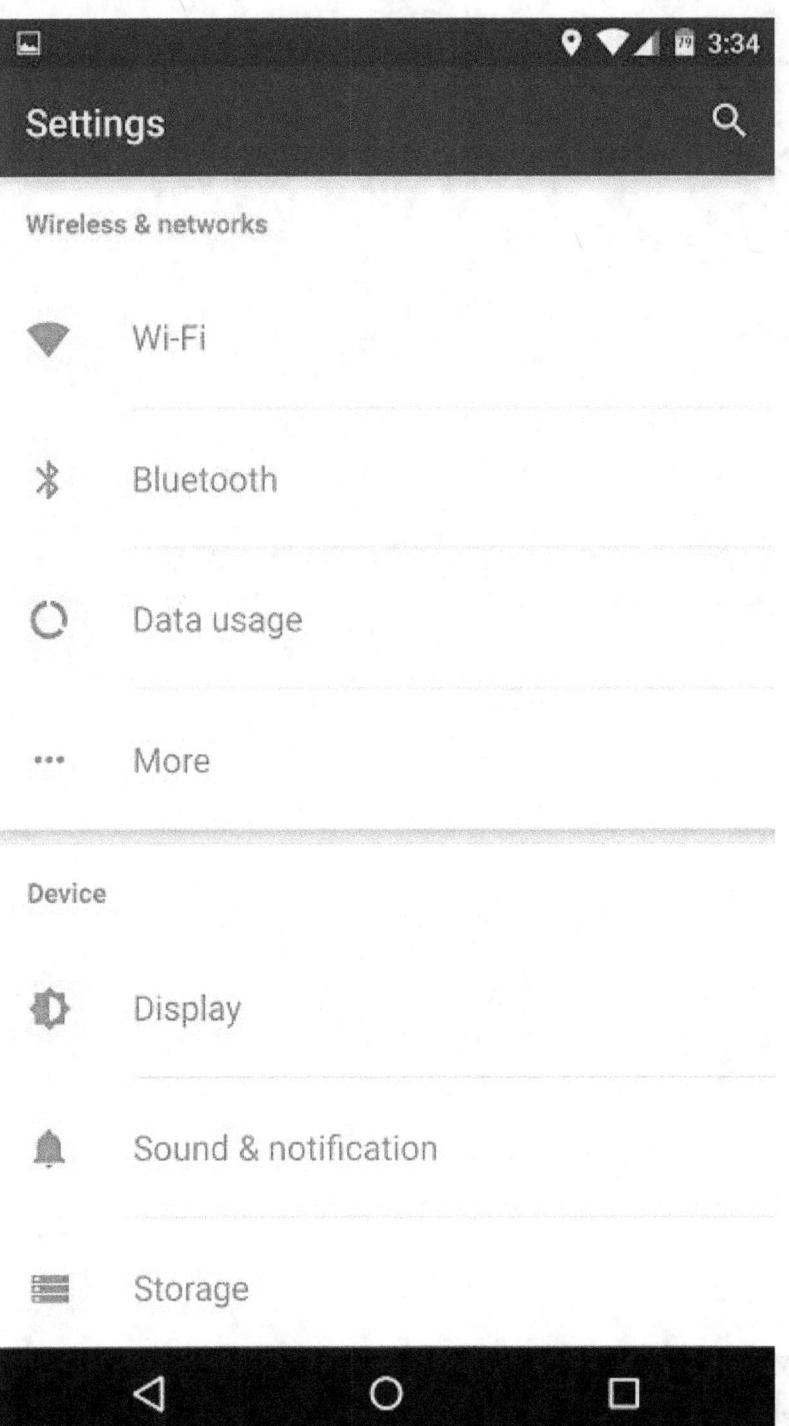

Figure 10: Settings Screen

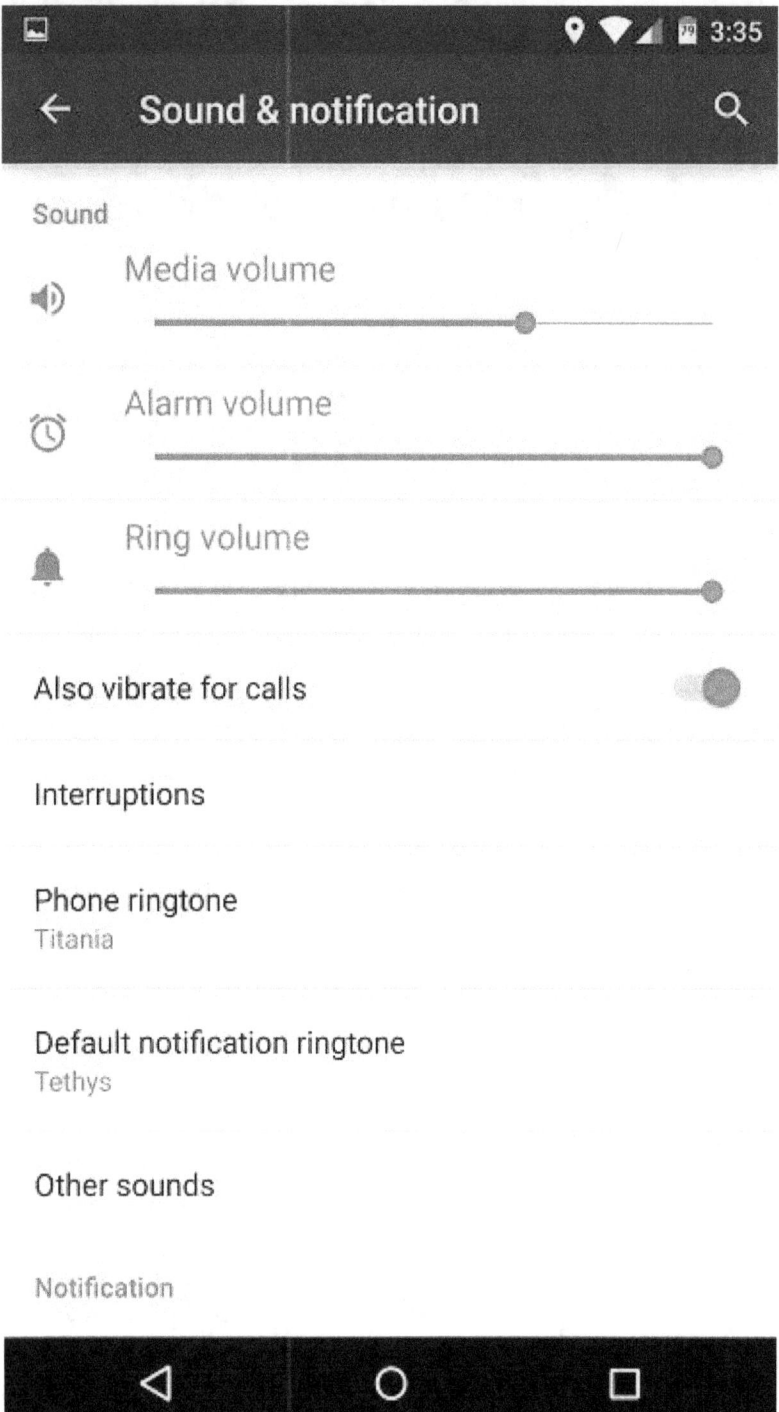

Figure 11: Sound & Notification Screen

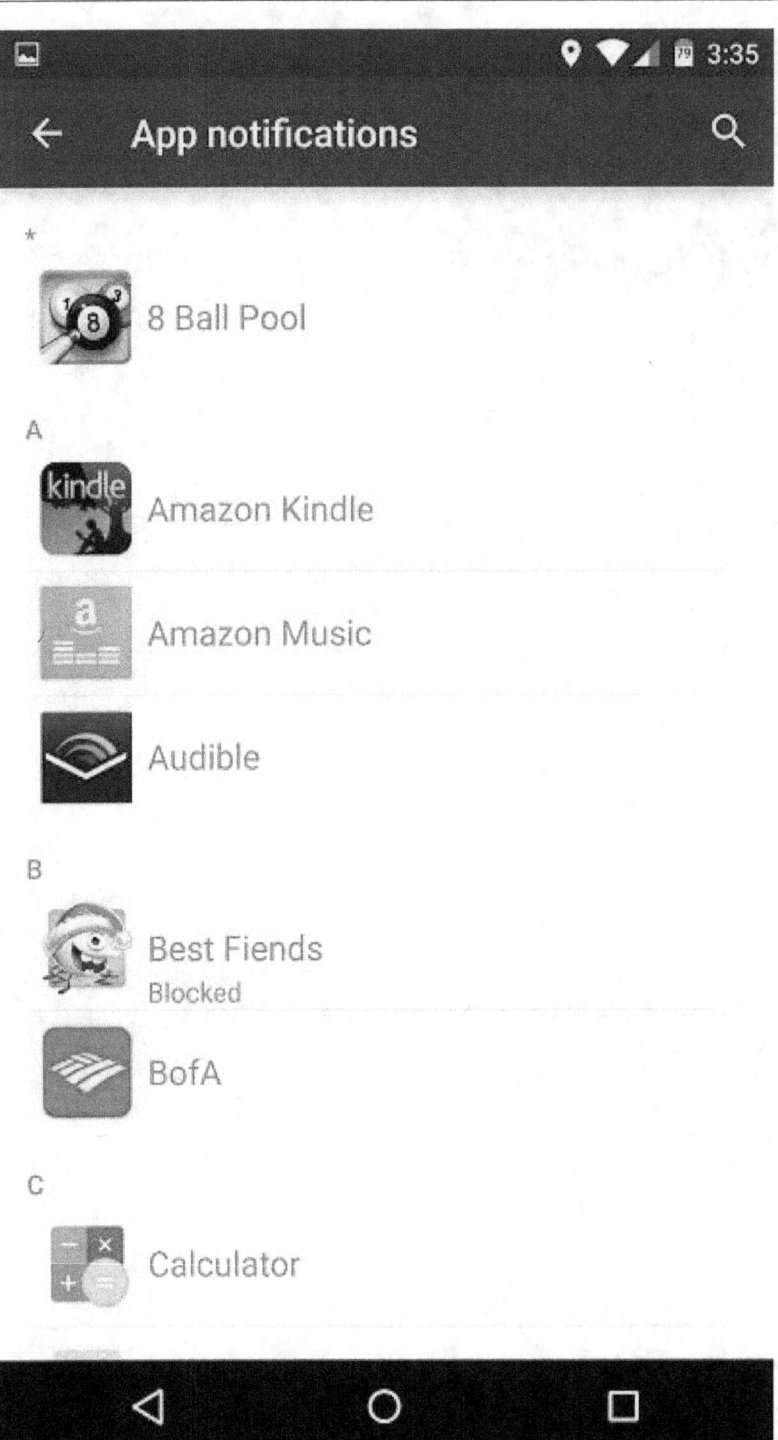

Figure 12: App Notifications Screen

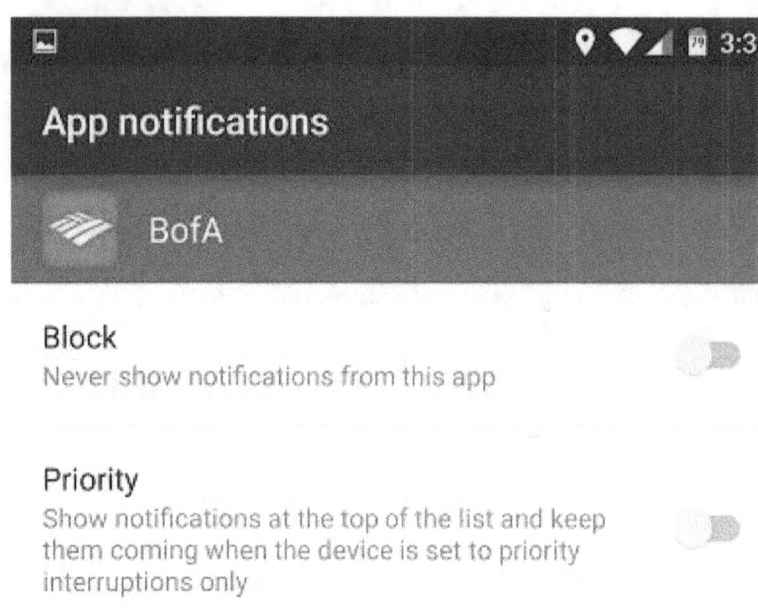

Figure 13: Application Notification Settings

Figure 14: Volume Bar

Making Calls (Smartphones Only)

Table of Contents

Note: The Hangouts application on tablets now allows you to make calls to domestic numbers. This feature is not covered in this guide.

1. Dialing a Number

Numbers that are not in your phonebook can be dialed on the keypad. To manually dial a phone number:

1. Touch the ![phone icon] icon at the bottom of the screen. The Speed Dial screen appears, as shown in **Figure 1**.

2. Touch the ![keypad icon] icon at the bottom of the screen. The Keypad appears, as shown in **Figure 2**.

3. Enter a phone number and touch the ![call button] button at the bottom of the screen. The phone calls the number.

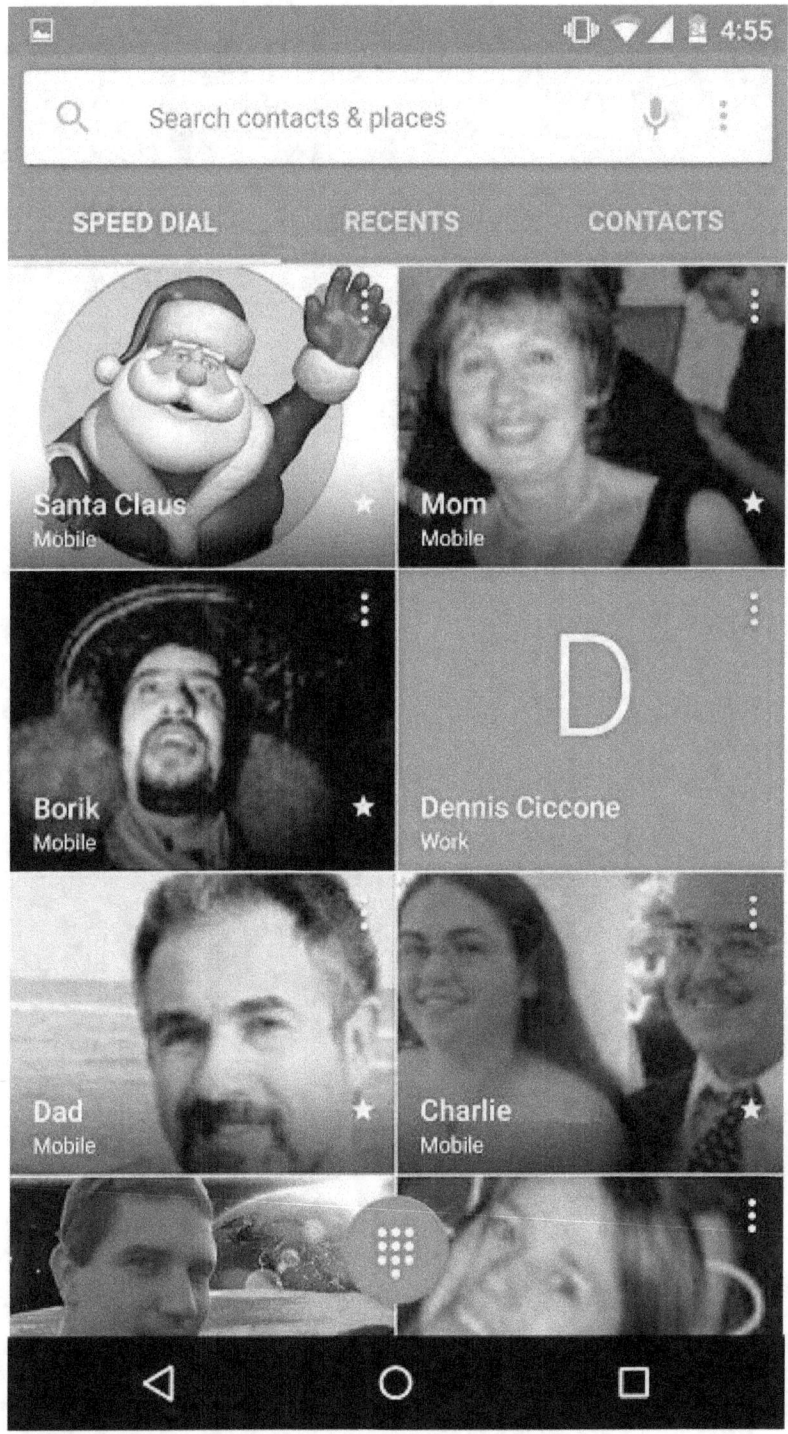

Figure 1: Speed Dial Screen

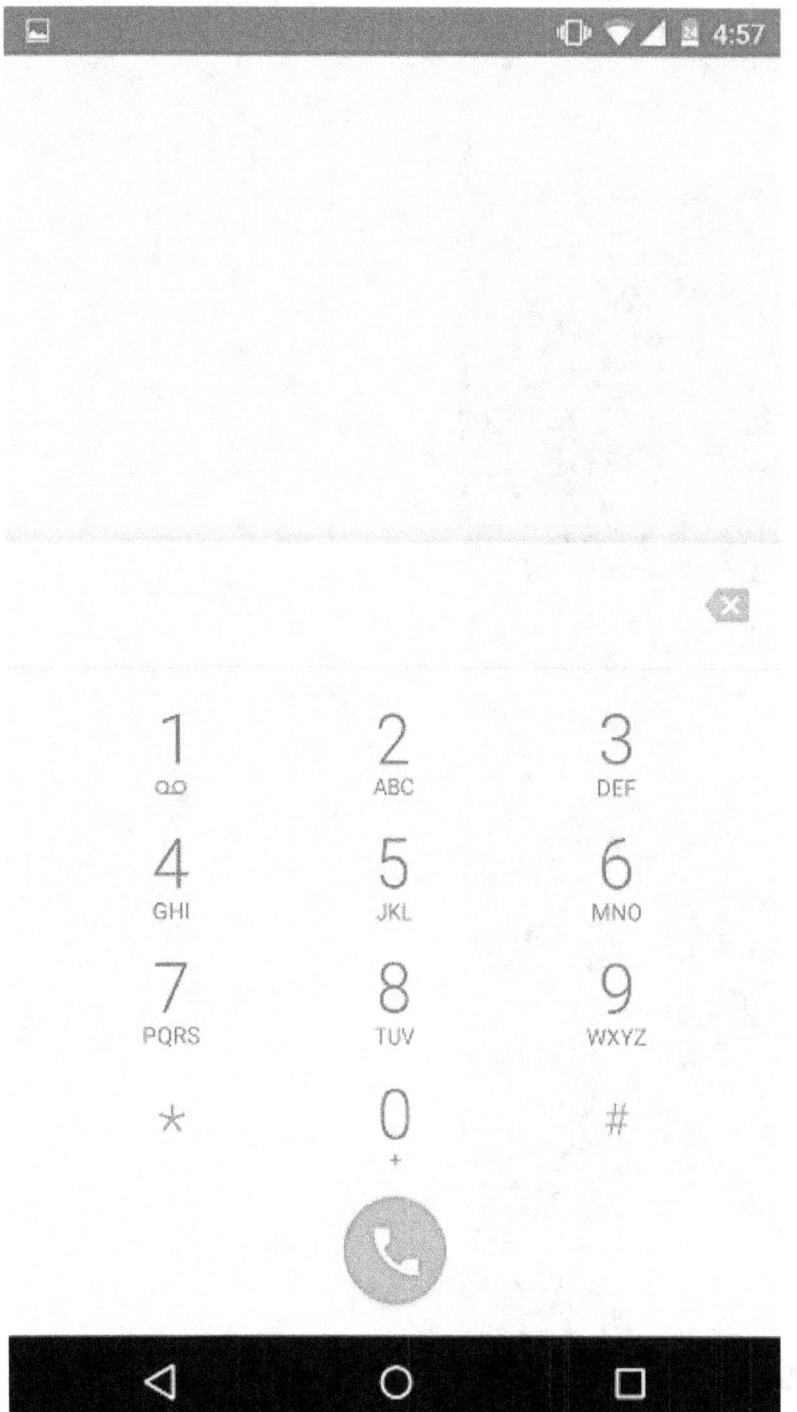

Figure 2: Phone Keypad

2. Calling a Contact

If a number is stored in your Phonebook, you may touch the name of a contact to dial the number. Refer to *"Adding a New Contact"* on page 189 to learn how to add a contact to the Phonebook. To call a contact already stored in your Phonebook:

1. Touch the icon at the bottom of the Home screen. The Phonebook appears, as shown in **Figure 3**. If you do not see the icon, touch the icon, and then touch the icon.
2. Touch a contact's name. The Contact Information screen appears, as shown in **Figure 4**.
3. Touch the number that you wish to call. The phone dials the number.

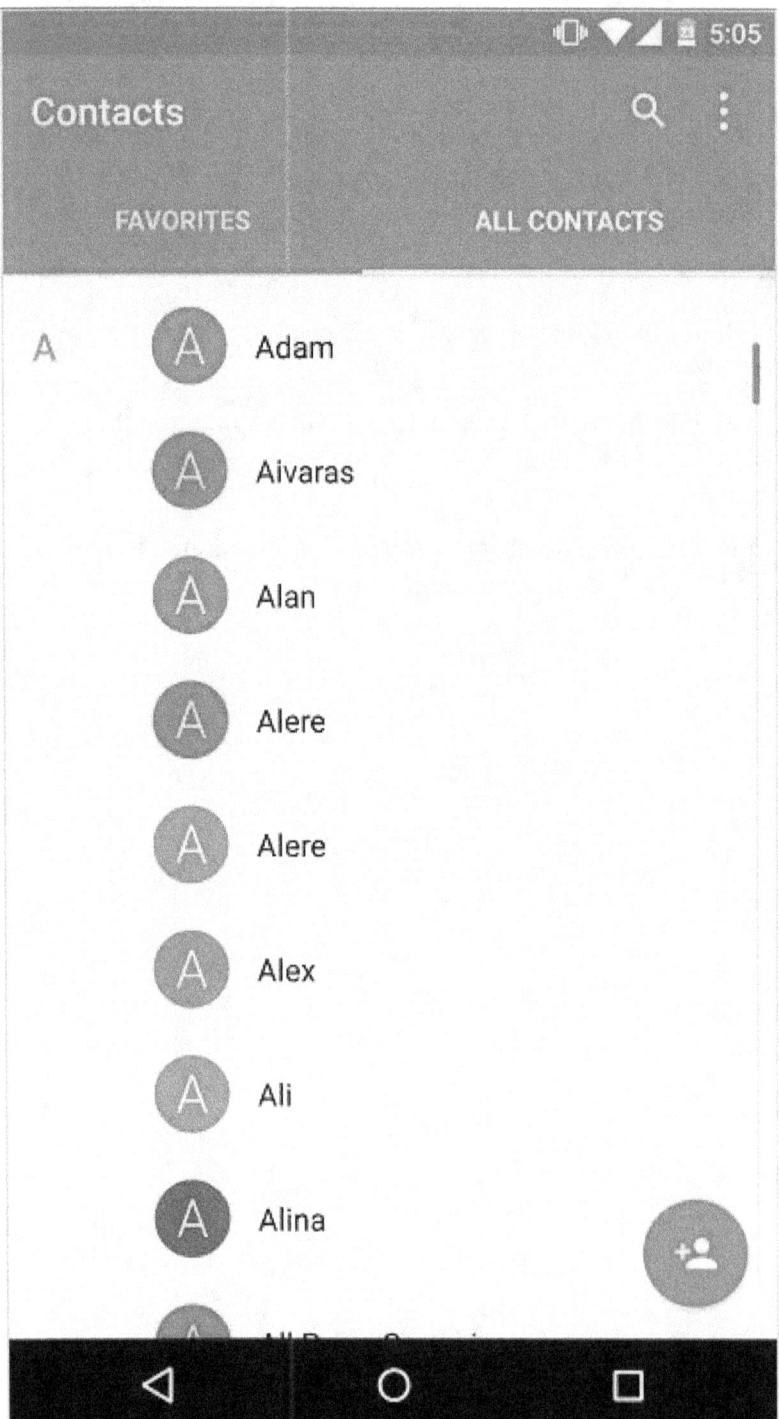

Figure 3: Phonebook

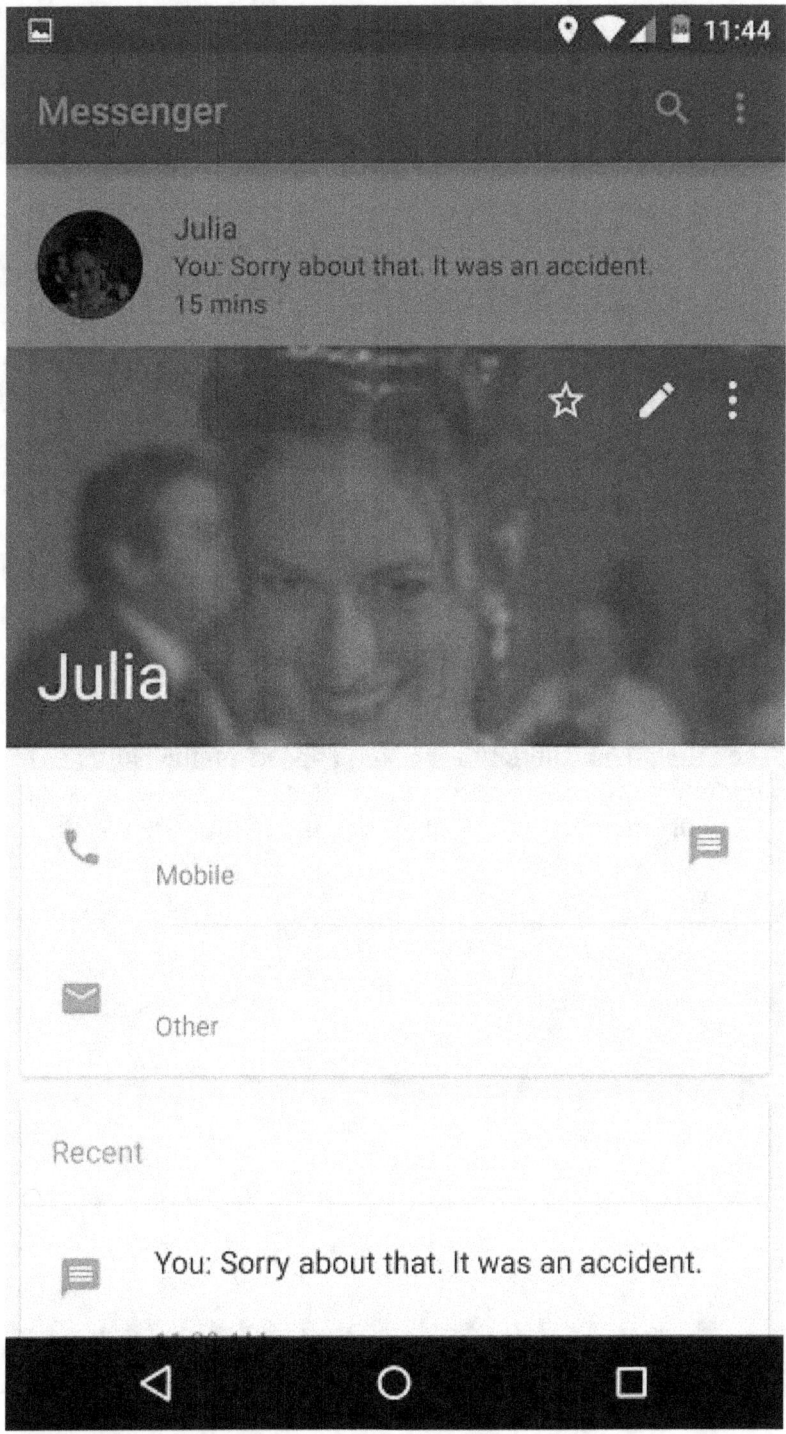

Figure 4: Contact Information Screen

3. Calling a Frequently Dialed Number

You can add a Direct Dial shortcut to the Home screen, which immediately dials a number stored in your phonebook when you touch the shortcut. To add and use a Direct Dial shortcut:

1. Touch an empty space on the home screen. The Home screen editing menu appears, as shown in **Figure 5**.
2. Touch **Widgets** at the bottom of the screen. A list of widgets appears, as shown in **Figure 6**.
3. Touch the screen and move your finger to the left. Additional widgets appear.
4. Touch the widget. A list of Contact Widget options appears.
5. Touch and hold the **Direct Dial** widget. The main Home screen appears, as shown in **Figure 7**. Do not release the screen yet.
6. Drag the icon to the desired location and release the screen. If you wish to place the Direct Dial icon on an alternate home screen, hold the icon over one of the other Home Screens. The icon is placed and the Phonebook appears.
7. Touch the name of a contact. The Direct Dial shortcut is set and appears on the Home screen, provided that there is only one number assigned to the contact. Otherwise, a list of phone numbers appears. Touch a phone number in the list to assign it to the Direct Dial.
8. Touch the **Direct Dial** icon. The number is dialed.

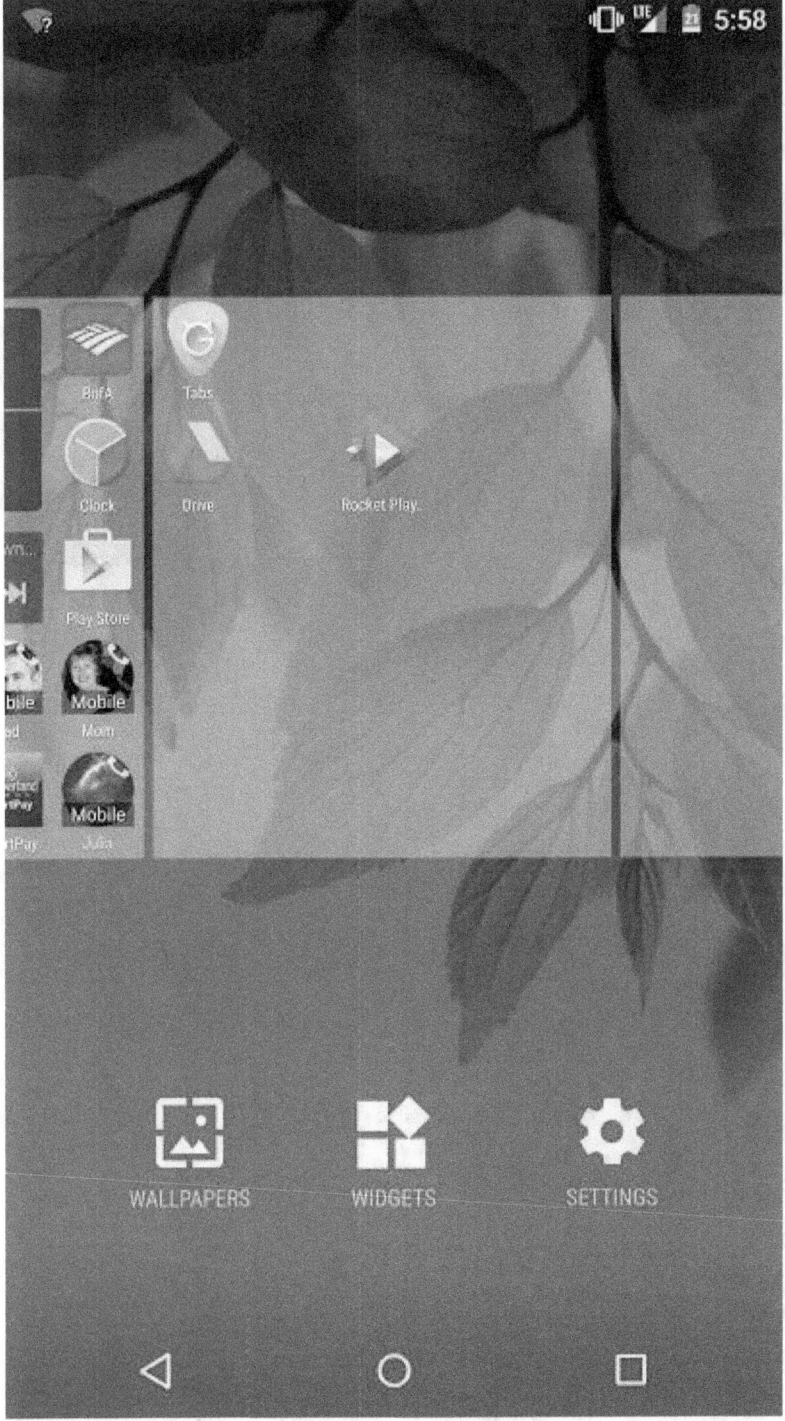

Figure 5: Home Screen Editing Menu

Figure 6: List of Widgets

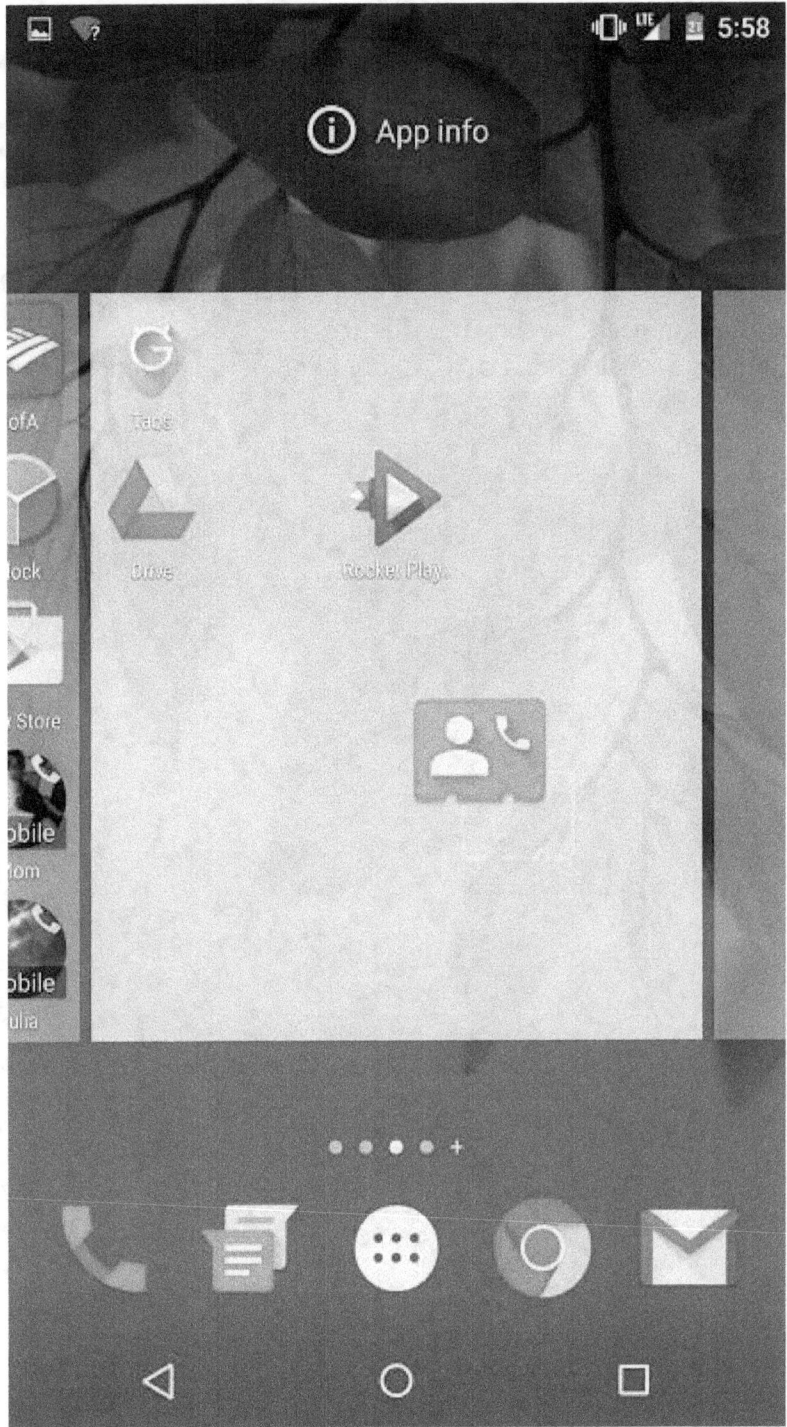

Figure 7: Home Screen while Adding the Direct Dial Icon

4. Returning a Recent Phone Call

After you miss a call, the phone notifies you of who called and at what time. The phone also shows a history of all recent calls. To view and return a missed call or redial a recently entered number:

1. Touch the icon at the bottom of the screen. The Speed Dial screen appears.
2. Touch **Recents**. A list of recent calls appears, as shown in **Figure 8**.
3. Touch the name of a contact, and then touch CALL BACK. The phone calls the selected contact.

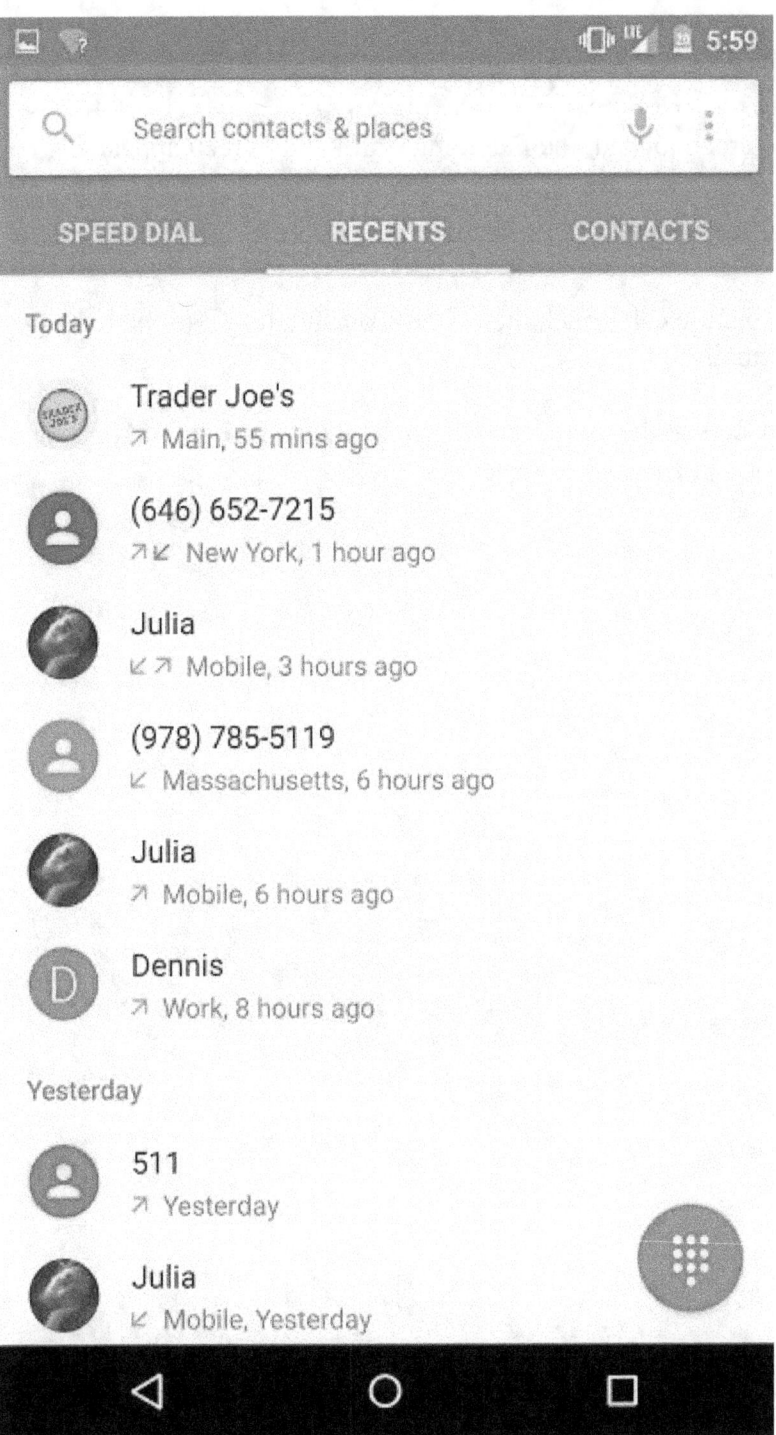

Figure 8: Full List of Recent Calls

5. Receiving a Voice Call

When receiving a voice call with the screen locked, the Incoming Call Lock Screen appears, as

shown in **Figure 9**. To answer the call, touch the　　　icon and drag it to the right side of the

screen. The call is connected. To decline the call, touch the　　　icon and drag it to the left side
of the screen. The call is sent to voicemail.

If the screen is unlocked, a pop-up appears at the top of the screen, as shown in **Figure 10**.
Touch **Answer** to answer the call, or touch **Dismiss** to reject it.

Figure 9: Incoming Call Screen

Figure 10: Incoming Call Popup

6. Using the Speakerphone during a Voice Call

The Galaxy S5 has a built-in Speakerphone, which is useful when calling from a car or when several people need to participate in a conversation. To use the Speakerphone during a phone call:

1. Place a phone call. The Calling Screen appears, as shown in **Figure 11**.

2. Touch the ◀ॐ icon. The speakerphone turns on.
3. Adjust the volume of the Speakerphone using the Volume Controls. Refer to *"Button Layout"* on page 12 to locate the Volume Controls.

4. Touch the ◀ॐ icon again. The speakerphone turns off.

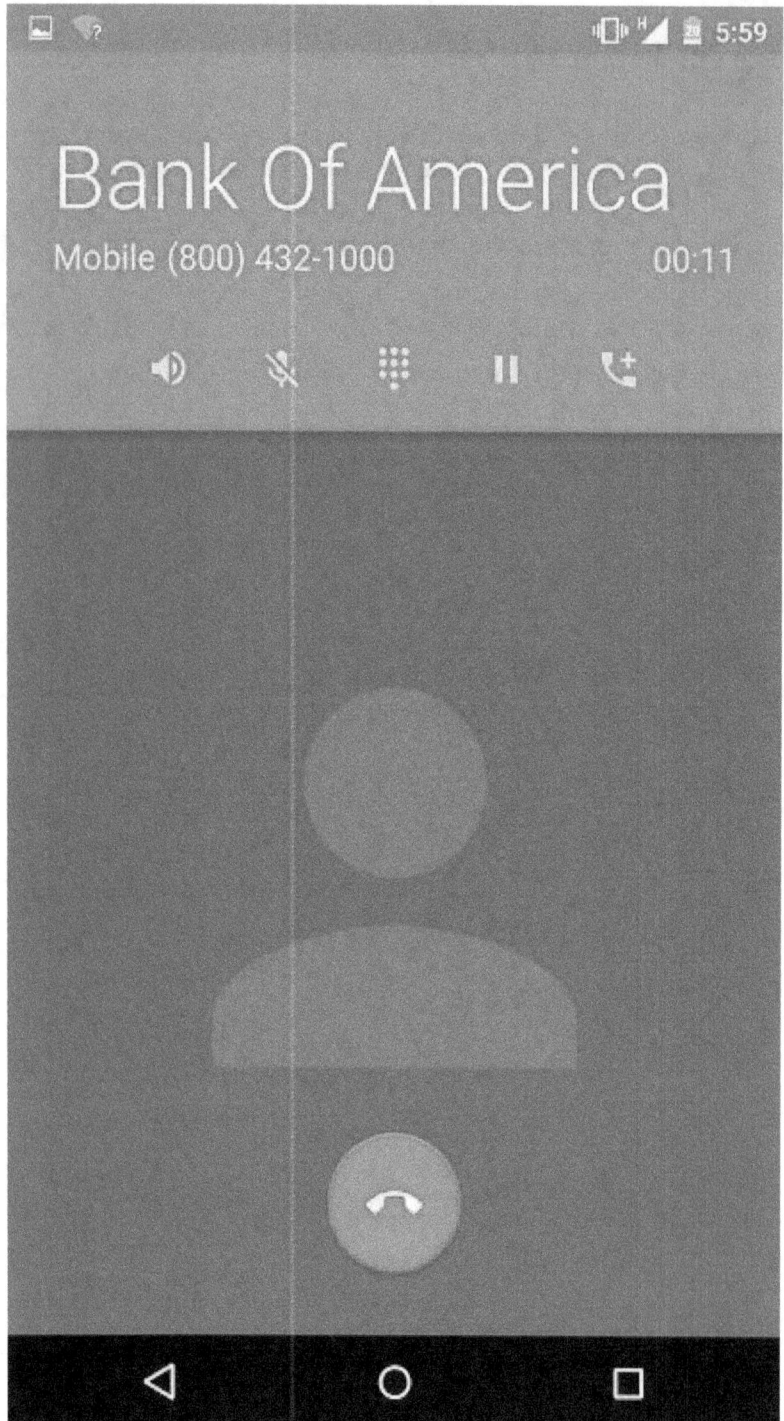

Figure 11: Calling Screen

7. Using the Keypad during a Voice Call

You may wish to use the keypad while on a call in order to input numbers in an automated menu or to enter an account number. To use the keypad during a voice call, place the call and touch the icon. The keypad appears, as shown in **Figure 12**. To hide the keypad, touch the icon again.

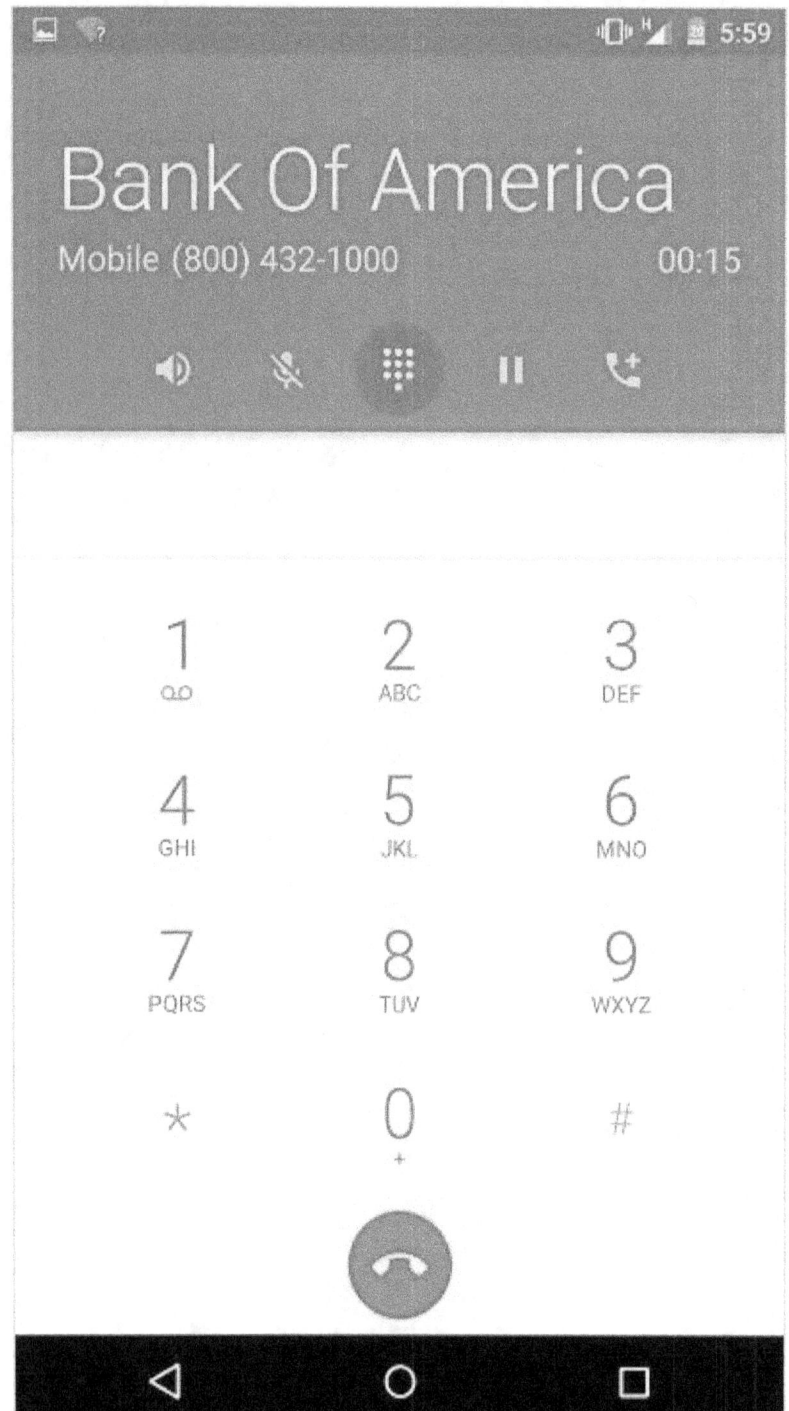

Figure 12: Phone Keypad While on a Call

8. Using the Mute Function during a Voice Call

During a voice call, you may wish to mute your side of the conversation. When mute is turned on, the person on the other end of the line will not hear anything on your side. To use Mute during a call, place a voice call and touch the [icon] icon. The phone mutes your voice and the caller(s) can no longer hear you, but you are still able to hear them. Touch the [icon] icon again. Mute is turned off.

9. Starting a Conference Call (Adding a Call)

To talk to more than one person at a time, place a new call without ending the current one. To add a call:

1. Place a call. The call is connected and the Calling screen appears.

2. Touch the [icon] icon. The keypad appears.

3. Dial a number and touch the [icon] button at the bottom of the screen. The phone dials the second number.

4. Touch the [icon] icon once connected. The calls are merged, and a three-person conference call is started.

10. Redialing the Last Dialed Number

You may redial the number that you last dialed by touching the [icon] button at the bottom of the phone keypad. The last dialed number appears above the keypad. Touch the [icon] button again. The number is redialed.

Text Messaging (Smartphones)

Table of Contents

1. Composing a New Text Message

Your phone can send text messages to other mobile phones. To compose a new text message:

1. Touch the ▤ icon at the bottom of the Home screen. The Messaging screen appears, as shown in **Figure 1**.

2. Touch the ✚ icon. The New Message screen appears, as shown in **Figure 2**. A list of frequently contacted people appears.

3. Touch the name of a contact in the list, or enter a phone number. Suggestions appear while typing. The addressee or phone number is entered.

4. Touch the check mark next to the contact's name or number. The Send message field appears.

5. Enter a message, and touch the ▷ button. The message is sent and appears as a conversation, sorted by send date, as shown in **Figure 3**.

Note: Refer to "Tips and Tricks" *on page 312 to learn how to schedule a text message to be sent at a later time.*

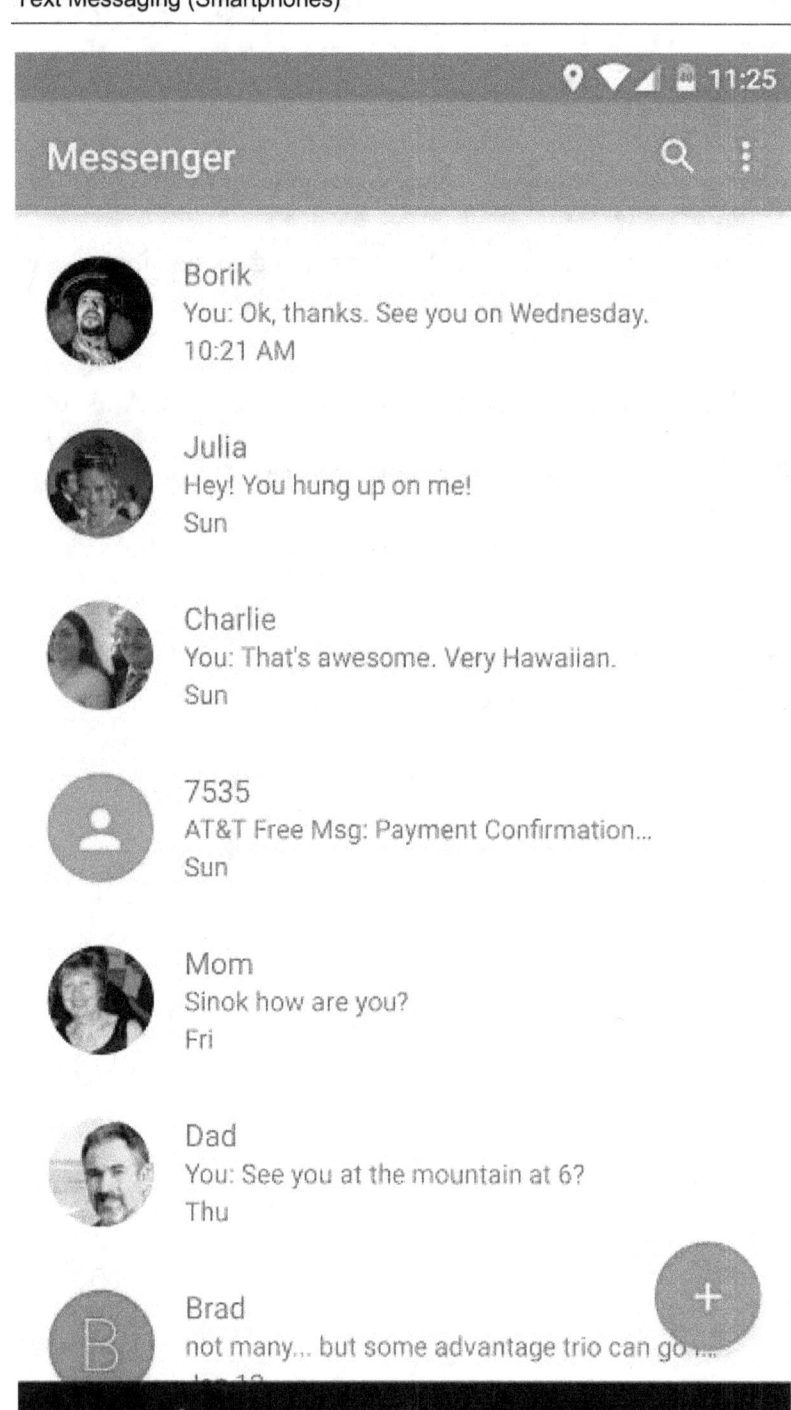

Figure 1: Messaging Screen

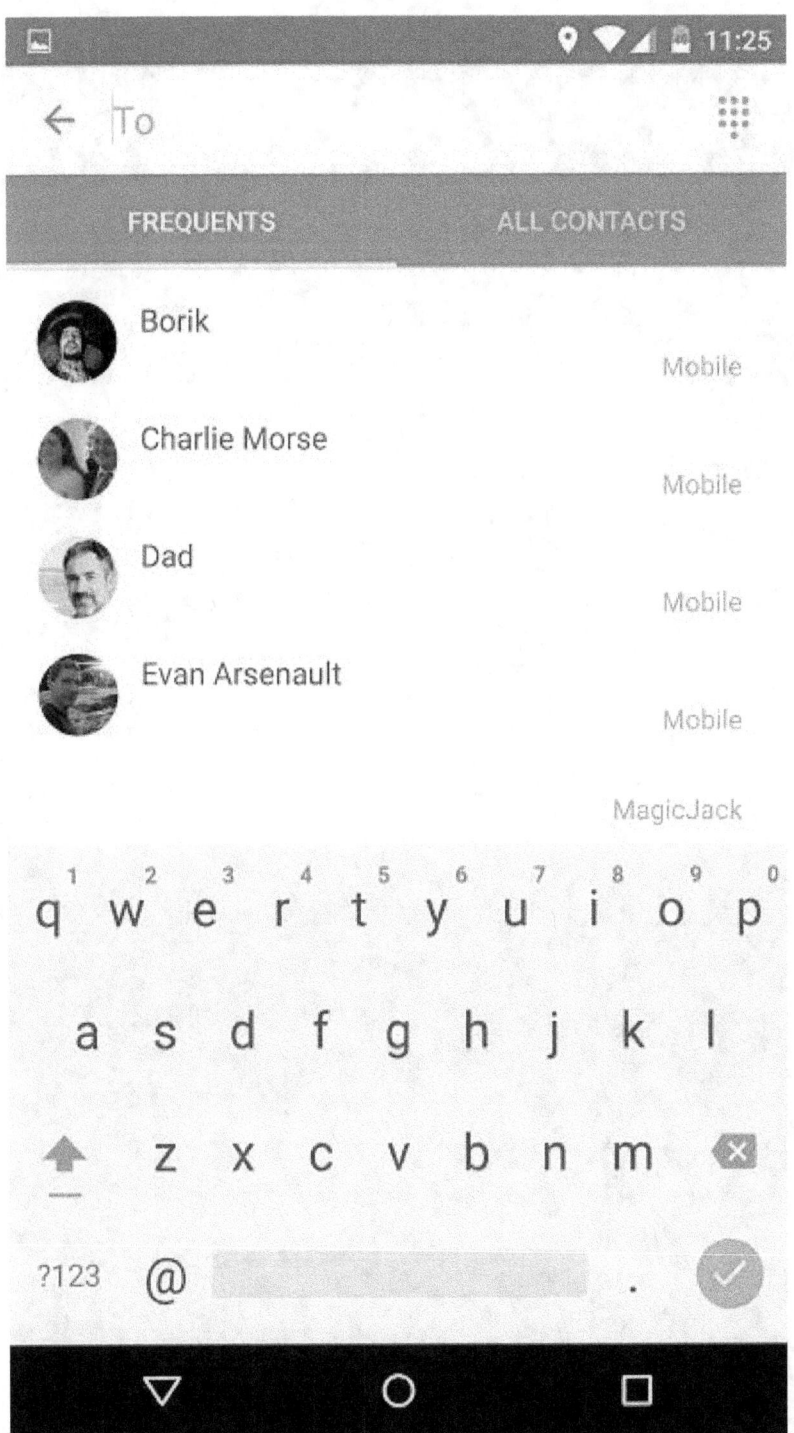

Figure 2: New Message Screen

Figure 3: Text Conversation

2. Copying, Cutting, and Pasting Text

The phone allows you to copy or cut text from one location and paste it to another. Copying leaves the text in its current location and allows you to paste it elsewhere. Cutting deletes the text from its current location and allows you to paste it elsewhere. To cut, copy, and paste text:

1. Touch and hold text on the screen. The Text options appear, as outlined in **Figure 4**. To learn how to compose a message, refer to *"Composing a New Text Message"* on page 50.
2. Touch one of the following options to perform the associated action:

- Select All - Selects all of the text in the field.

- Removes the text while copying it to the clipboard. Touch and hold any white field, even in an outside application, and touch Paste to enter the cut text.

- Leaves the text in the field while copying it to the clipboard. Touch and hold any white field, even in an outside application, and touch Paste to enter the copied text.

Note: The 'cut' and 'copy' options only become available when text is selected.

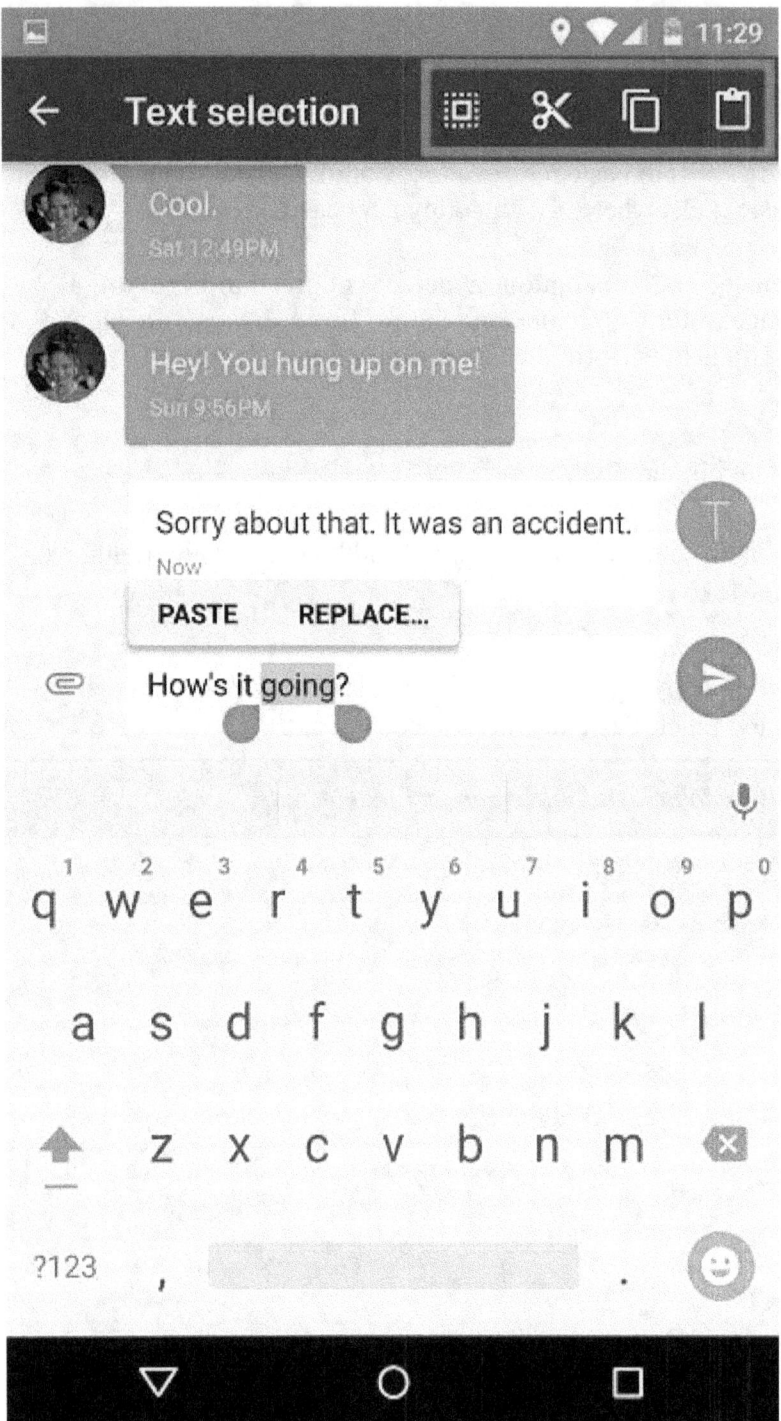

Figure 4: Text Options

3. Using the Auto-Complete Feature

While typing a text message, the device automatically makes suggestions to auto-complete words, which appear above the virtual keyboard, as outlined in **Figure 5**. This is especially useful when a word is very long. To accept a suggestion, touch the word. The word is inserted into the current message.

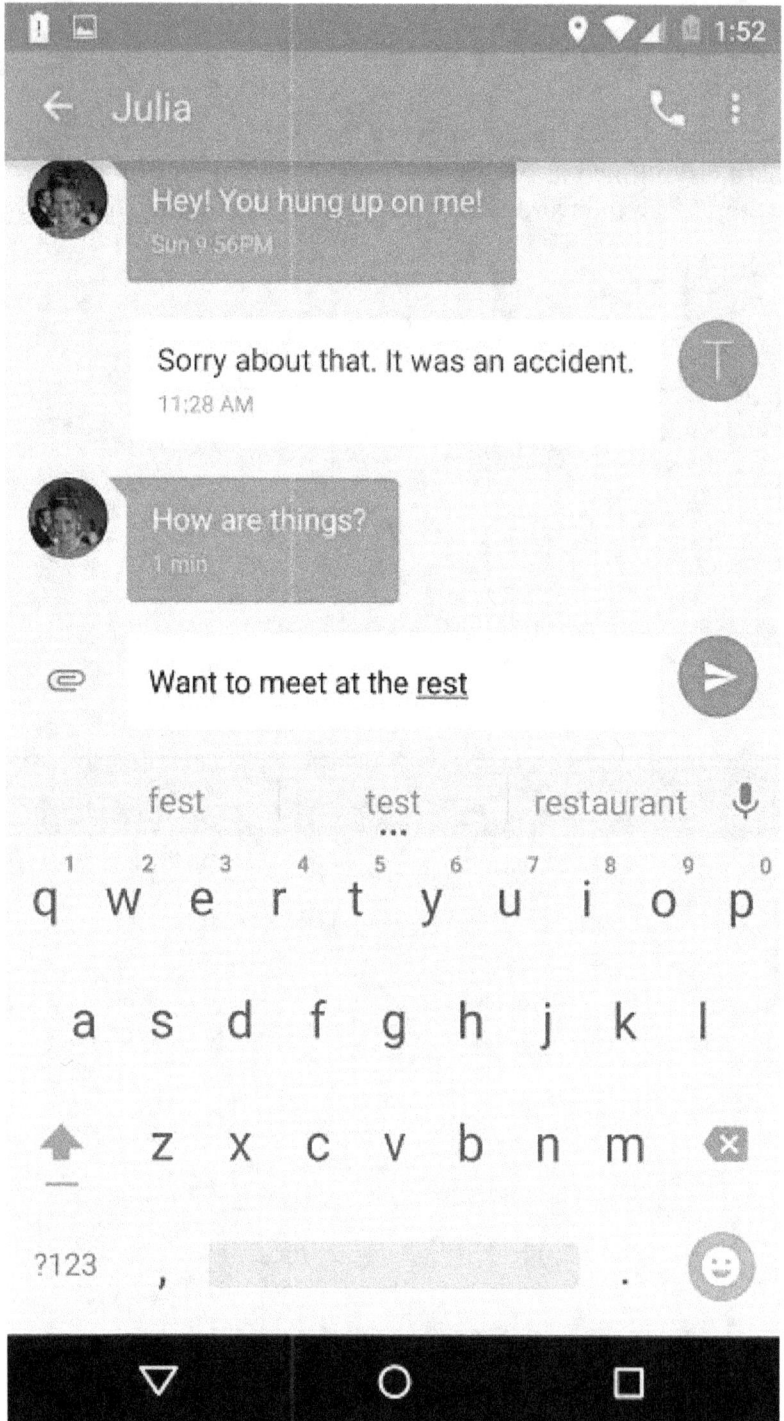

Figure 5: Auto Suggestions

4. Switching to another Language

While entering a text message, you can switch your keyboard to display a non-English keyboard. Before switching to another keyboard, you must add it via the Keyboard Settings screen. Refer to *"Changing the Input Method"* on page 301 to learn how. To switch to another language, touch the spacebar and slide your finger to the left or right. The alternate keyboard appears.

5. Receiving Text Messages

The phone can receive text messages from any other mobile phone, including non-smartphones. When receiving a text, the phone vibrates twice, plays a sound, or both, depending on the settings. Refer to *"Changing the Notification Ringtone"* on page 262 to learn how to set text message notifications.

If the screen is locked, the text message alert appears on the screen, as shown in **Figure 6**. Touch the text message twice to open the text conversation.

To open a newly received text message when the screen is unlocked, touch the status bar at the top of the screen and drag it down (the bar where the time, battery, and signal bars are located). The Notifications screen appears, as shown in **Figure 7**. Touch the message. The new text message opens.

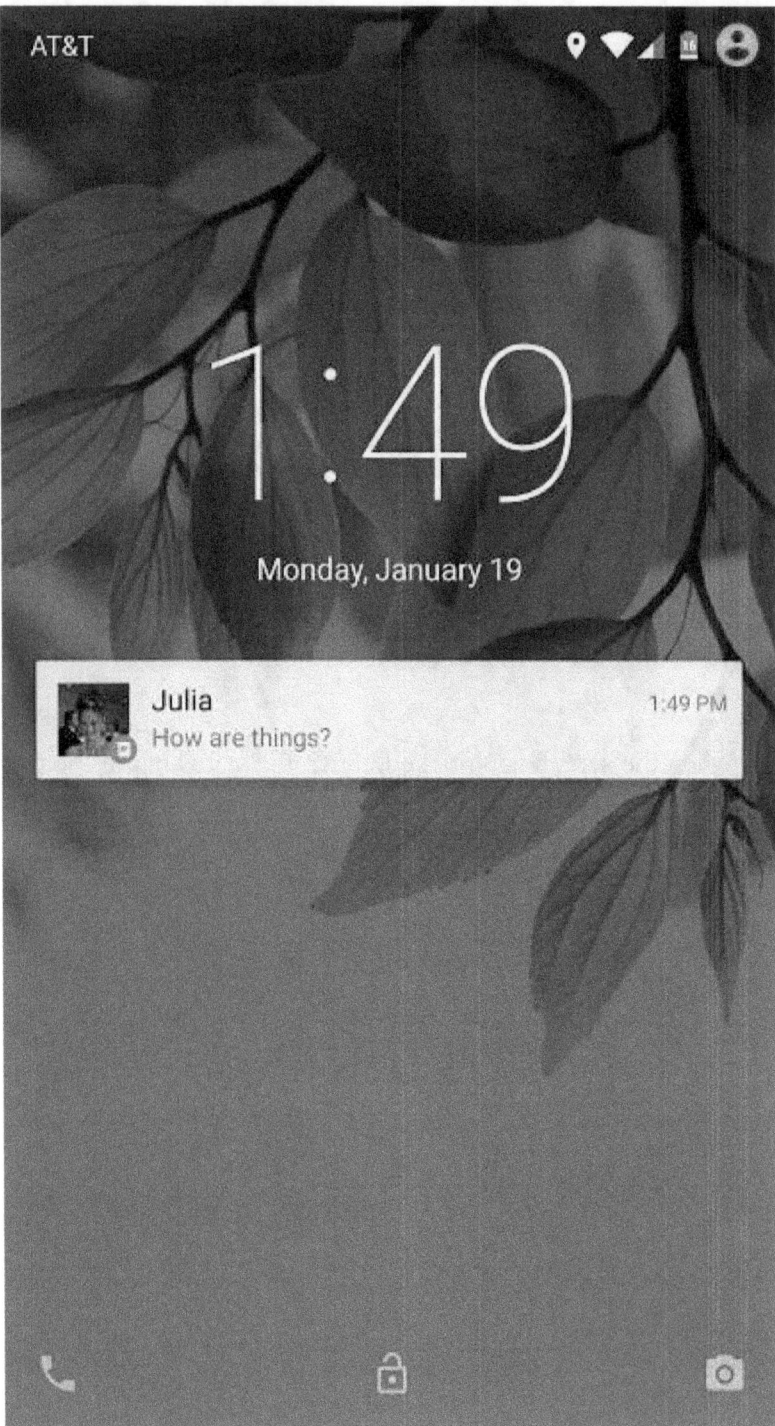

Figure 6: Text Message on the Lock Screen

Figure 7: Notifications Screen

6. Reading Text Messages

You may read any text messages that you have received, provided that you have not deleted them.

To read stored text messages, touch the icon. The Messaging screen appears. Touch a conversation. The conversation opens.

7. Forwarding Text Messages

The forwarding feature on the phone allows a text message to be copied in full and sent to other recipients. To forward a text message:

1. Touch the   icon. The Messaging screen appears.
2. Touch a conversation. The Conversation opens.
3. Touch and hold a text message. The Message options appear, as outlined in **Figure 8**.

4. Touch the   icon at the top of the screen. The Forward Message screen appears, with a list of the most frequently contacted people.

5. Touch the name of a contact, or touch the   icon to add a different one. A conversation with the selected contact is created, or an existing conversation appears, and the original message is pasted in the message field.

6. Touch the   button. The text message is forwarded.

Figure 8: Message Options

8. Calling the Sender from within a Text

After receiving a text message from a contact, you may call that person without exiting the text

message. To call someone while viewing a text conversation, touch the icon at the top of the screen. The device automatically dials the contact's number.

9. Viewing Sender Information from within a Text

You can look up a contact's details without exiting the Messaging application. To view the information of the person who sent you a text message touch the letter next to the conversation between you and that contact, or touch the person's picture, if one is assigned. The Contact Information screen appears, as shown in **Figure 9**. Touch the top of the screen to hide the contact's information.

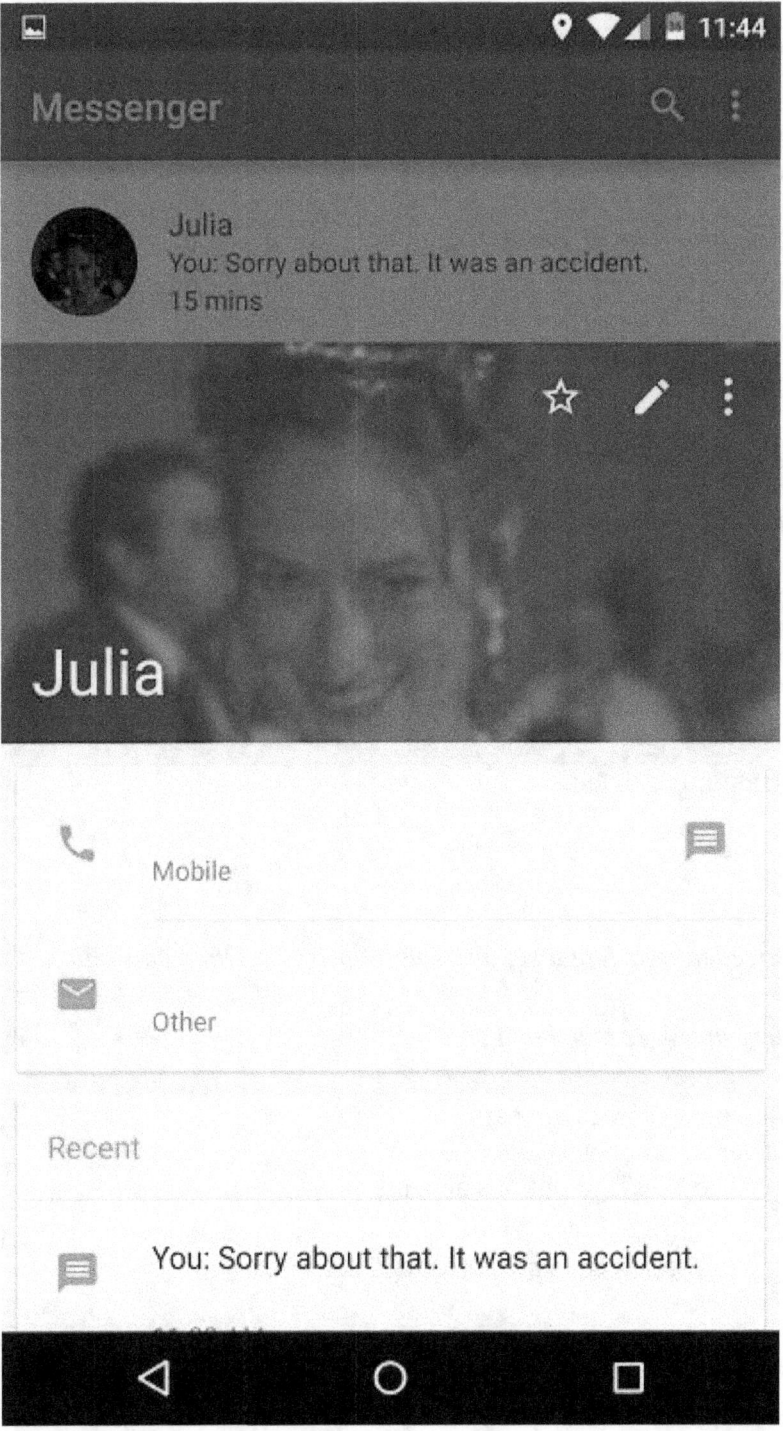

Figure 9: Contact Information Screen

10. Deleting Text Messages

The device can delete separate text messages or an entire conversation, which is a series of text messages between you and one or more contacts.

Warning: Once deleted, text messages cannot be restored.

To delete an entire conversation:

1. Touch the  icon. The Messaging screen appears.

2. Touch and hold a conversation. The Conversation is selected and a ✓ mark appears next to it, as shown in **Figure 10**. Touch any additional conversations that you would like to delete.

3. Touch the 🗑 icon in the upper right-hand corner of the screen. A Confirmation dialog appears.

4. Touch **DELETE**. The conversation is deleted.

To delete a separate text message:

Warning: There is no confirmation needed to delete a separate text message. Once you touch the 🗑 ***icon in step 4 below, the text message is deleted forever.***

1. Touch the 🗑 icon. The Messaging screen appears.
2. Touch a conversation. The conversation opens.
3. Touch and hold a text message. The Message options appear.

4. Touch the 🗑 icon at the top of the screen. The message is deleted.

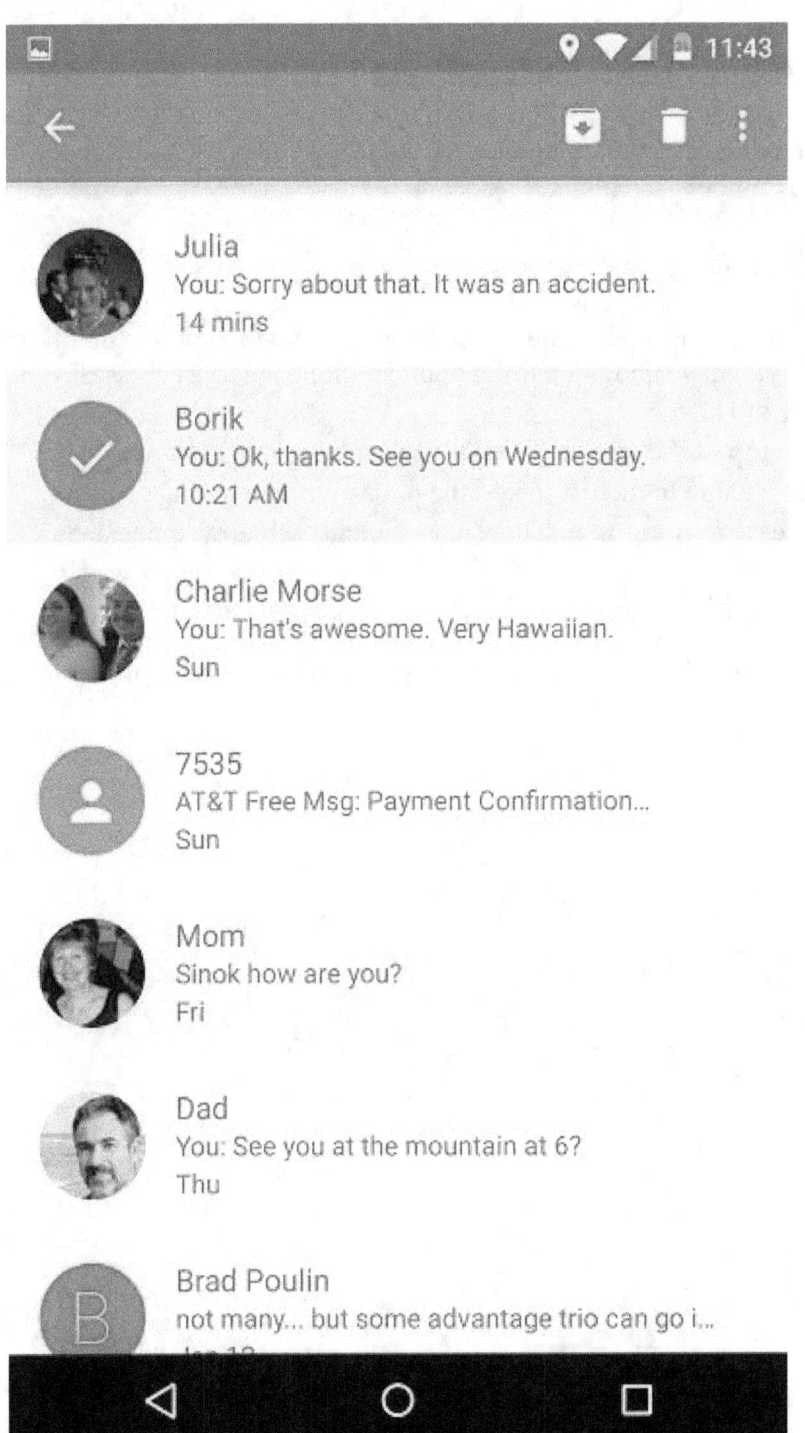

Figure 10: Selected Conversation

11. Adding Texted Phone Numbers to Contacts

A phone number contained in a text message may be immediately added to the phonebook as a new contact. To save a texted phone number as a contact:

1. Touch the [icon] icon. The Messaging screen appears.
2. Touch a conversation. The conversation opens.
3. Touch the phone number in the text message. The keypad appears, with the phone number pasted in the number field. If you have another calling application installed, such as Skype, you must touch **Phone** before the keypad appears.
4. Touch **Add to contacts** at the top of the screen. The phonebook appears, as shown in **Figure 11**. You may touch a name in the list to add the phone number to an existing contact. Otherwise, touch **Create new contact**. The Create Contact window appears, as shown in **Figure 12**.
5. Enter the name of the contact, and fill in any other fields, as necessary. Then, touch the [icon] icon at the top of the screen. The new contact is saved to the phonebook.

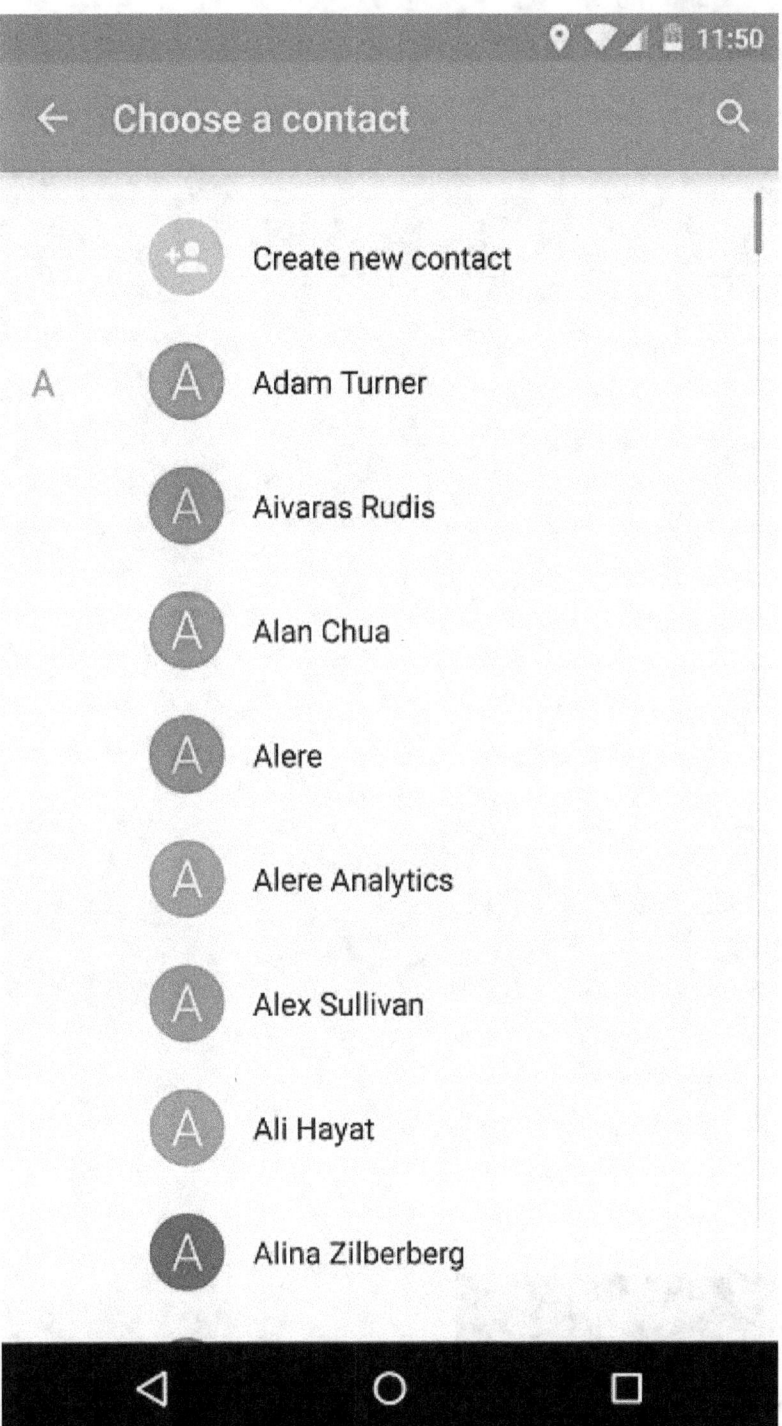

Figure 11: Phonebook

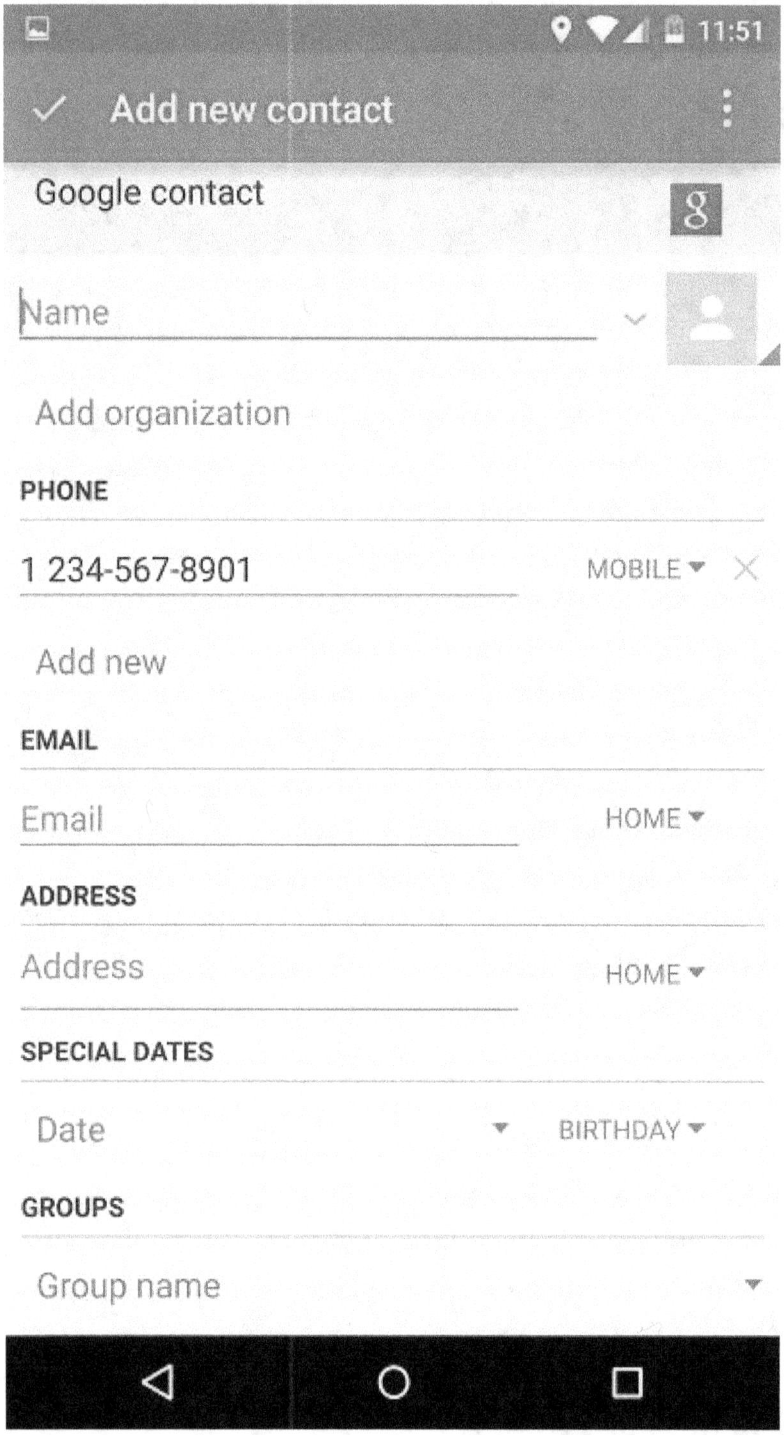

Figure 12: Create Contact Window

12. Adding an Attachment to a Text Message

A picture, video, or other file can be attached to any text message. To send a text message with an attachment:

1. Refer to *"Composing a New Text Message"* on page 50 and follow steps 1-3.

2. Touch the ⬭ icon to the left of the 'Enter message' field. The camera turns on, as shown in **Figure 13**. If you previously attached a photo from the gallery or a voice recording, the corresponding screen appears in the lower half of the screen.

3. Refer to one of the following sections to learn how to attach the associated media:
   - Attaching a Picture
   - Attaching a Video
   - Attaching a Voice Recording

4. Touch and hold an attachment to view it, or touch the ✕ icon to remove it.

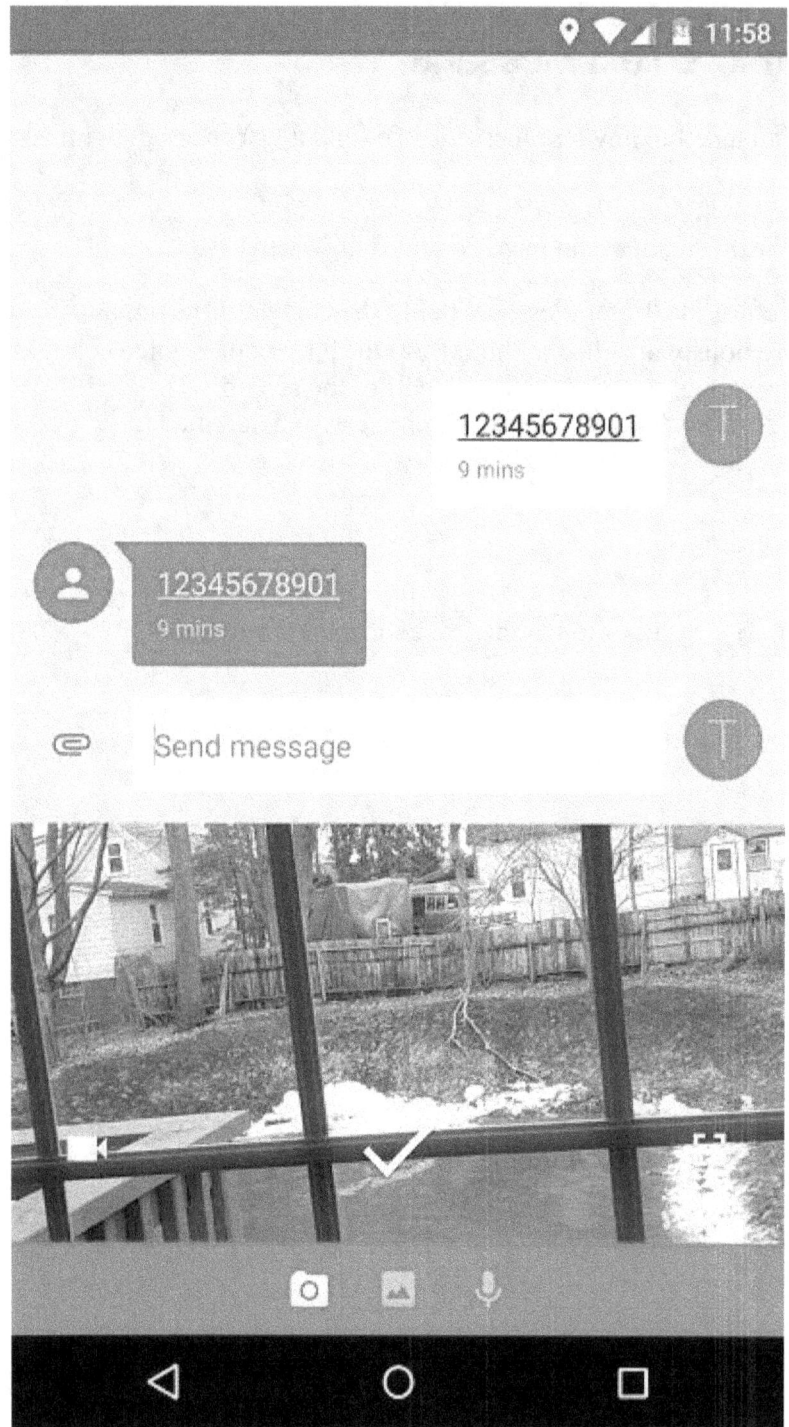

Figure 13: Camera On

13. Attaching a Picture

The device can send media messages containing pictures. To attach a picture to a text message:

1. Refer to *"Adding an Attachment to a Text Message"* on page 71 and follow steps 1-2. The Attachment menu appears.
2. Follow the steps in the appropriate section below:

Taking and Attaching a Picture

Touch the 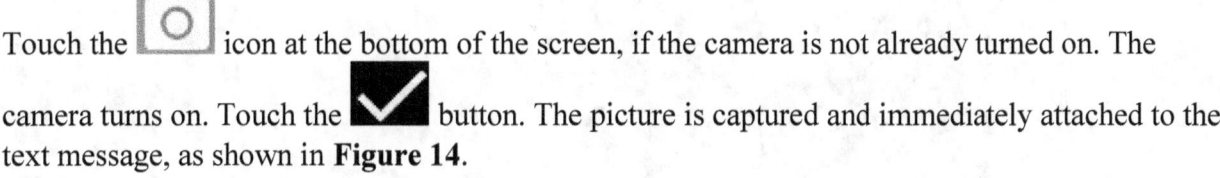 icon at the bottom of the screen, if the camera is not already turned on. The camera turns on. Touch the 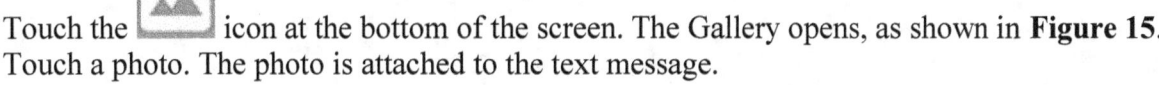 button. The picture is captured and immediately attached to the text message, as shown in **Figure 14**.

Attaching a Picture from a Photo Album

Touch the icon at the bottom of the screen. The Gallery opens, as shown in **Figure 15**. Touch a photo. The photo is attached to the text message.

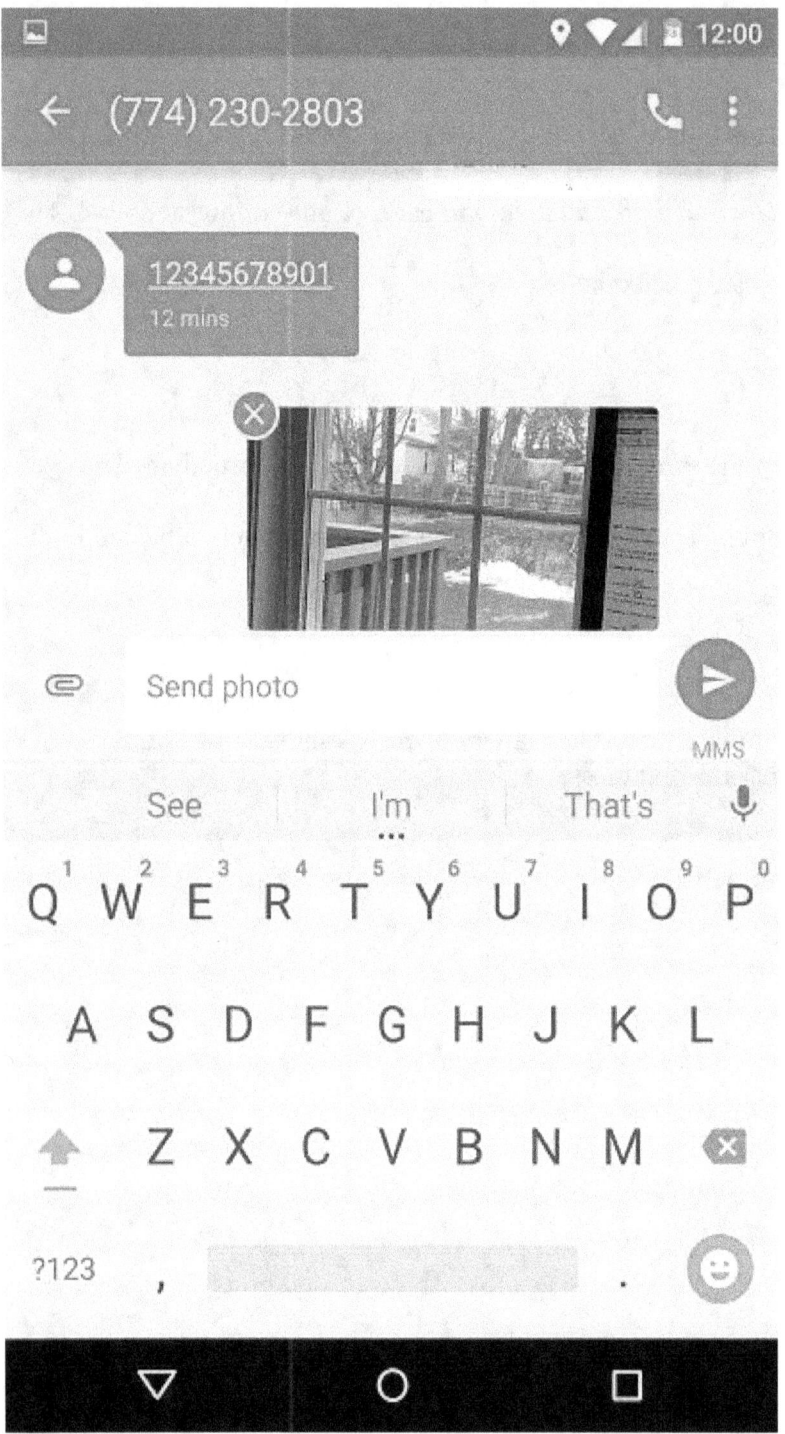

Figure 14: Text Message with Picture Attached

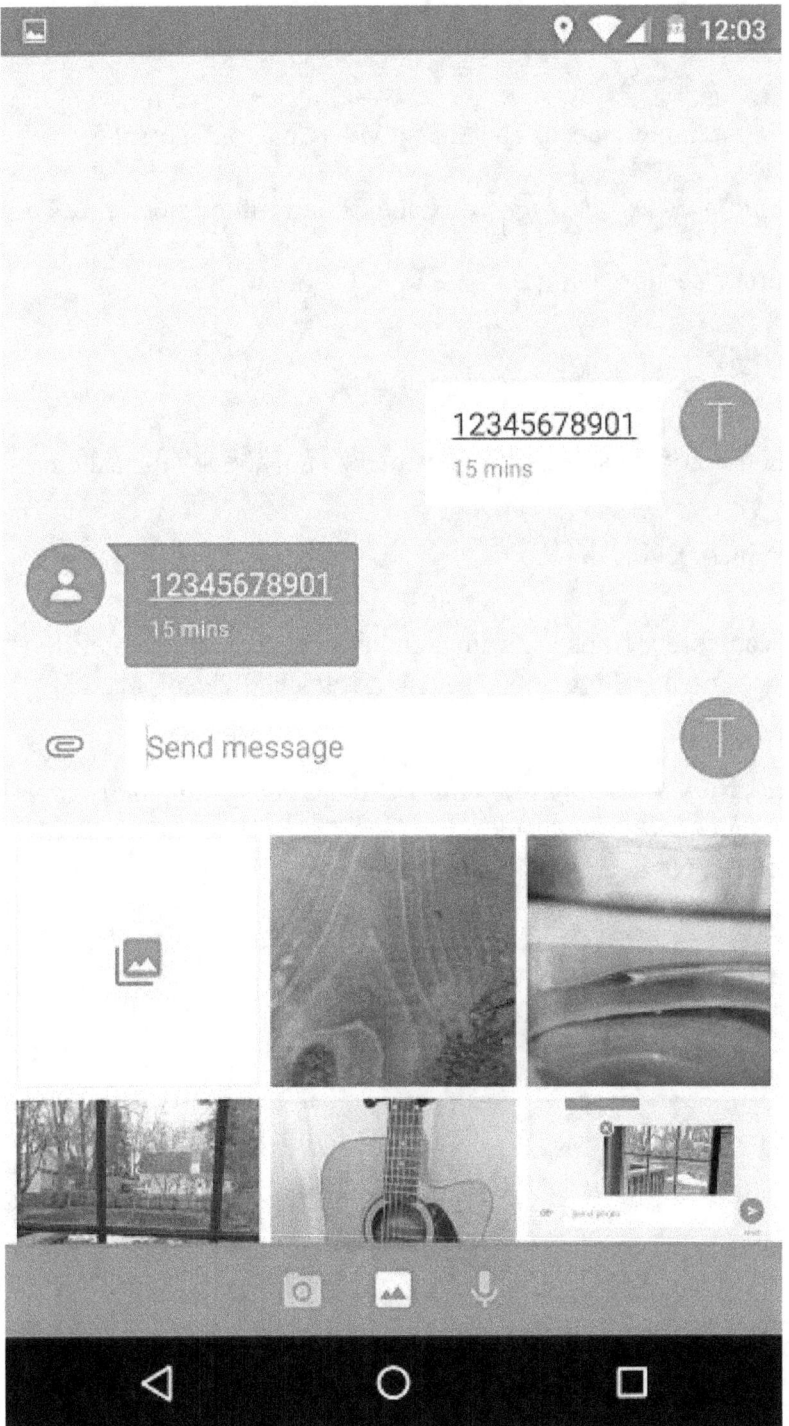

Figure 15: Gallery

14. Attaching a Video

The device can send media messages containing videos. To attach a video to a text message:

1. Refer to *"Adding an Attachment to a Text Message"* on page 71 and follow steps 1-2. The Attachment menu appears.
2. Follow the steps in the appropriate section below:

Attaching a Video from the Camcorder

1. Touch the [icon] icon at the bottom of the screen, if the camera is not already turned on. The camera turns on.

2. Touch the [button] button. The video begins to record.

3. Touch the [button] button. The camcorder stops recording, and the video is immediately attached to the text message, as shown in **Figure 16**. Touch the attached video once to preview it.

Note: The camcorder will automatically stop recording when the video has reached the maximum size limit. Attaching videos from the gallery is not supported.

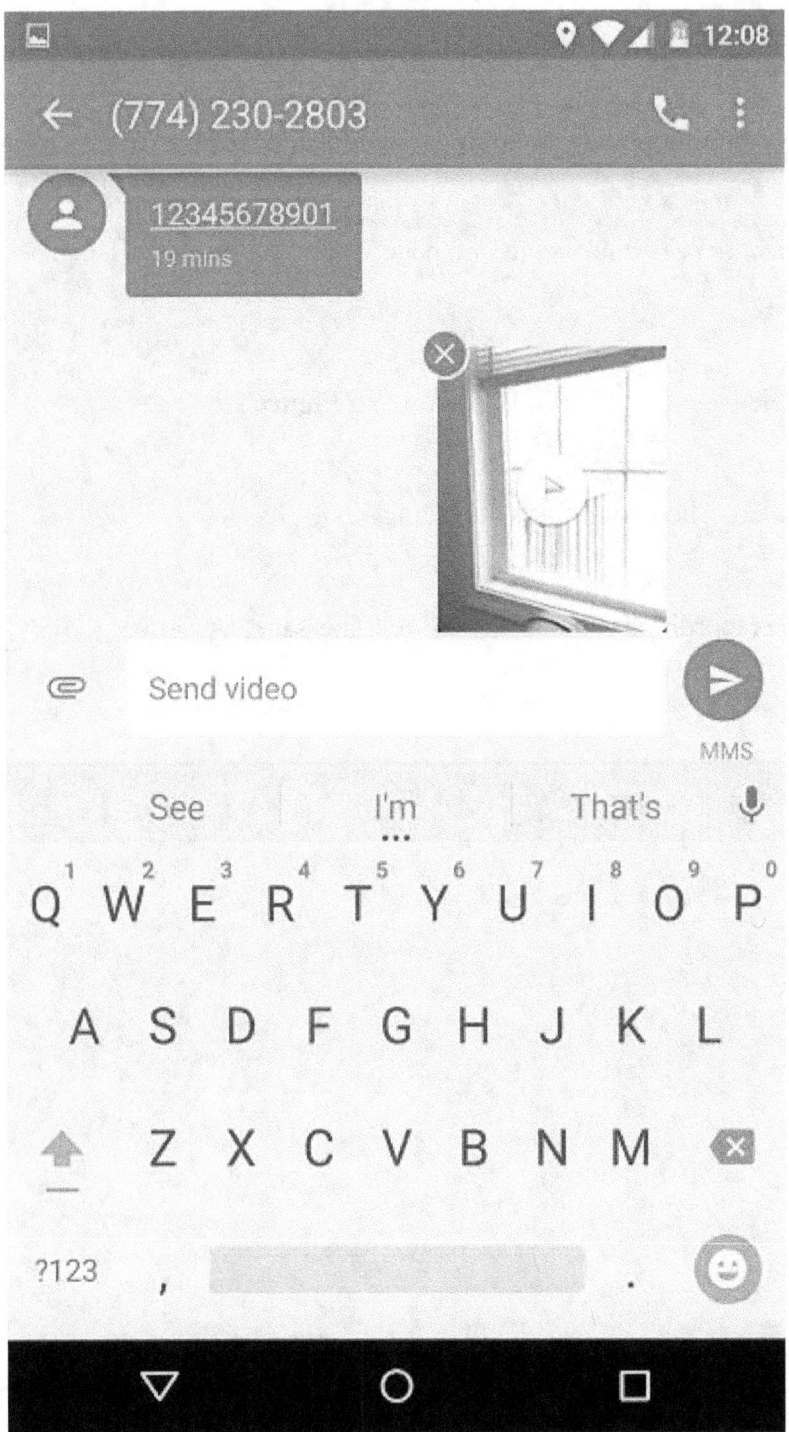

Figure 16: Text Message with Video Attached

15. Attaching a Voice Recording

The device can send media messages containing voice recordings. To attach a voice recording to a text message:

1. Refer to *"Adding an Attachment to a Text Message"* on page 71 and follow steps 1-2. The Attachment menu appears.

2. Touch the ![mic icon] icon. The voice recorder turns on, as shown in **Figure 17**.

3. Touch and hold the ![mic icon] button. The phone starts recording.

4. Release the ![mic icon] button. The recording is attached to the text message, as shown in **Figure 18**.

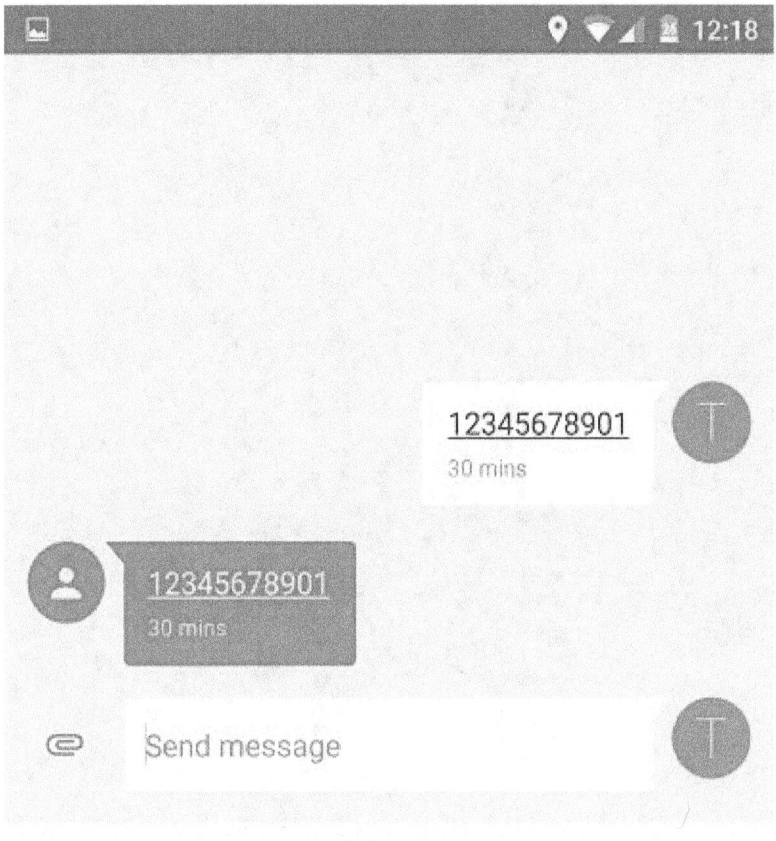

Tap + Hold

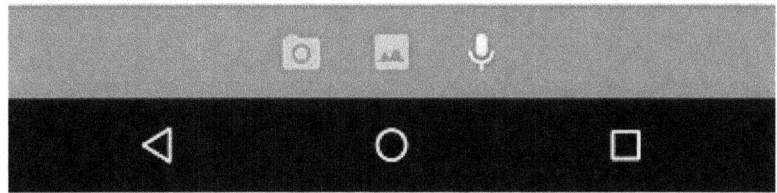

Figure 17: Voice Recorder

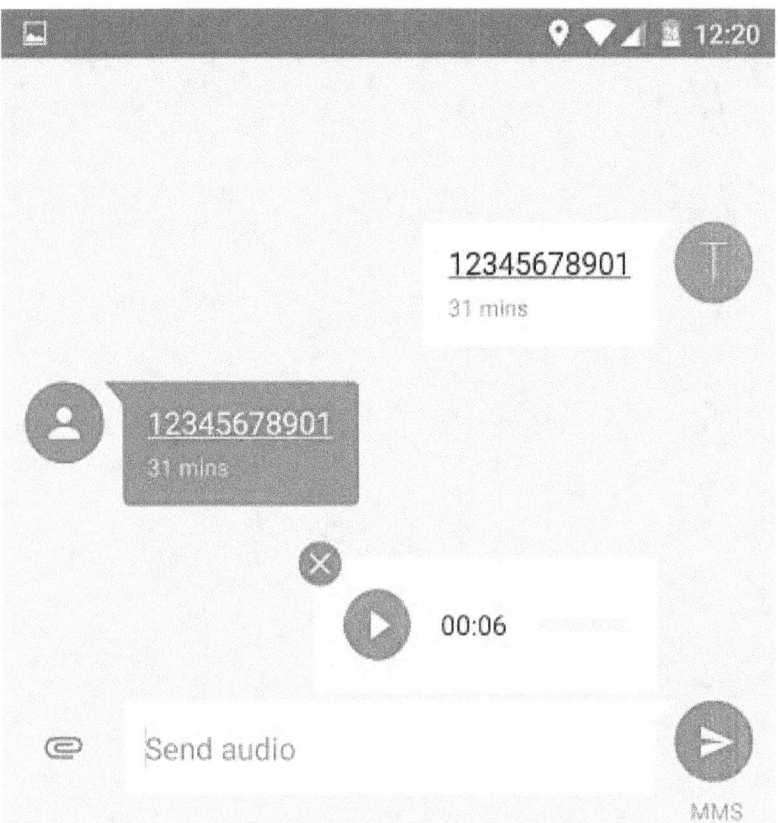

Figure 18: Text Message with Voice Recording Attached

16. Saving Attachments from Text Messages

After receiving an attachment in a text message, it can be saved to your device. To save an attachment from a text message:

1. Touch the icon. The Messaging screen appears.
2. Touch a conversation. The conversation opens.
3. Touch and hold the attachment in the text message. The Attachment options appear, as outlined in **Figure 19**.

4. Touch the icon at the top of the screen. The attachment is saved to the phone. If the attachment is a voice recording, you may open it using the

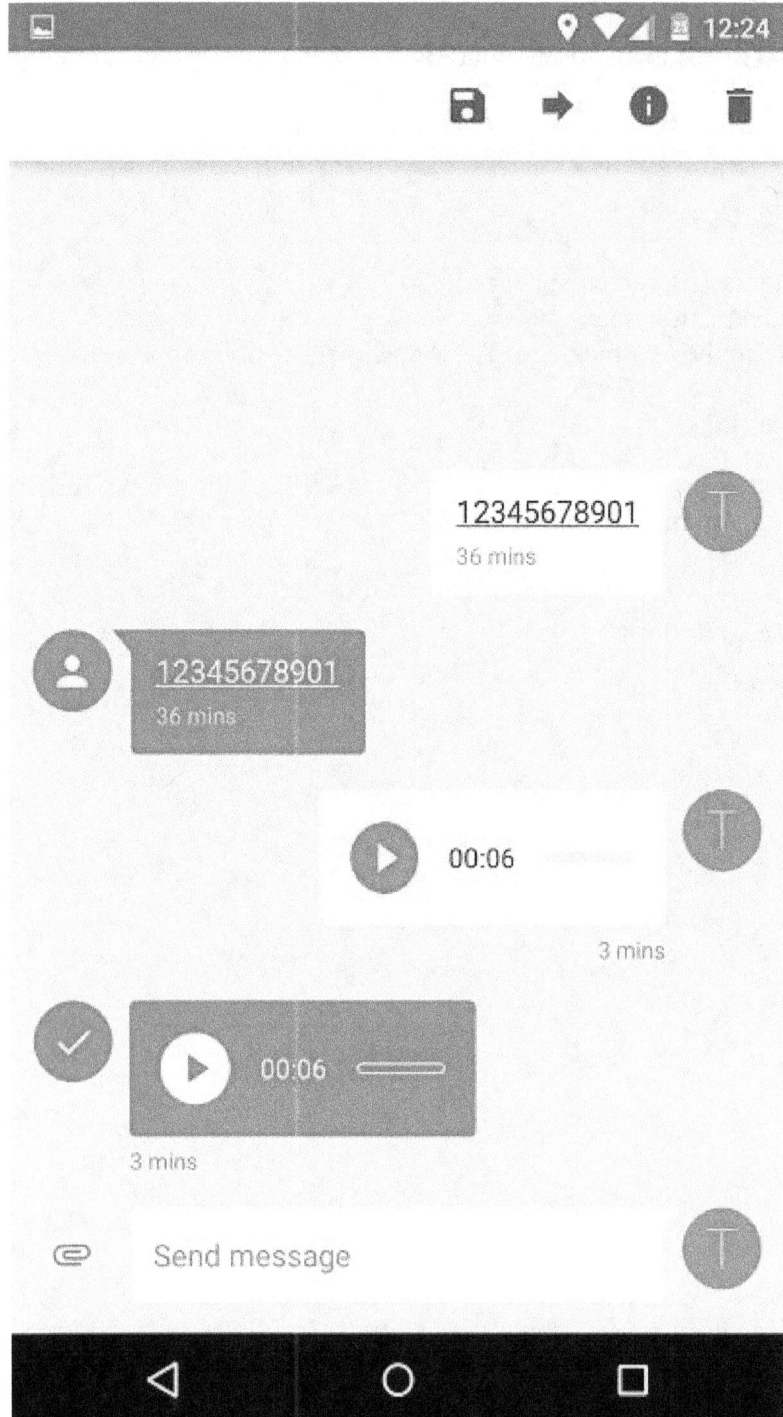

Figure 19: Attachment Options

17. Archiving a Text Conversation

You may wish to remove a text conversation from the Messaging screen, but save it on your phone for future reference. To archive a conversation, touch it and move your finger to the left or right until the conversation has disappeared. The conversation is archived.

To restore a conversation from the archive, touch the icon at the top of the screen, and then

touch **Archived** to view the archive. Touch and hold a conversation, and then touch the icon. The conversation is now visible on the Messaging screen.

18. Turning Off Text Message Notifications for a Specific Contact

If someone is annoying you, you may want to temporarily stop receiving text message notifications from a specific person. To turn off notifications for a specific contact:

1. Touch and hold the conversation. The Conversation menu appears.

2. Touch the icon at the top of the screen, and then touch **Notifications off**. The icon appears next to the contact's name, and notifications are turned off.
3. To turn notifications on, repeat steps 1-1, but touch **Notifications on** instead. The notifications are turned on.

Managing Users

Table of Contents

1. Adding a User

The device allows you to have multiple user profiles, each with different settings and applications. To add a user to the device:

1. Touch the ⠿ icon on the Home screen, and then touch the ⚙ icon. The Settings screen appears, as shown in **Figure 1**. Refer to *"Tips and Tricks"* on page 312 to learn how to quickly access the Settings screen.
2. Touch **Users**. The Users Settings screen appears, as shown in **Figure 2**.
3. Touch **Add user**. A confirmation dialog appears.
4. Touch **OK**. Touch **Set Up Now** in the following dialog. The Lock screen appears, and you can now set up the new user.
5. Unlock the screen by swiping up. The Welcome screen appears.
6. Touch the right arrow at the bottom of the screen. The Google Account screen appears, as shown in **Figure 3**.
7. Enter your Google credentials, or touch **CREATE A NEW ACCOUNT**. Otherwise, touch **SKIP** to do this later. The Google Services screen appears.
8. Touch each service that you want to turn on. Touch **Next** when you are finished. The Google Now screen appears, as shown in **Figure 4**.
9. Touch **Yes, I'm** in or **Skip** to turn Google Now on or off, respectively. Touch **Next** when you are finished. The new user account is set up and ready to use.

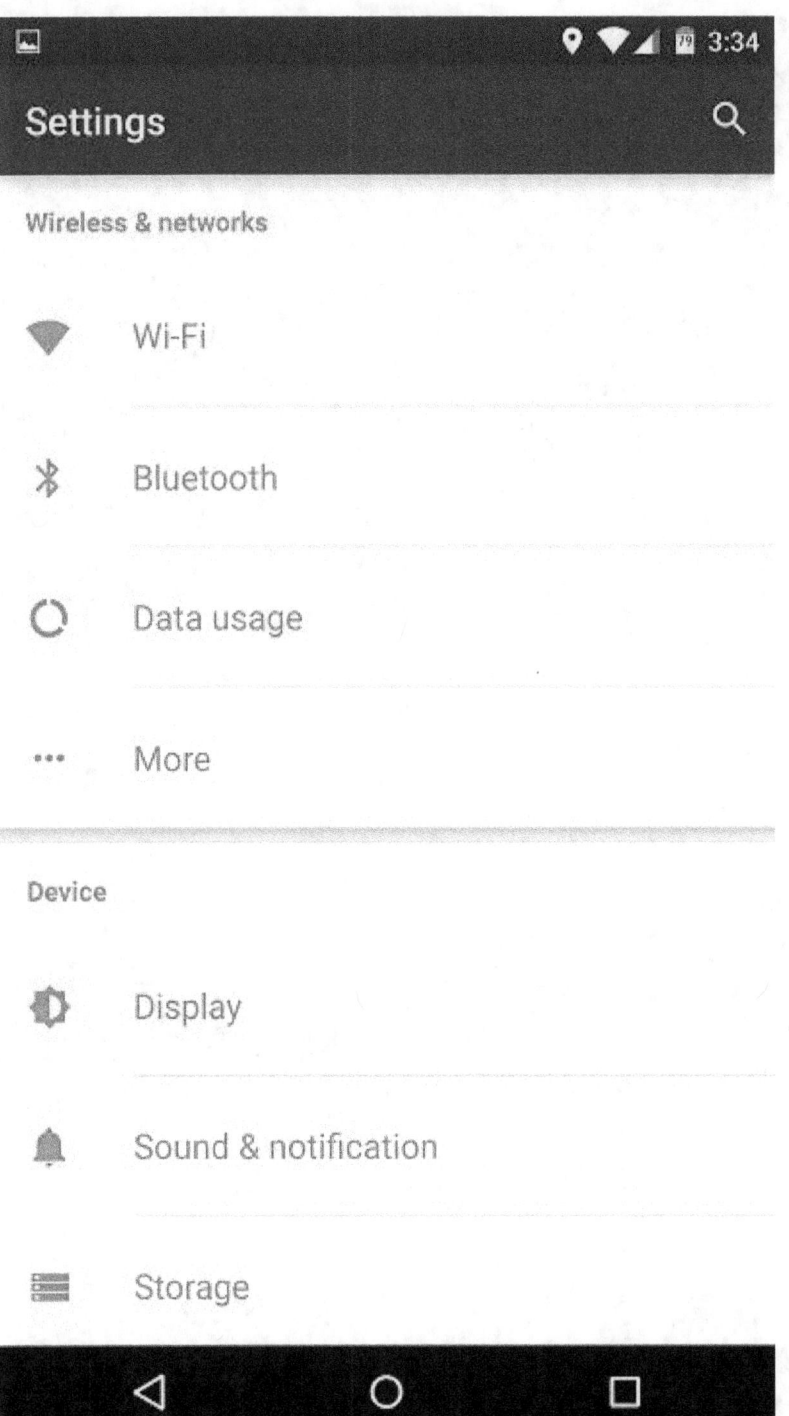

Figure 1: Settings Screen

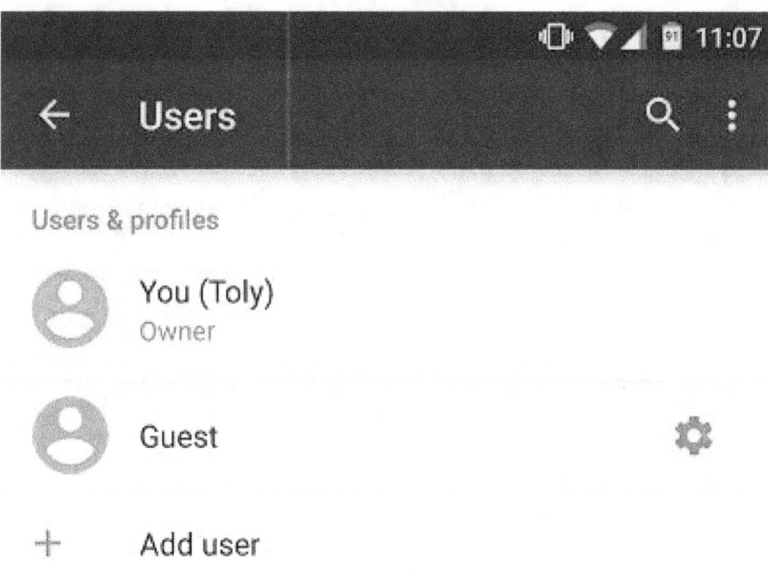

Figure 2: Users Settings Screen

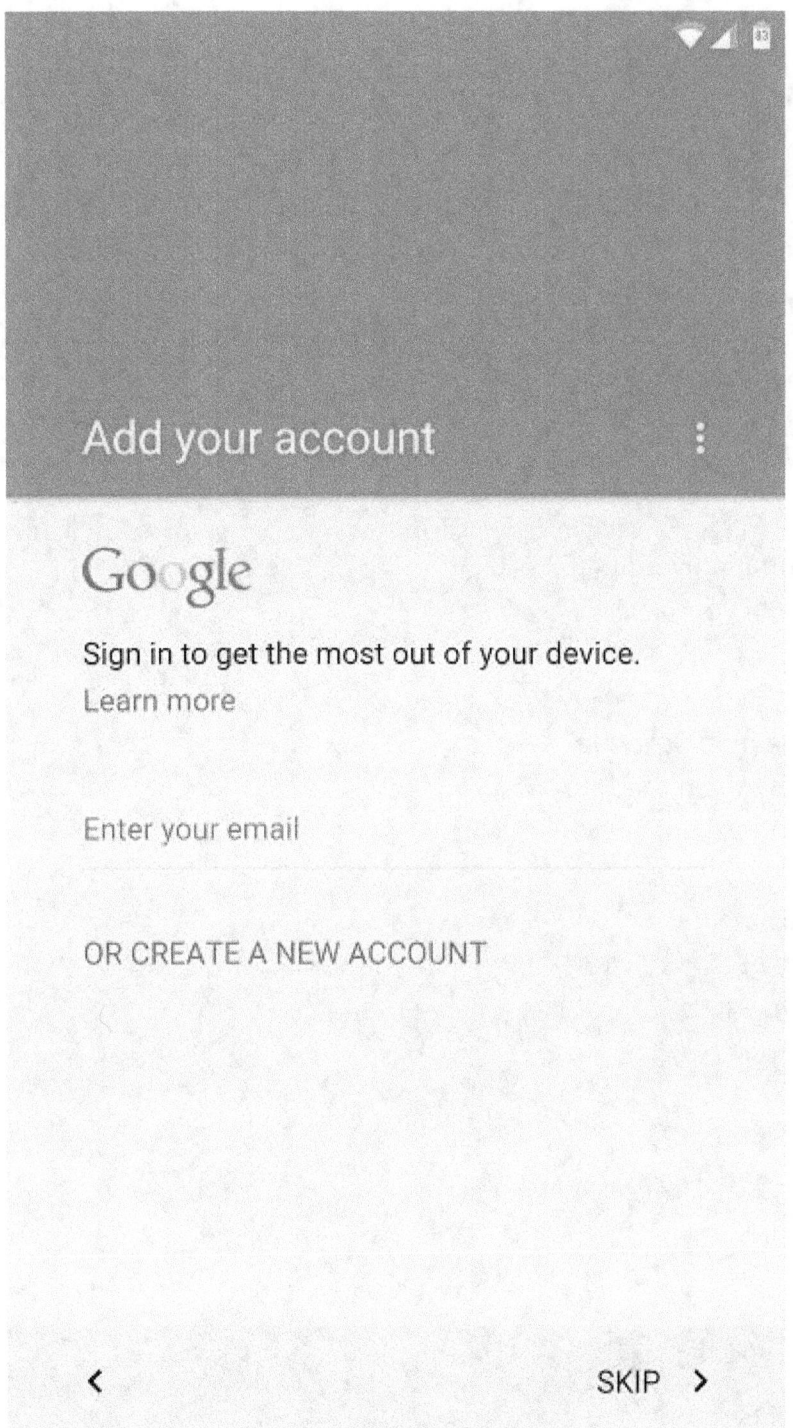

Figure 3: Google Account Screen

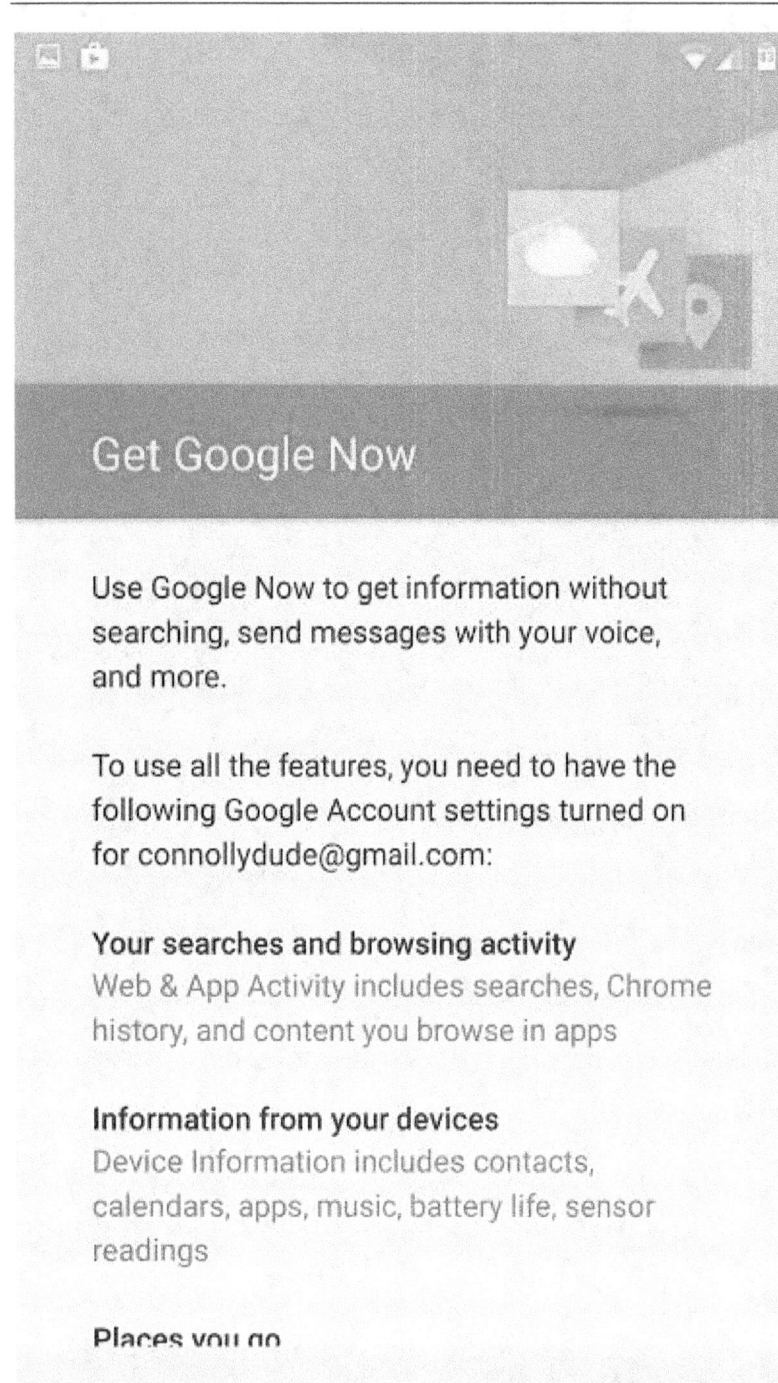

Figure 4: Google Now Screen

2. Deleting a User Profile

If a particular user no longer needs to use the device, you may delete their profile. To delete a user profile:

Warning: Deleting a user profile permanently erases all of the user's settings and files that have not been uploaded to the Cloud.

1. Touch the icon on the Home screen, and then touch the icon. The Settings screen appears.
2. Touch **Users**. The Users Settings screen appears.
3. Touch the icon next to a user's name. The User Information screen appears, as shown in **Figure 5**.
4. Touch **Remove user**. A confirmation dialog appears.
5. Touch **DELETE**. The user profile is deleted.

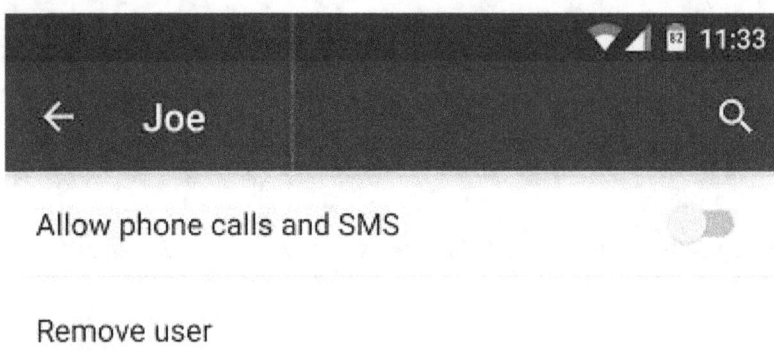

Allow phone calls and SMS

Remove user

Figure 5: User Information Screen

3. Switching Users

You can switch between users at any time. To switch to a different user:

1. Touch the top of the screen when the device is locked or unlocked, and slide your finger down. The Notifications screen appears. If the device is unlocked, you will need to slide your finger down twice.

2. Touch the icon. A list of available users appears, as shown in **Figure 6**.

3. Touch the name of the user. The device switches to the selected user. Repeat steps 1-3 to switch back to the first user.

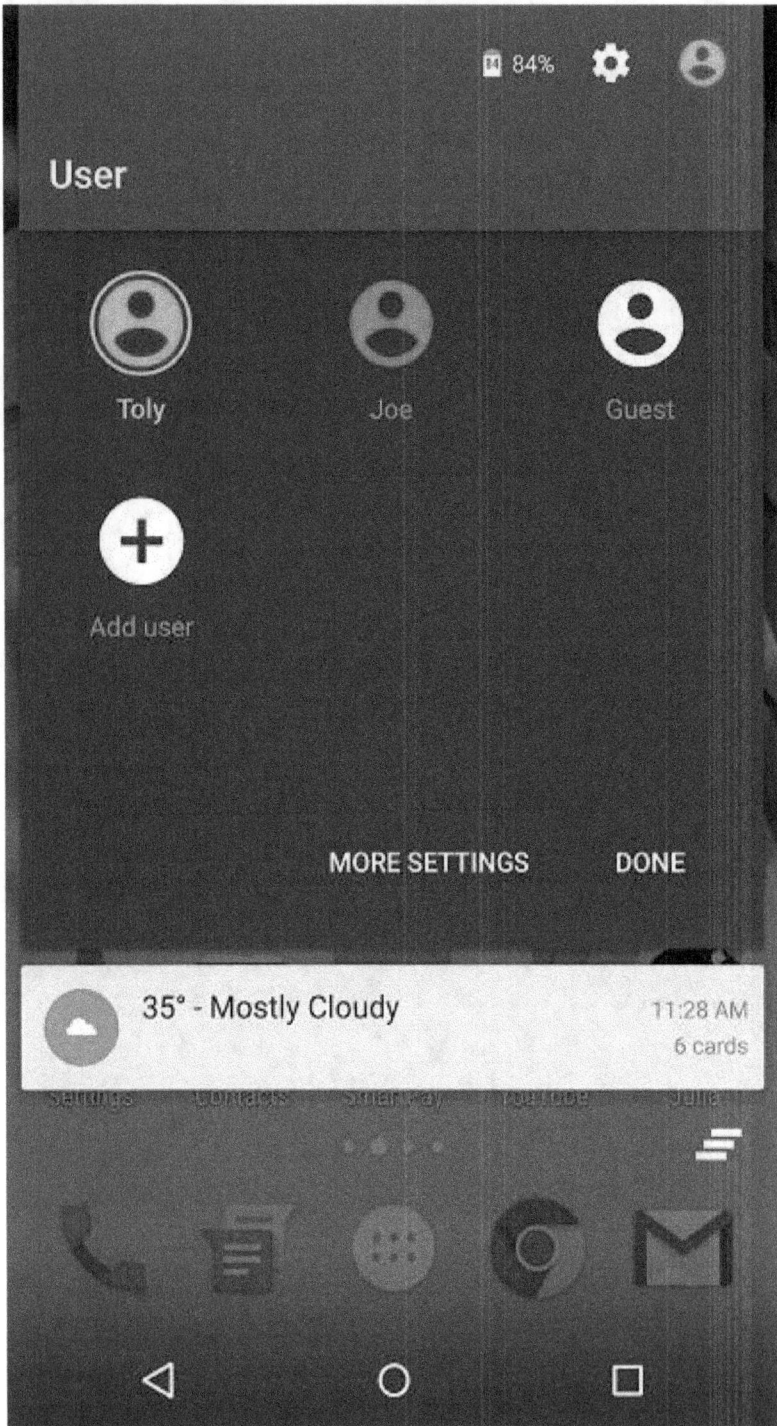

Figure 6: List of Available Users

4. Using the Device as a Guest

If you do not want to create a separate user account, you can have someone use the device as a guest. A guest receives a clean slate, as if he or she just started using the device. They do not have access to the main user's applications, contacts, or any other personal data. In addition, a guest's progress is saved, and the option to continue from where the guest last left off is given when logging back in as a guest. To use the device as a guest:

1. Touch the top of the screen when the device is locked or unlocked, and slide your finger down. The Notifications screen appears. If the device is unlocked, you will need to slide your finger down twice.

2. Touch the icon. A list of available users appears.
3. Touch **Guest**. The Guest account is ready to use.
4. If you have used the Guest account on the device in the past, a Welcome Back window appears. Touch **YES, CONTINUE** to retain your applications and settings from the last time that you used the account. Otherwise, touch **START OVER**.

5. Using Application Pinning for Children

Lollipop devices let you pin, or lock, a single application, which prevents the user from leaving that application. This is especially useful for allowing your children to use the device without worrying about their surfing the web or checking your email. To use application pinning:

1. Touch the 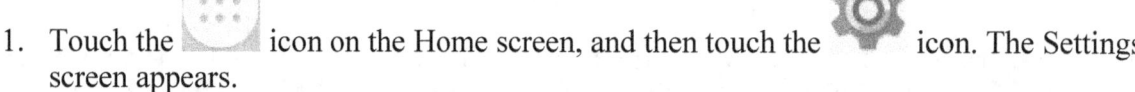 icon on the Home screen, and then touch the icon. The Settings screen appears.
2. Touch **Security**. The Security Settings screen appears, as shown in **Figure 7**.
3. Touch **Screen Pinning**. The Screen Pinning screen appears, as shown in **Figure 8**.
4. Touch **Off**. The feature is turned on.
5. Open the application that you want to pin. Then, touch the key. A list of all recent applications appears, as shown in **Figure 9**.
6. Touch the screen and move your finger up. The icon becomes visible.
7. Touch the icon. A confirmation dialog appears.
8. Touch **START**. The application is pinned. To exit the pinned application, touch and hold the and the keys at the same time.

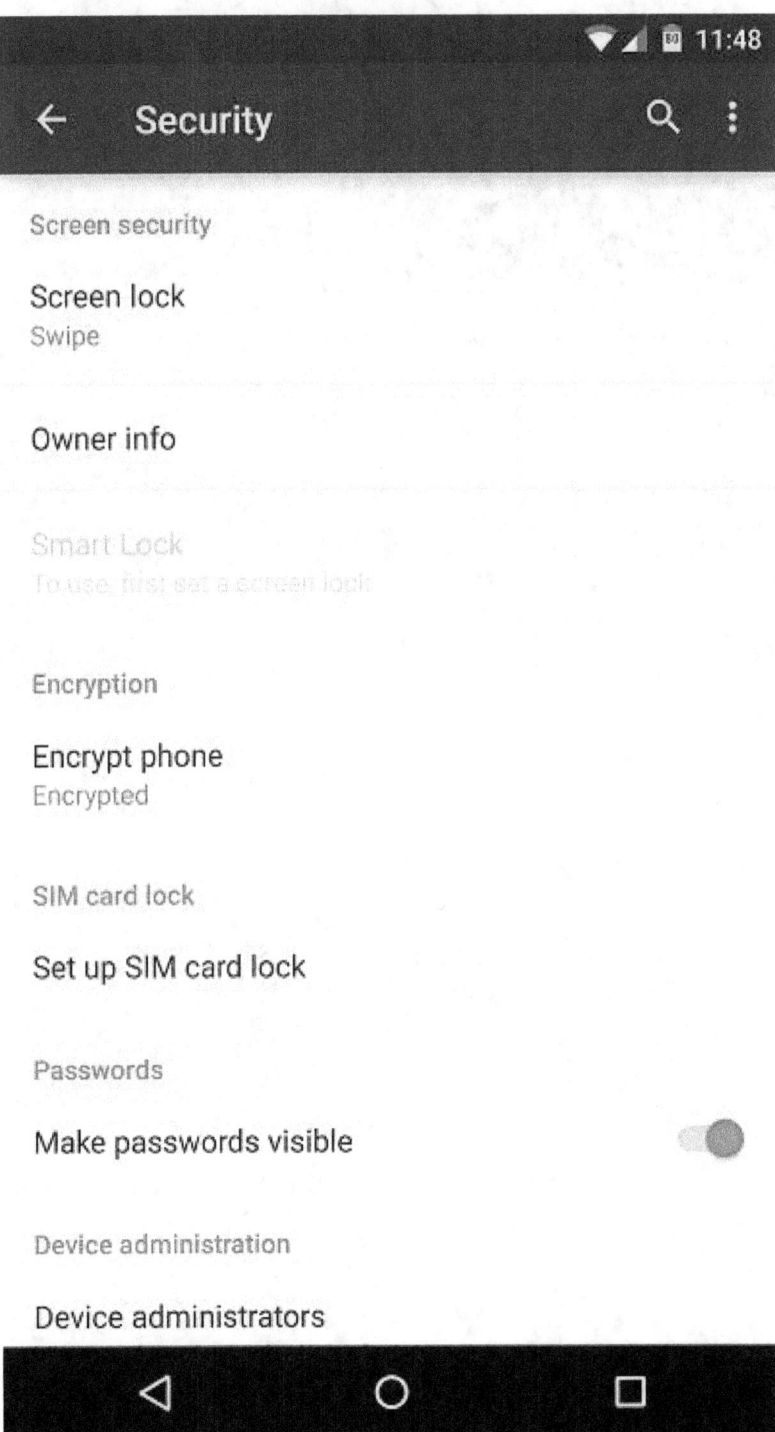

Figure 7: Security Settings

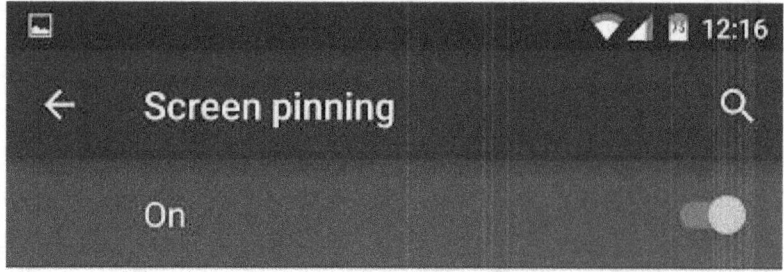

When turned on, you can use
screen pinning to keep the current
screen in view until you unpin.

To use screen pinning:

1. Make sure screen pinning is
turned on.

2. Open the screen you want to pin.

3. Touch Overview.

4. Touch the pin icon.

Figure 8: Screen Pinning Screen

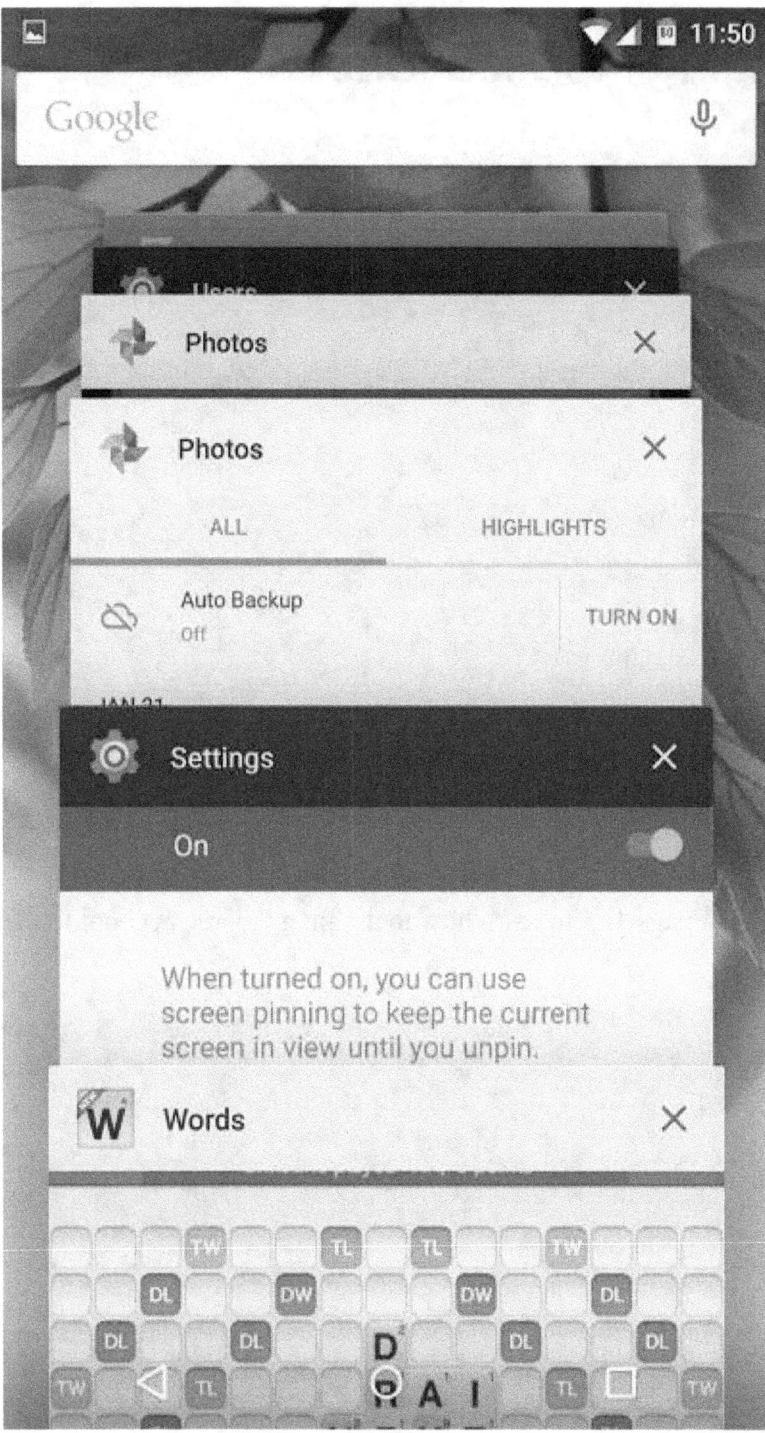

Figure 9: List of Recent Applications

Managing Applications

Table of Contents

1. Setting Up a Google Account

In order to buy applications, you will need to assign a Google account to the device. Refer to *"Setting Up the Gmail Application"* on page 165 to learn how to assign a Google account to the device.

2. Searching for Applications

There are two ways to search for applications; perform a manual search or browse them by category.

Manual Search

To search for an application manually:

1. Touch the ▶ icon on the Home screen, or touch the icon and then touch the ▶ icon. The Play Store opens, as shown in **Figure 1**.

2. Touch the 🔍 icon at the top of the screen. The Search field and the keyboard appear.

3. Enter the name of an application and touch the key. All matching results appear, as shown in **Figure 2.**
4. Touch **Apps** in the upper left-hand corner of the screen, as outlined in **Figure 1**. The Application results appear.
5. Touch the name of an application. A description of the application appears. Refer to *"Purchasing Applications"* on page 105 to learn how to buy the selected application.

Browse by Category
View applications by genre, such as games, travel, or productivity. To browse applications by category:

1. Touch the icon on the Home screen, or touch the icon and then touch the icon. The Play Store opens.
2. Touch **Apps** on the left-hand side of the screen, as outlined in **Figure 1**. The Featured Applications screen appears, as shown in **Figure 3**.
3. Touch the screen and move your finger to the right. A list of application categories appears, as shown in **Figure 4**.
4. Touch a category. The top applications in the selected category appear, as shown in **Figure 5**.
5. Touch the name of an application. A description of the application appears. Refer to *"Purchasing Applications"* on page 105 to learn how to buy the selected application.

Note: Some applications, such as games, may have sub-categories (i.e. racing, puzzle, arcade). For these cases, repeat steps 3 and 4 to browse the sub-categories.

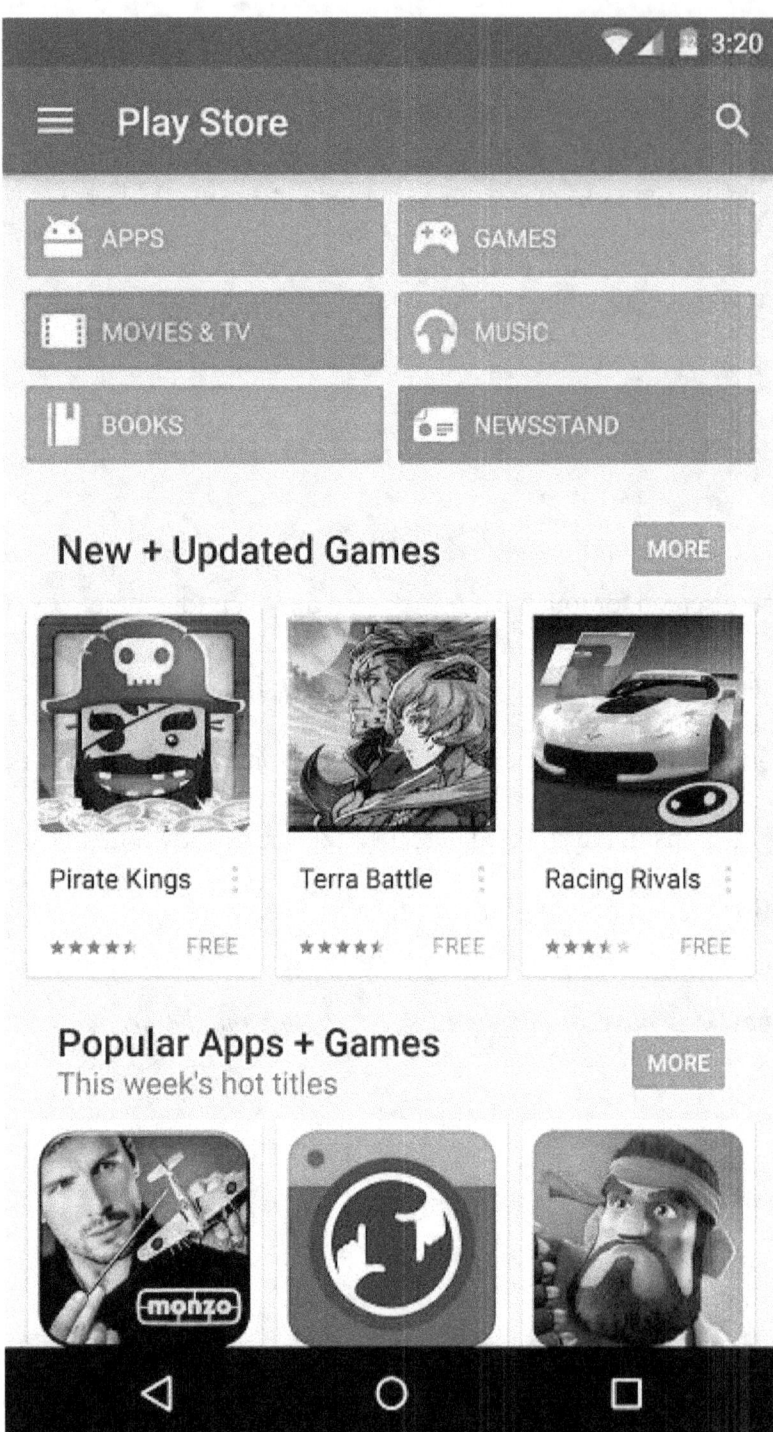

Figure 1: Play Store

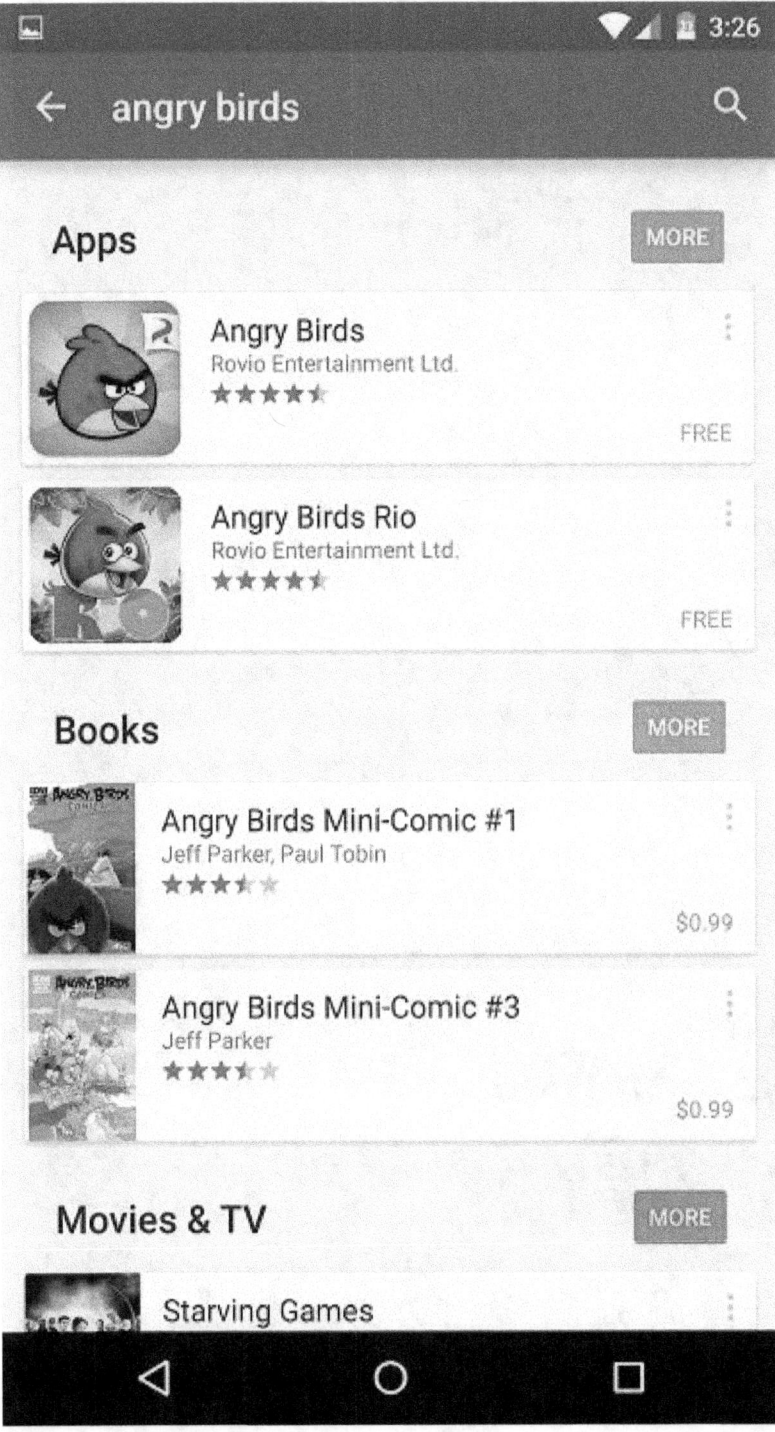

Figure 2: Market Search Results

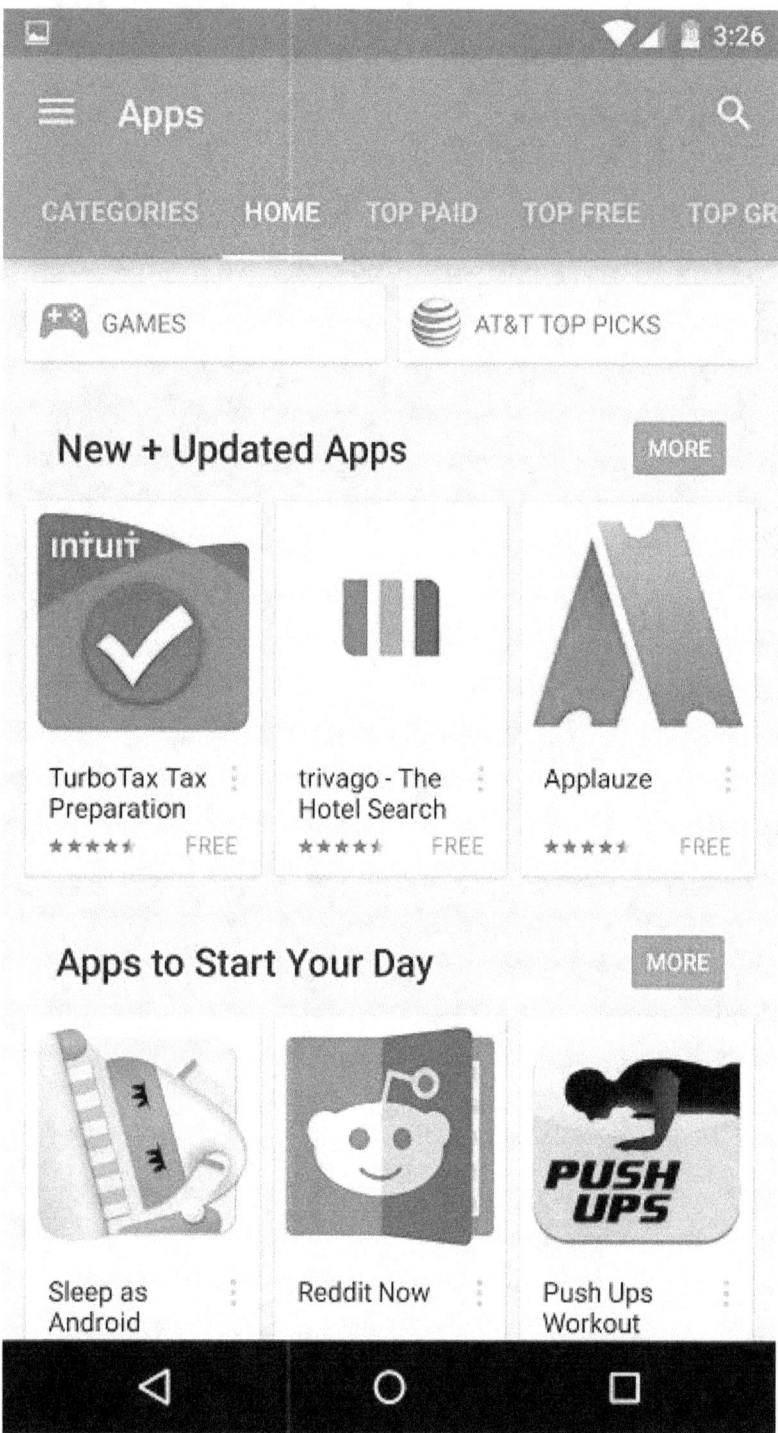

Figure 3: Featured Applications Screen

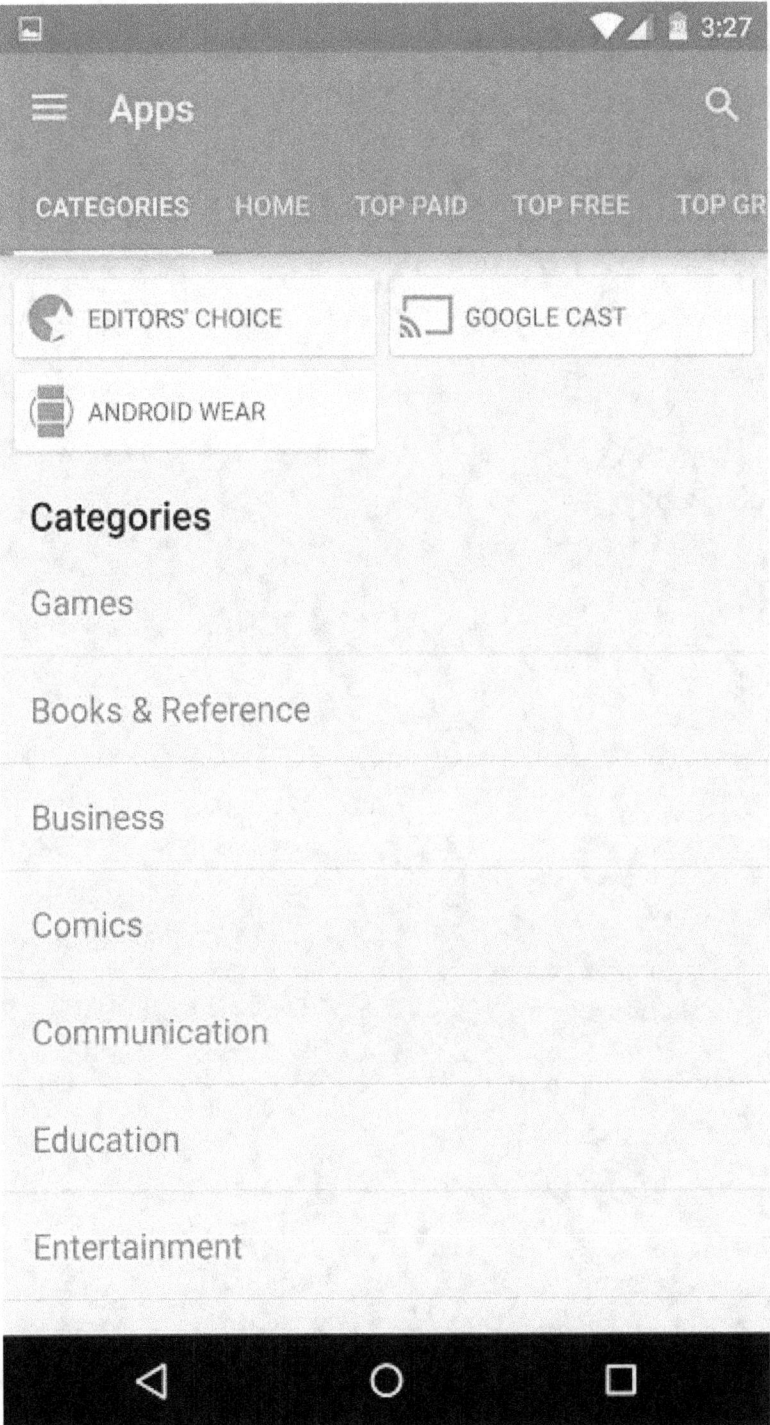

Figure 4: List of Application Categories

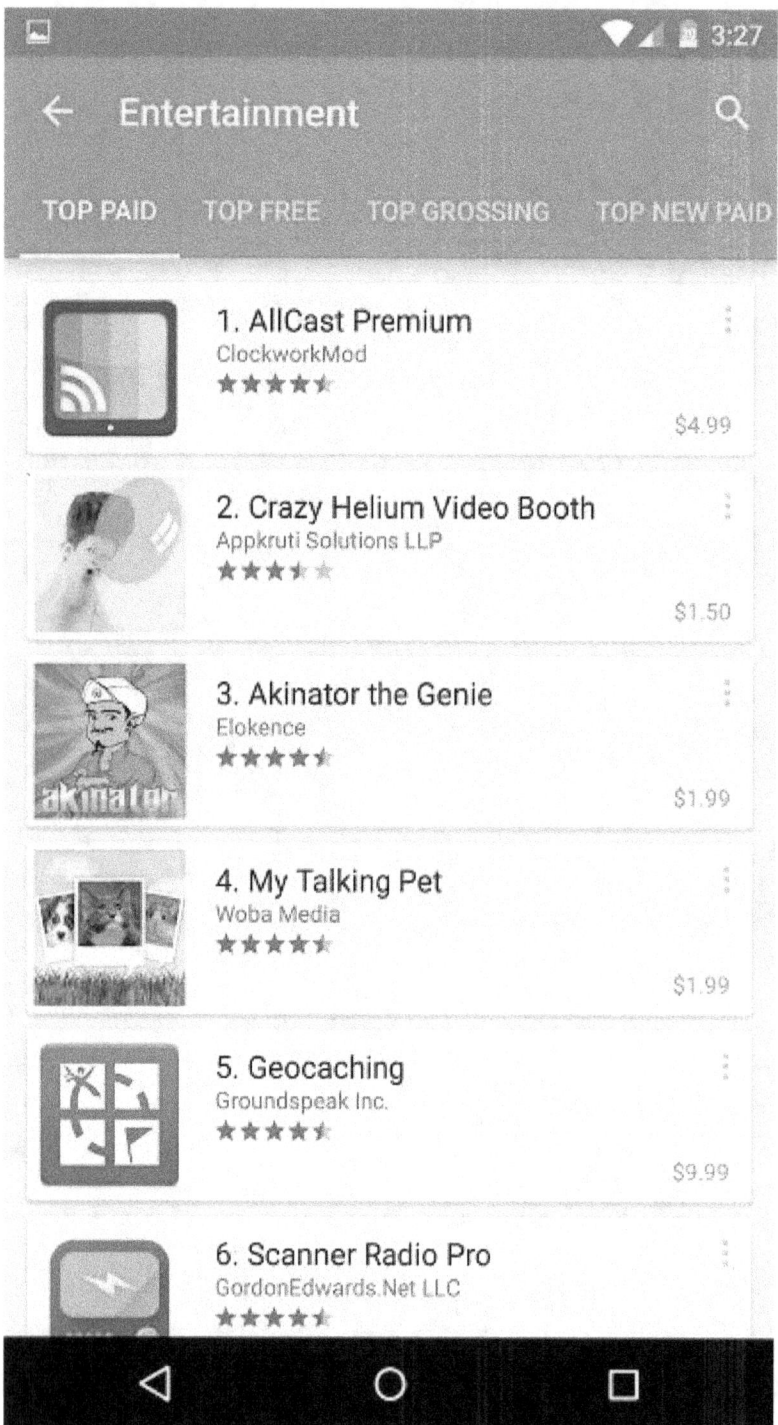

Figure 5: List of Top Applications in a Category

3. Purchasing Applications

Applications can be purchased directly from the device using the Play Store. To buy an application:

1. Touch the ▶ icon on the Home screen, or touch the ⊞ icon and then touch the ▶ icon. The Play Store opens.
2. Find the application that you wish to purchase. Refer to *"Searching for Applications"* on page 98 to learn how.
3. Touch the name of an application. The Application Description screen appears, as shown in **Figure 6** (free application) and **Figure 7** (paid application).
4. Follow the appropriate instructions below to download the application:

Installing Free Applications

1. Touch the ░INSTALL░ button. A warning appears regarding the application's access to various parts of the device, called the Permissions window, as shown in **Figure 8**.
2. Touch the ░ACCEPT░ button. The application is downloaded and installed. The download progress is shown on the Application Description screen while the application is downloading.
3. Touch **Open**. The application opens. Refer to *"Types of Home screen Objects"* on page 17 and *"Organizing Home screen Objects"* on page 19 to learn more about accessing applications.

Installing Paid Applications

1. Touch the price of the application. The Permissions window appears, as shown in **Figure 8**. Touch the ░ACCEPT░ button.
2. Enter your credit card information, which Google Checkout requests the first time that you purchase an application. The information is saved and the Purchase Confirmation screen appears. On all subsequent purchases, the Purchase screen appears, as shown in **Figure 9**.
3. Touch **Buy**. If this is the first time that you are purchasing an application, the Password Confirmation dialog appears.
4. Enter your password and touch **OK**. The application is purchased, downloaded, and installed. The download progress is shown on the Application Description screen while the application is downloading.
5. Touch **Open**. The application opens. Refer to *"Types of Home screen Objects"* on page 17 and *"Organizing Home screen Objects"* on page 19 to learn more about accessing applications.

Figure 6: Application Description Screen (Free Application)

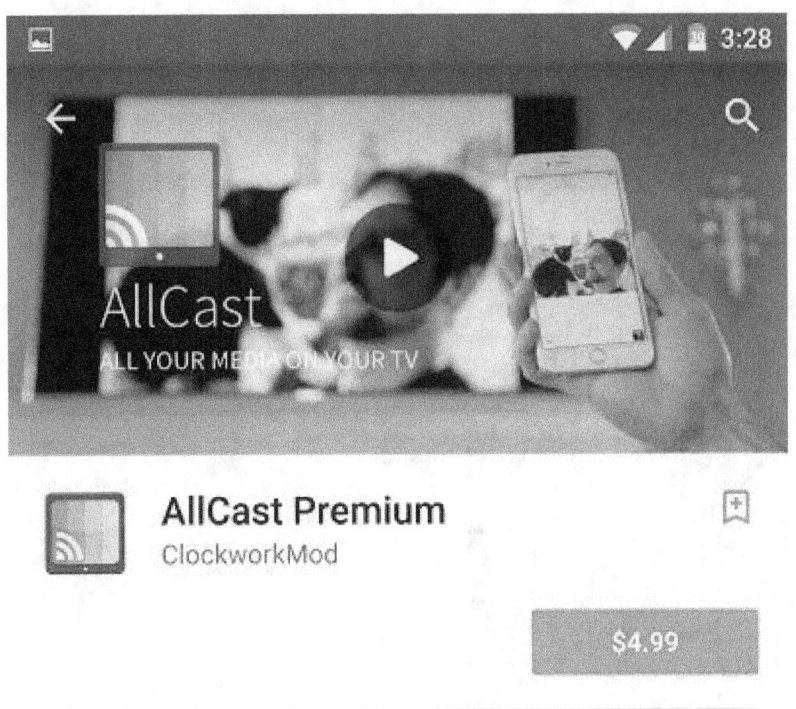

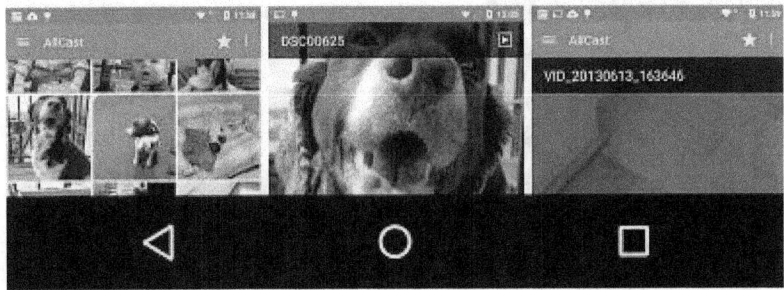

Figure 7: Application Description Screen (Paid Application)

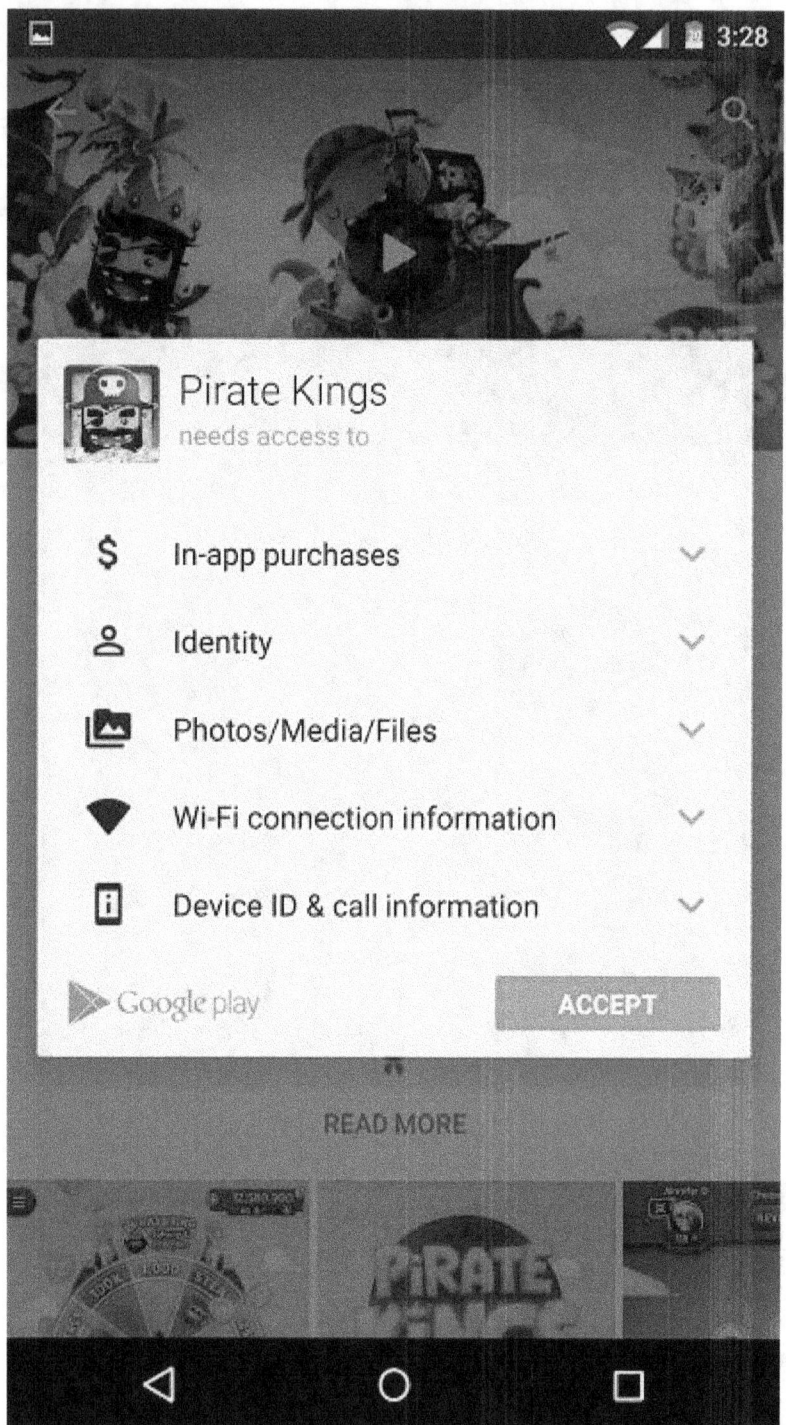

Figure 8: Permissions Window

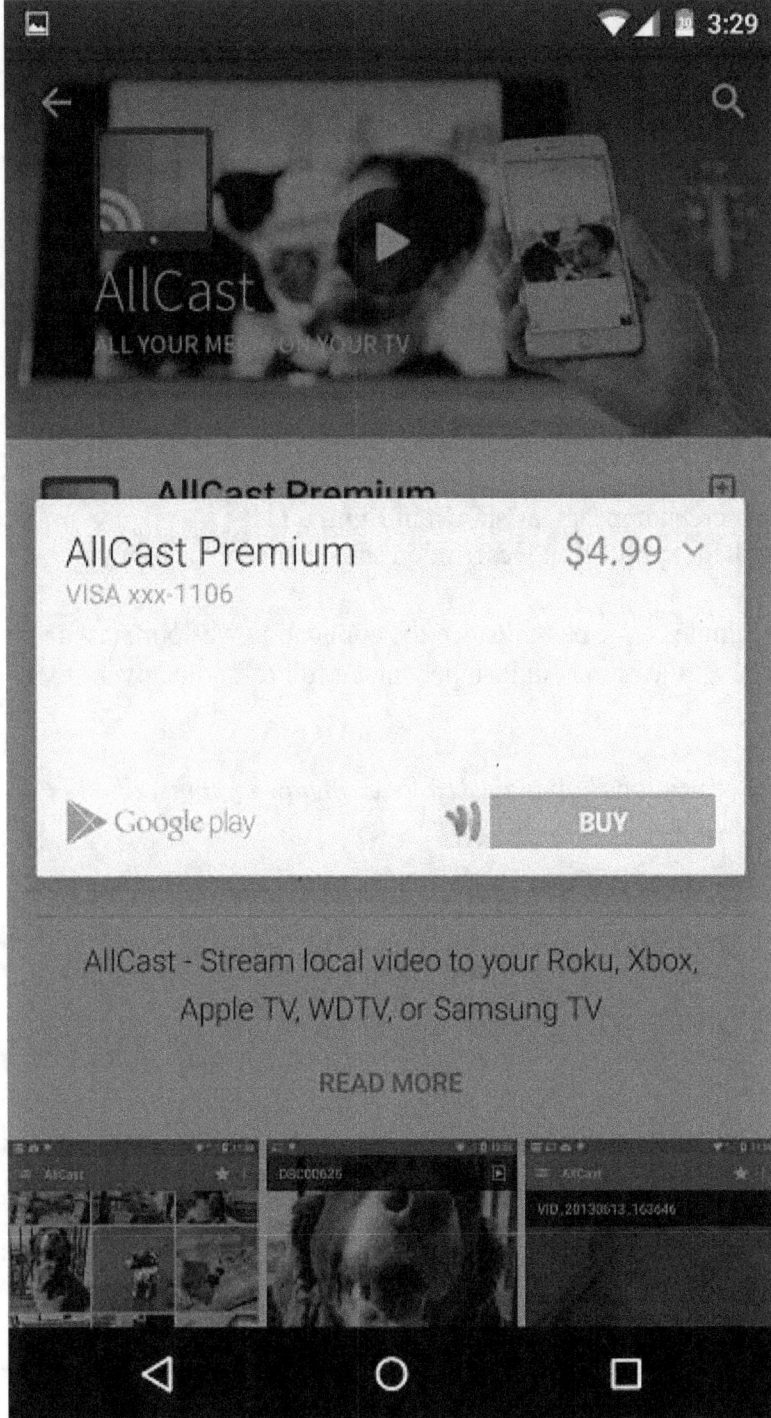

Figure 9: Purchase Screen

4. Uninstalling an Application

Within the first 15 minutes of purchasing an application, it can be uninstalled for a full refund. After 15 minutes have passed, the following instructions only apply to uninstalling an application with no refund. An application that you have purchased can always be re-downloaded for free, unless you touch **Refund**, in which case you need to purchase the application again. To uninstall an application:

1. Touch the icon on the Home screen, or touch the icon and then touch the icon. The Play Store opens.
2. Touch the left-hand side of the screen, and slide your finger to the right. The Play Store menu appears, as shown in **Figure 10**.
3. Touch **My apps**. The My Apps screen appears, as shown in **Figure 11**.
4. Touch an application. The Installed Application Description screen appears, as shown in **Figure 12**.
5. Touch **Refund** if less than 15 minutes have passed since the application was purchased. Otherwise, touch **Uninstall**. The application is uninstalled, and a full refund is given if you touched Refund.

Note: Refer to "Quickly Uninstalling Applications" *on page 313 to learn how to uninstall an application without opening the Play Store.*

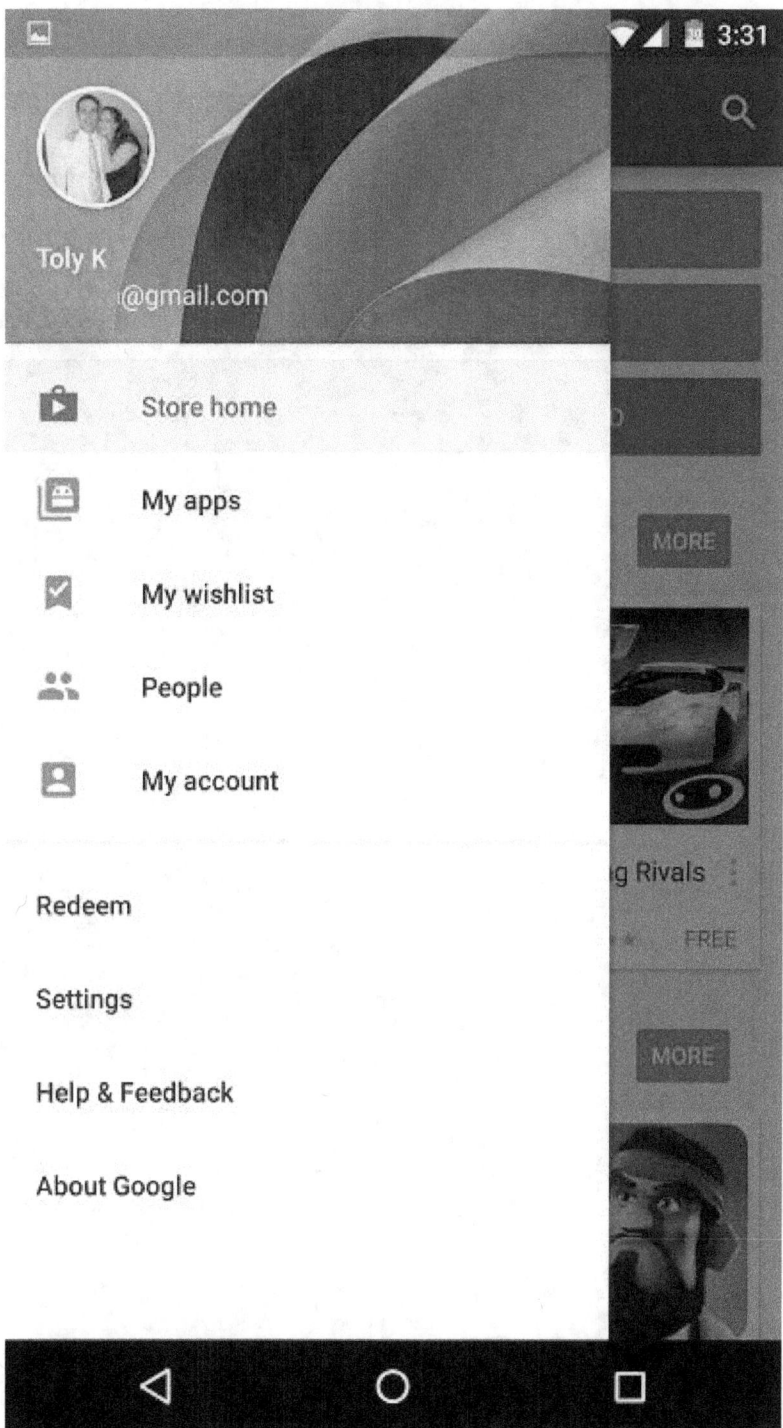

Figure 10: Play Store Menu

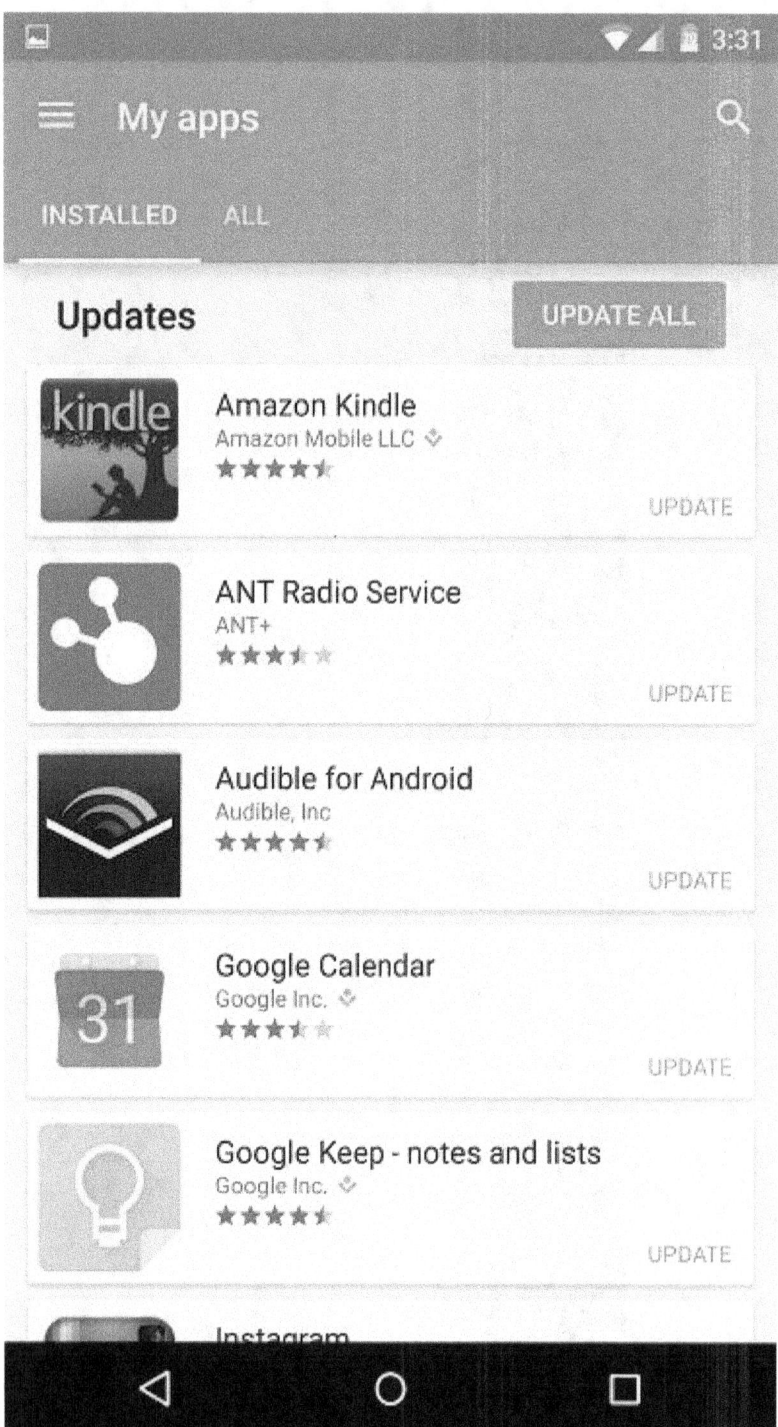

Figure 11: My Apps Screen

Figure 12: Installed Application Description Screen

5. Sharing an Application via Email

The device allows you to share applications with friends via email. When sharing an application, a link to the application's page in the Play Store is sent. Those with whom links are shared will still need to pay for the shared applications that they purchase. To share an application via email:

1. Touch the ▶ icon on the Home screen, or touch the ⦙⦙⦙ icon and then touch the ▶ icon. The Play Store opens.
2. Find the application that you wish to share. If you already own the application that you wish to share, touch the left side of the screen in the Play Store, and then touch **My apps** to browse your installed applications. Otherwise, refer to *"Searching for Applications"* on page 98 to learn how to find an application for sale in the Play Store.
3. Touch the name of an application. The Application Description screen appears.
4. Scroll down and touch the ◁ icon. A list of sharing options appears.
5. Touch the M icon in the list of sharing options. A new email is composed with a link to the shared application pasted into the message, as shown in **Figure 13**.
6. Enter the recipient's email address. The email address is entered.
7. Touch the ▷ button. The email is sent, sharing the application with the selected recipient.

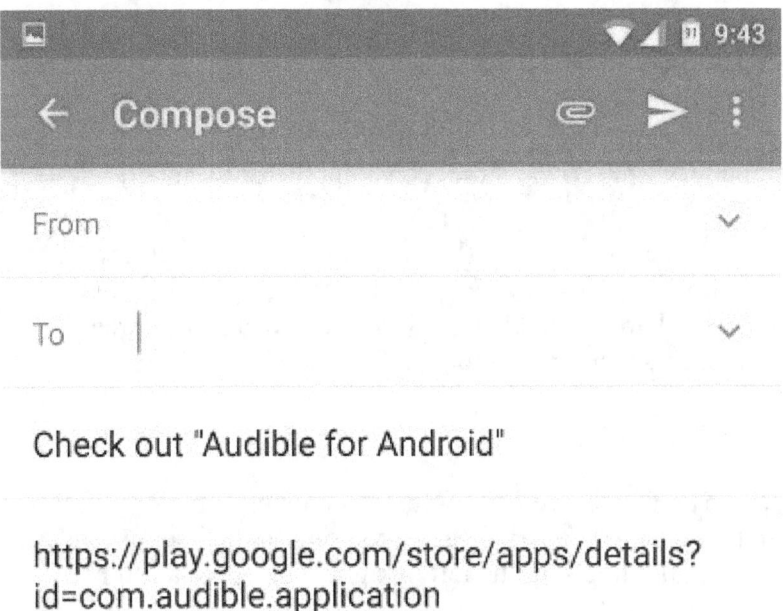

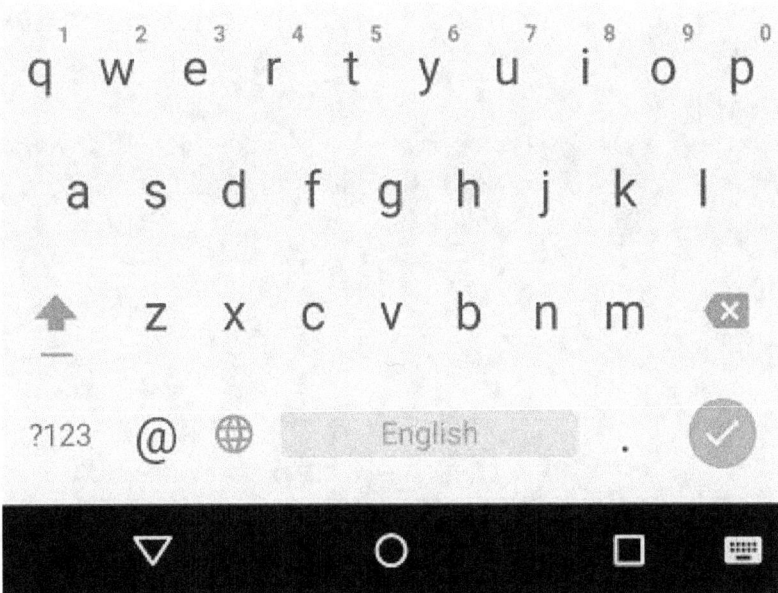

Figure 13: New Email with a Link to the Shared Application

6. Viewing Recently Opened Applications

Most applications will keep running in the background even after they are exited, and some require a considerable amount of memory and battery life. To view the recent applications, touch

the ■ key at any time. The Overview screen appears, as shown in **Figure 14**. Overview creates multiple cards for a single application, if necessary. For example, when you compose a new email, both your inbox and the new email appear in Overview, and you can switch freely between the two. When using a Web browser, separate tabs appears in separate windows in Overview.

Closing Open Applications
To speed up the performance of the device and conserve battery life, try closing some or all of these applications while they are not in use. To close an application running in the background, touch and hold an application in Overview, and drag it to the left or right. The application is closed.

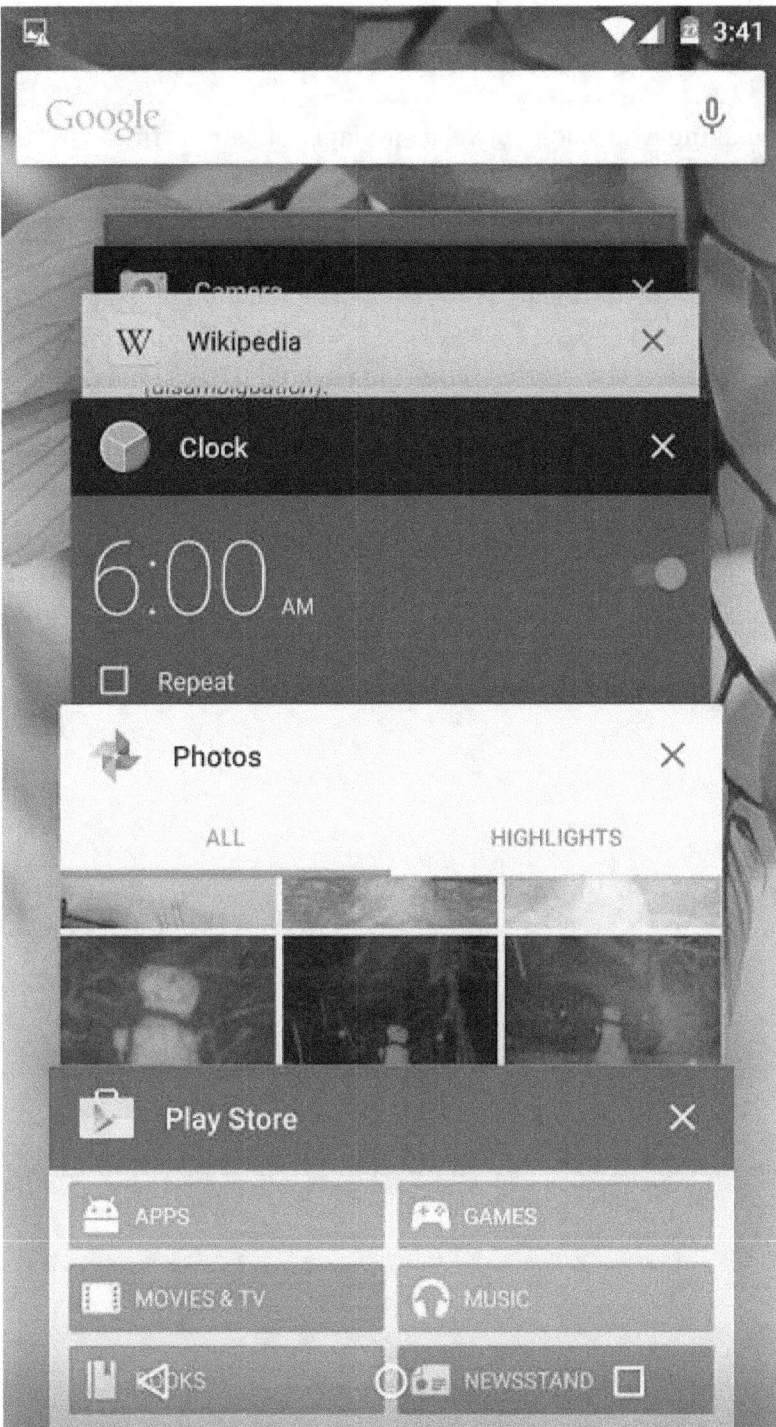

Figure 14: Open Applications Screen

7. Reading User Reviews

Reading user reviews may help when making a decision between similar applications from different developers. To read user reviews for an application:

1. Touch the ▶ icon on the Home screen, or touch the ⦂⦂⦂ icon and then touch the ▶ icon. The Play Store opens.
2. Find an application. Refer to *"Searching for Applications"* on page 98 to learn how.
3. Touch the name of the application. The Application Description screen appears.
4. Touch the screen and move your finger up to scroll to the bottom of the page. The reviews for the current application are found below the application screenshots, as shown in **Figure 15**.

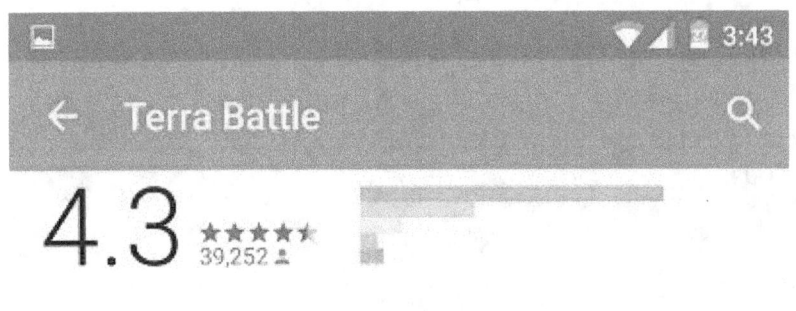

Aaron Bates
★★★★★ 01/26/2015

Fun game

I have been having a blast with this game. Best part is I don't feel like I have to spend money on it to make progress. For 5 free energy enter th

Jeremy Shayne Gagnon
★★★★★ 01/24/2015

It's like,

If final fantasy and chess had a baby together, this would be it. You'll need skills, but no bills. No cash is need to fully enjoy the game. Ent

Uzoma Okeke
★★★☆☆ 01/29/2015
Samsung Galaxy S3

Problem with server times

Have absolutely no idea what is considered daily. Log in at 10p est and apparently it's a new day. Same with 7p. But the events change on

Figure 15: User Reviews

8. Managing Payment Methods

Add a credit card to your Google account to purchase applications or other media from the Play Store. To manage your payment methods:

1. Touch the ▶ icon on the Home screen, or touch the ⊞ icon and then touch the ▶ icon. The Play Store opens.
2. Touch the left-hand side of the screen, and slide your finger to the right. The Play Store menu appears.
3. Touch **My account**. The My Account screen appears, as shown in **Figure 16**.
4. Touch **Add payment method**. The Payment Method Selection menu appears, as shown in **Figure 17**.
5. Touch the type of payment that you want to use. Enter the credit card or other information on the following screens. If using PayPal, you will only need to enter the email address and password associated with your account.

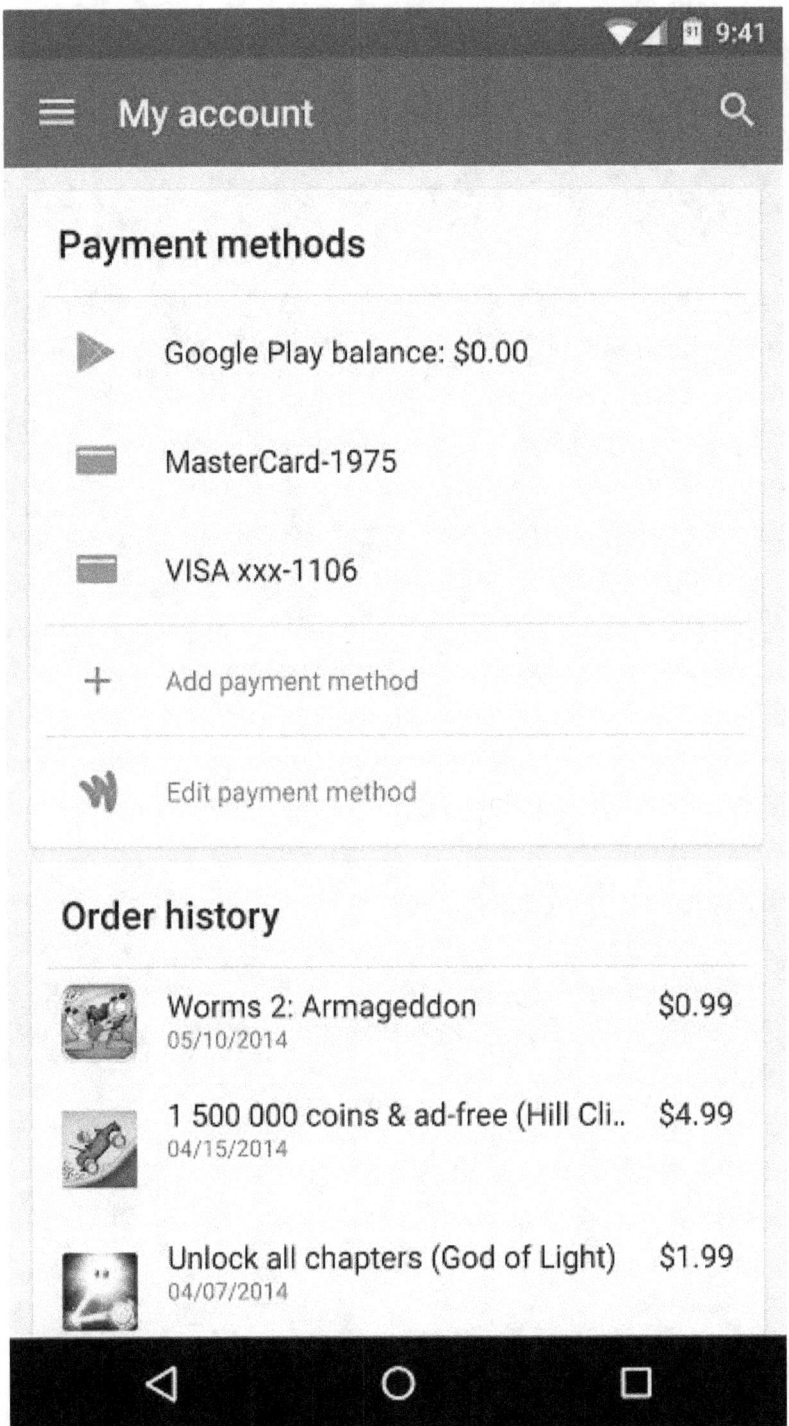

Figure 16: My Account Screen

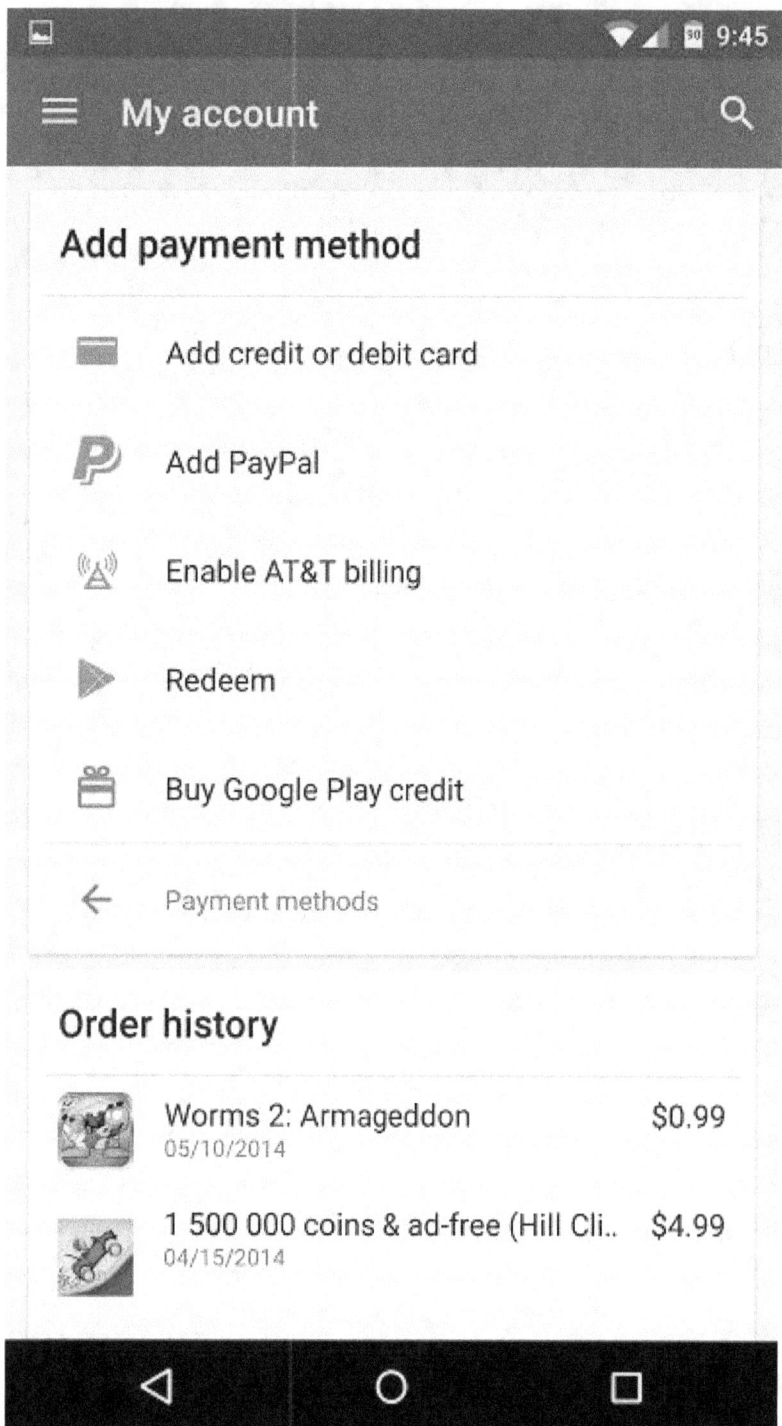

Figure 17: Payment Method Selection Menu

9. Redeeming a Play Store Gift Card

When you receive a Play Store gift card, you must redeem it before using it to purchase media in the Play Store. Redeeming a gift card adds the balance on the card to your Play Store account. When you have used the entire balance, your regular payment method is used to purchase media. To redeem a Play Store gift card:

1. Touch the ▶ icon on the Home screen, or touch the ⋮⋮ icon and then touch the ▶ icon. The Play Store opens.
2. Touch the left-hand side of the screen, and slide your finger to the right. The Play Store menu appears.
3. Touch **Redeem**. The Code Redemption screen appears, as shown in **Figure 18**.
4. Enter the code on your Play Store gift card. You may need to scratch the code field to access it, as indicated on the card.
5. Touch **Redeem**. The gift card is redeemed, and the card balance is added to your Play Store balance.

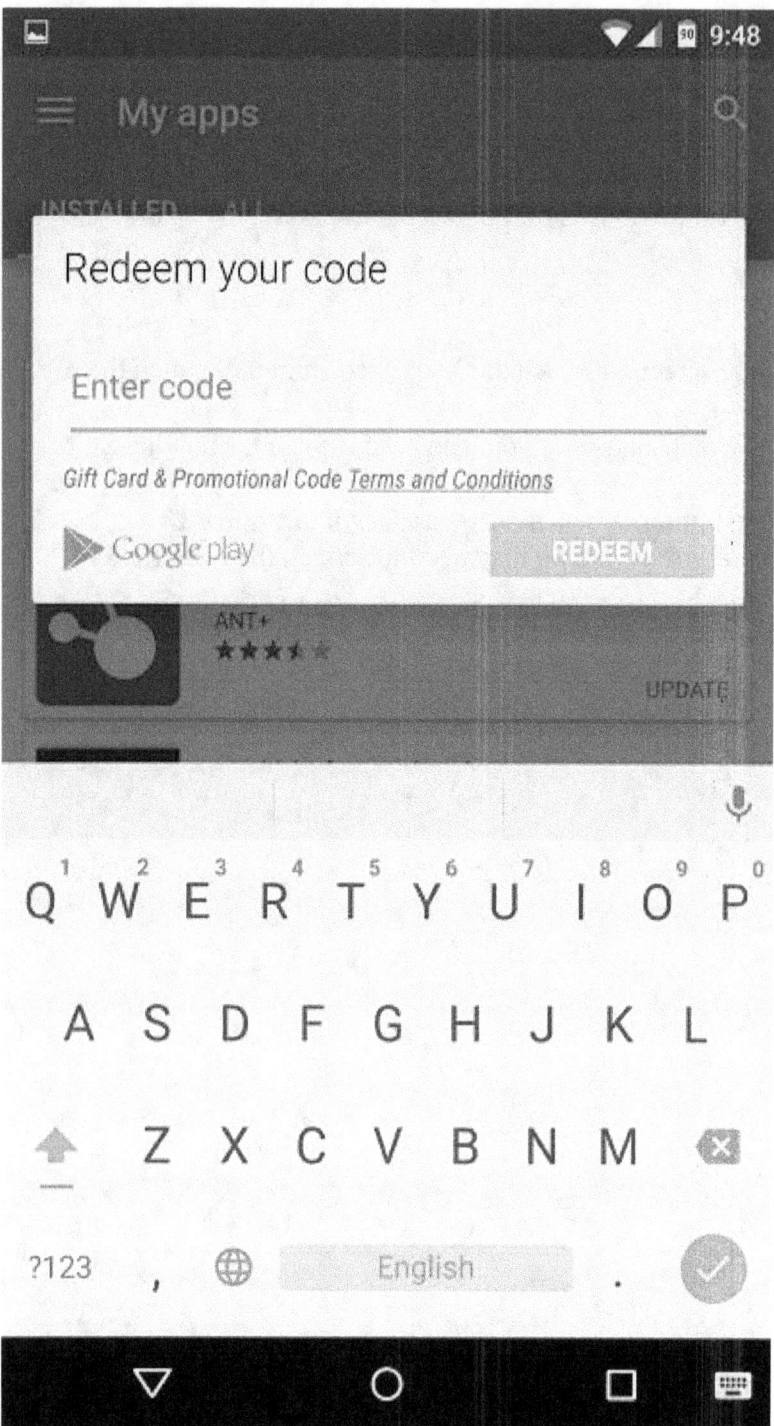

Figure 18: Code Redemption Screen

10. Viewing Your Friends' Favorite Applications

Adding your friends to your Google Plus circles lets you view the applications that they have purchased and reviewed. To view your friends' favorite applications:

1. Touch the ▶ icon on the Home screen, or touch the ⠿ icon and then touch the ▶ icon. The Play Store opens.
2. Touch the left-hand side of the screen, and slide your finger to the right. The Play Store menu appears.
3. Touch **People**. The People screen appears, as shown in **Figure 19**.
4. Touch **More** next to 'From familiar faces' to view a list of applications that are recommended by your friends. You can also add new friends by scrolling down and touching the name of a friend under 'Follow people on Play'.

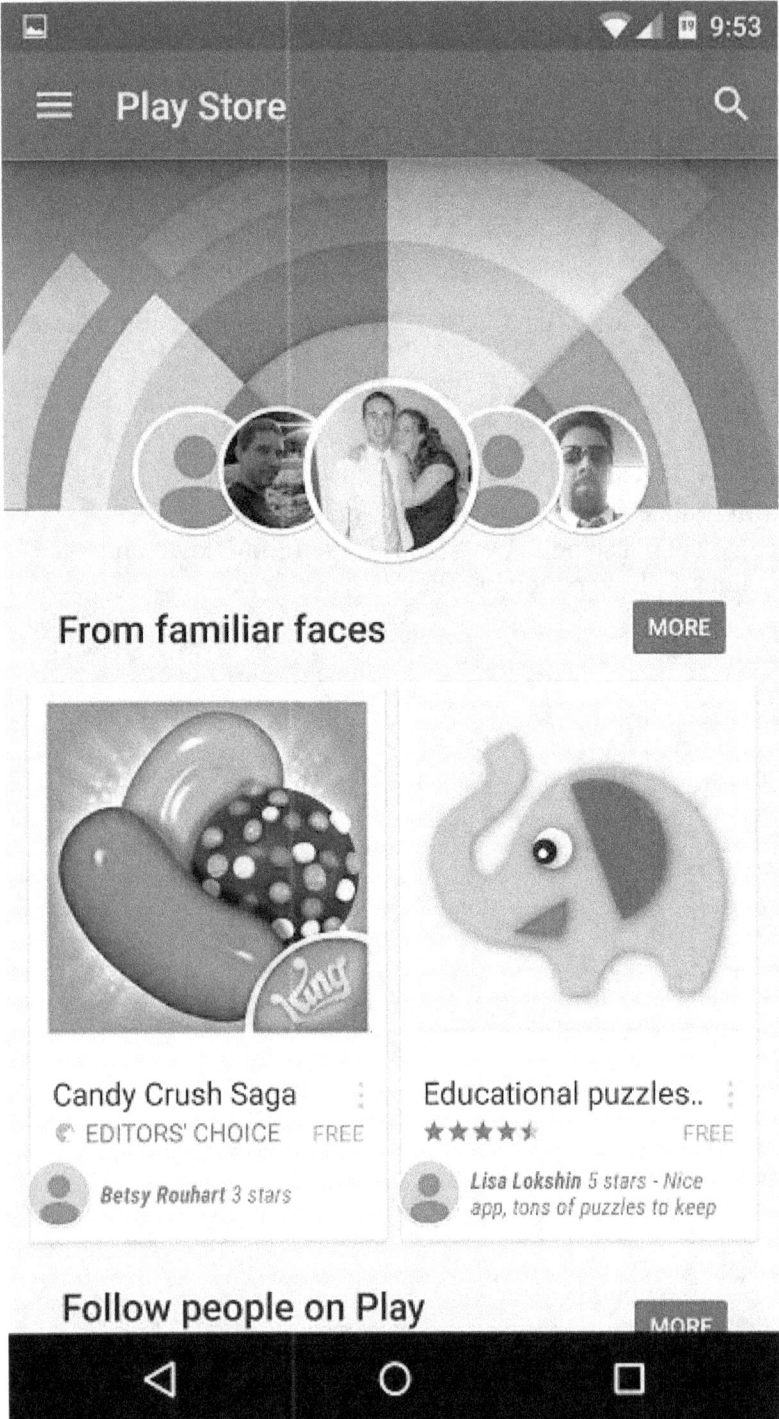

Figure 19: People Screen

Taking Pictures and Capturing Videos

Table of Contents

1. Taking a Picture

Lollipop devices have rear-facing and front-facing cameras of varying quality (depending on the device). To take a picture:

- Touch the icon to turn the camera on. The camera turns on, as shown in **Figure 1**.
- To switch to the front-facing camera, touch the … icon on the screen, located in the lower or upper right-hand corner of the screen, depending on the screen's orientation. The Camera options appear, as shown in **Figure 2**. Touch the icon. The device switches to the front camera. To switch to the rear-facing camera, touch the … icon, and then touch the icon.
- Touch the button to take a picture. A picture is captured and stored in the photo library.

Note: Refer to "Browsing Pictures" *on page 143 to learn how to browse the pictures in your Gallery.*

Figure 1: Camera Turned On

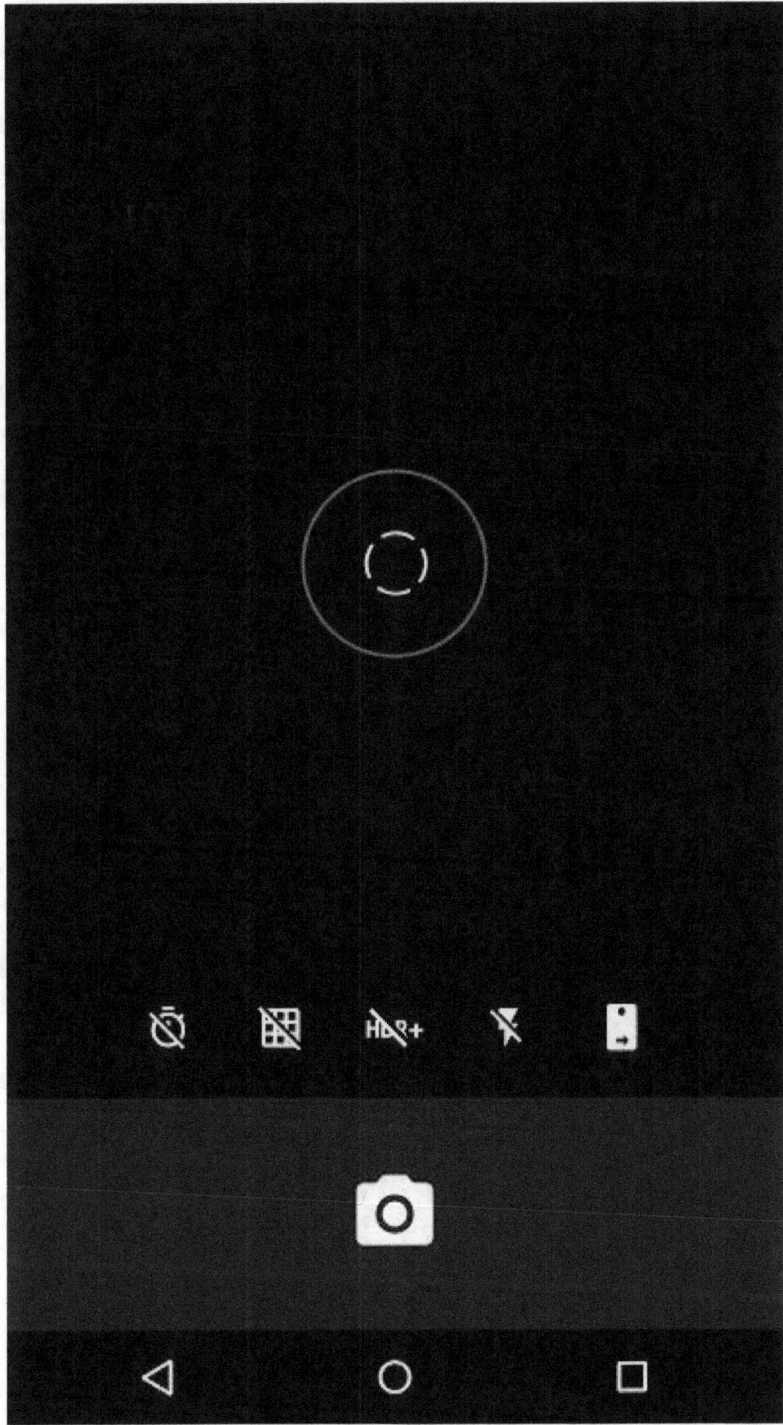

Figure 2: Camera Options

2. Using the Digital Zoom

While taking pictures, use the camera's built-in Digital Zoom feature if the subject of the photo is far away. Digital Zoom can also be used while recording a video. To zoom in, touch the screen with two fingers and move them apart. To zoom out, touch the screen with two fingers spread apart and move them together.

Note: Because of its digital nature, the zoom function will not provide the best resolution, and the image may look fuzzy. It is recommended to be as close as possible to the subject of the photo or video.

3. Turning the Photo Location On or Off

The device can store the location where a photo was captured. However, you may choose to turn this feature off. To turn the photo location feature on or off while the camera is turned on:

1. Touch the left side of the screen, and slide your finger to the right. The Camera Menu appears, as shown in **Figure 3**.
2. Touch the icon. The Camera Settings screen appears, as shown in **Figure 4**.
3. Touch **Save location**. Photo location is turned on.
4. Touch **Save location** again. Photo location is turned off.

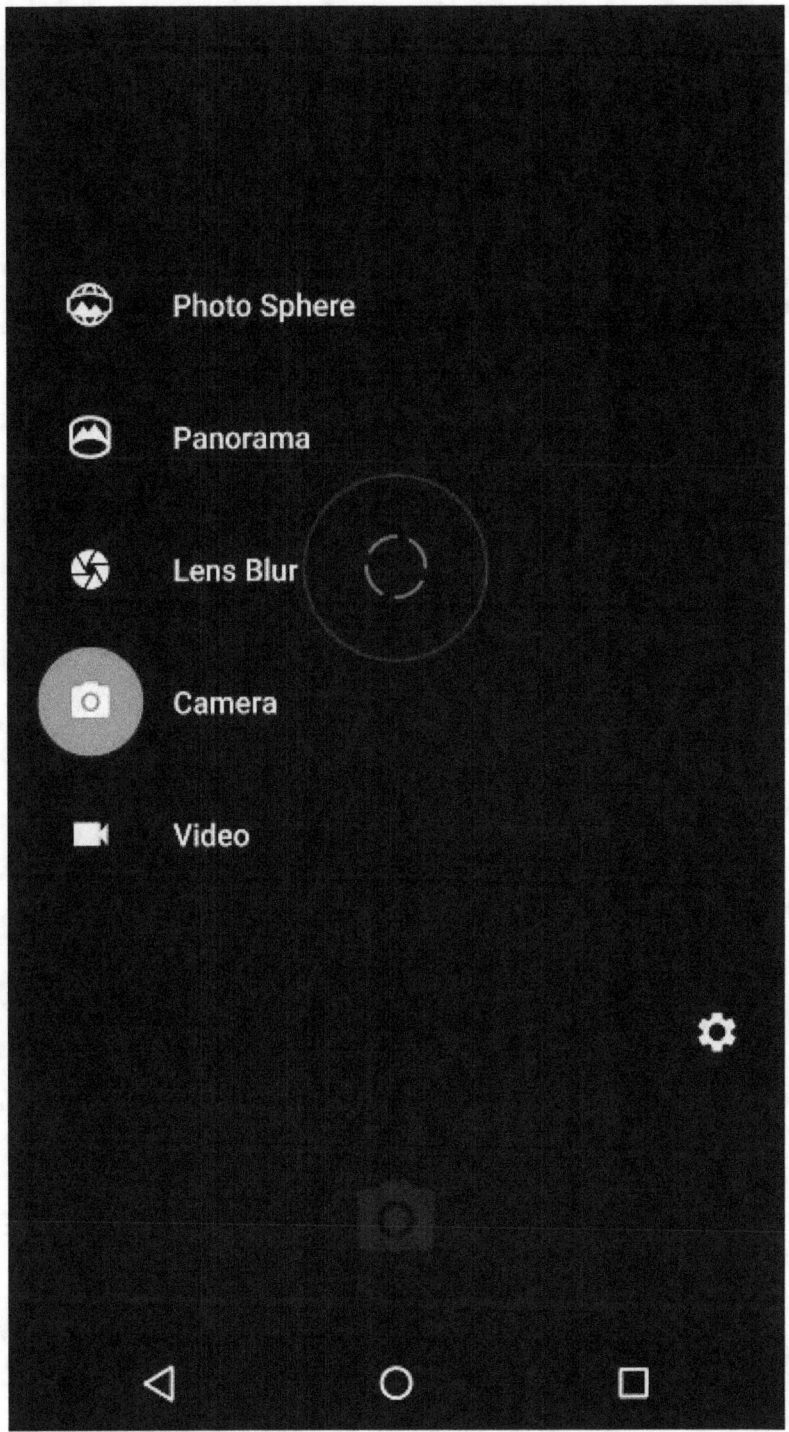

Figure 3: Camera Menu

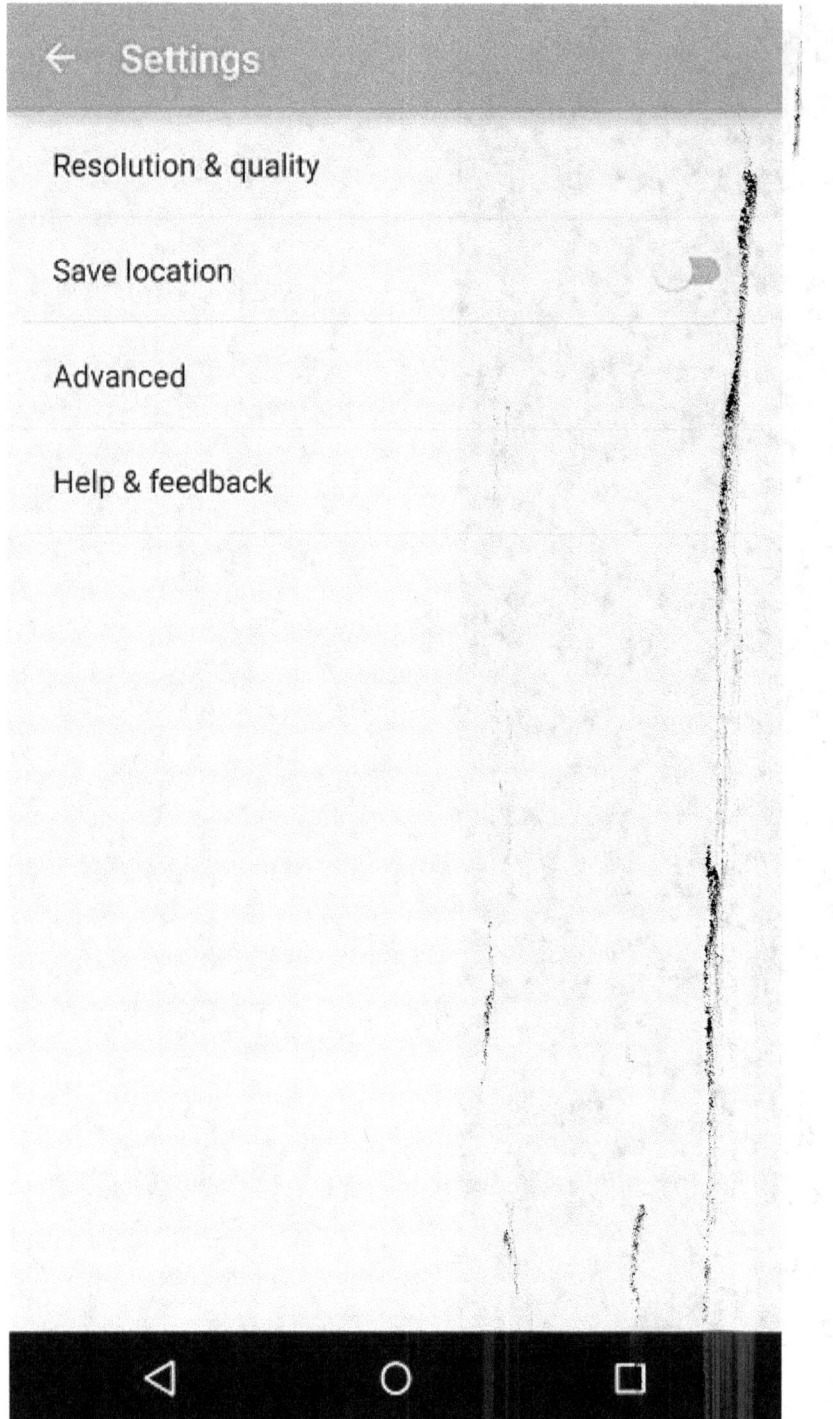

Figure 4: Camera Settings Screen

4. Turning the Countdown Timer On or Off

If you would like to capture a picture of several people, including yourself, you may wish to set a timer. To turn the countdown timer on or off when the camera is turned on:

1. Touch the **...** icon on the screen. The Camera Options appear.

2. Touch the [icon] icon. '3s' appears, which stands for three seconds.
3. Touch **3s** to view the time options. Touch the ten-second option to turn off the timer.

5. Setting the Picture Size

You may set the resolution of a photo or video before you take it. A higher resolution will produce a higher quality photo or video, but will take up more memory. To set the size of a picture:

1. Touch the left side of the screen, and slide your finger to the right. The Camera Menu appears.

2. Touch the [icon] icon. The Camera Settings screen appears.
3. Touch **Resolution & quality**. The Resolution Settings screen appears, as shown in **Figure 5**.
4. Touch one of the following options to set the corresponding resolution:
   - **Back camera photo** - Set the resolution for photos captured using the rear-facing camera
   - **Front camera photo** - Set the resolution for photos captured using the front-facing camera
   - **Back camera video** - Set the resolution for videos captured using the rear-facing camera
   - **Front camera video** - Set the resolution for videos captured using the front-facing camera

5. Touch the [icon] key to return to the camera. The resolution settings are saved until the next time that you change them, or until you reset the device to factory defaults.

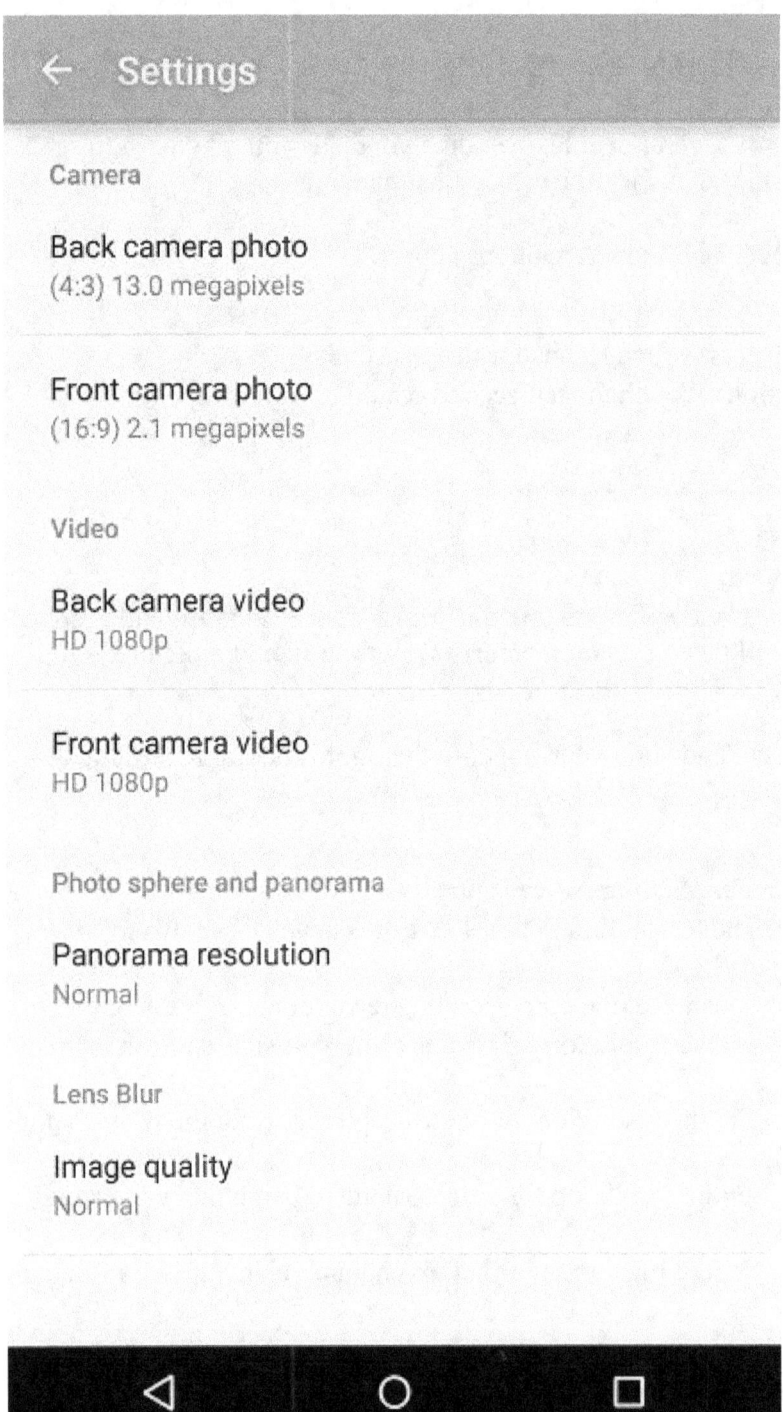

Figure 5: Resolution Settings Screen

6. Adjusting the Exposure

You may adjust the amount of light that is allowed to enter the camera lens, a concept known as the exposure. This will make a picture lighter or darker, depending on the setting. To adjust the exposure:

1. Touch the left side of the screen, and slide your finger to the right. The Camera Menu appears.

2. Touch the [icon] icon. The Camera Settings screen appears.

3. Touch **Advanced**. The Manual Exposure screen appears.

4. Touch **Manual exposure**. The feature is turned on, and you can now adjust the exposure when taking a picture.

5. Touch the [icon] key twice to return to the camera. Then, touch the **...** icon. The Camera options appear.

6. Touch the [icon] icon. The Exposure options appear, as shown in **Figure 6**.

7. Touch one of the options, which range from -2 to +2. The exposure is set.

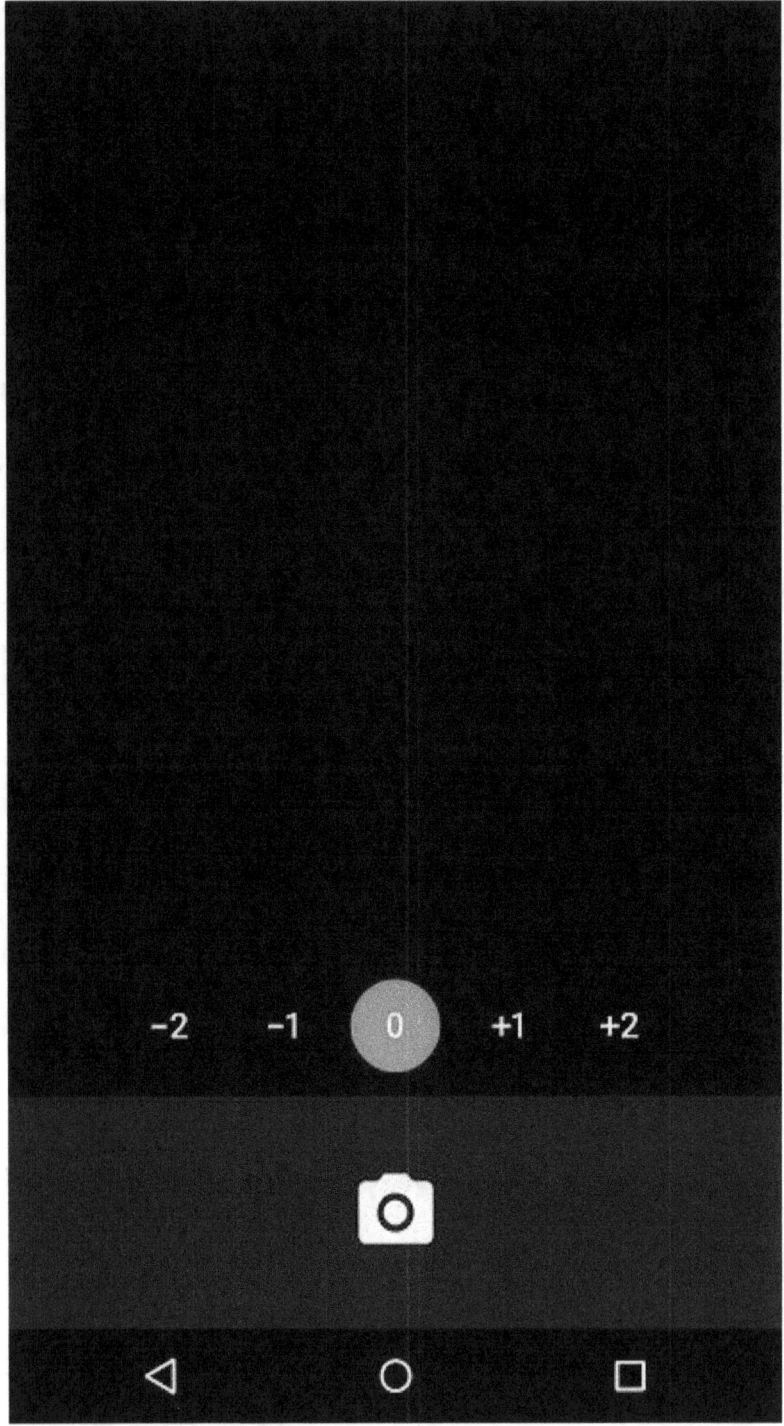

Figure 5: Exposure Options

7. Creating a Spherical Panorama

The camera on the device allows you to take a 360-degree panoramic photo by capturing several images and automatically patching them together. To take a panorama while the camera is turned on:

1. Touch the left side of the screen, and slide your finger to the right. The Camera Menu appears.
2. Touch the ⬛ icon. The Panorama instructions appear on the first time that you use this feature.
3. Touch **Next**, and then touch **OK, GOT IT**. The camera is ready to capture a 360-degree panorama, as shown in **Figure 7**.
4. Align the circle in the middle of the screen with the first frame of your panorama, and touch the ⬛ button at the bottom of the screen. The camera captures the first image. There is no need to touch any buttons.
5. Move the device in any direction and align the circle in the middle of the screen with the next dot. Try to stay in one place and simply rotate with the device. The camera captures another image. Repeat step 4 until you have captured all of the space around you.
6. Touch the check mark at the bottom of the screen. The spherical panorama is rendered and stored in your photo library.

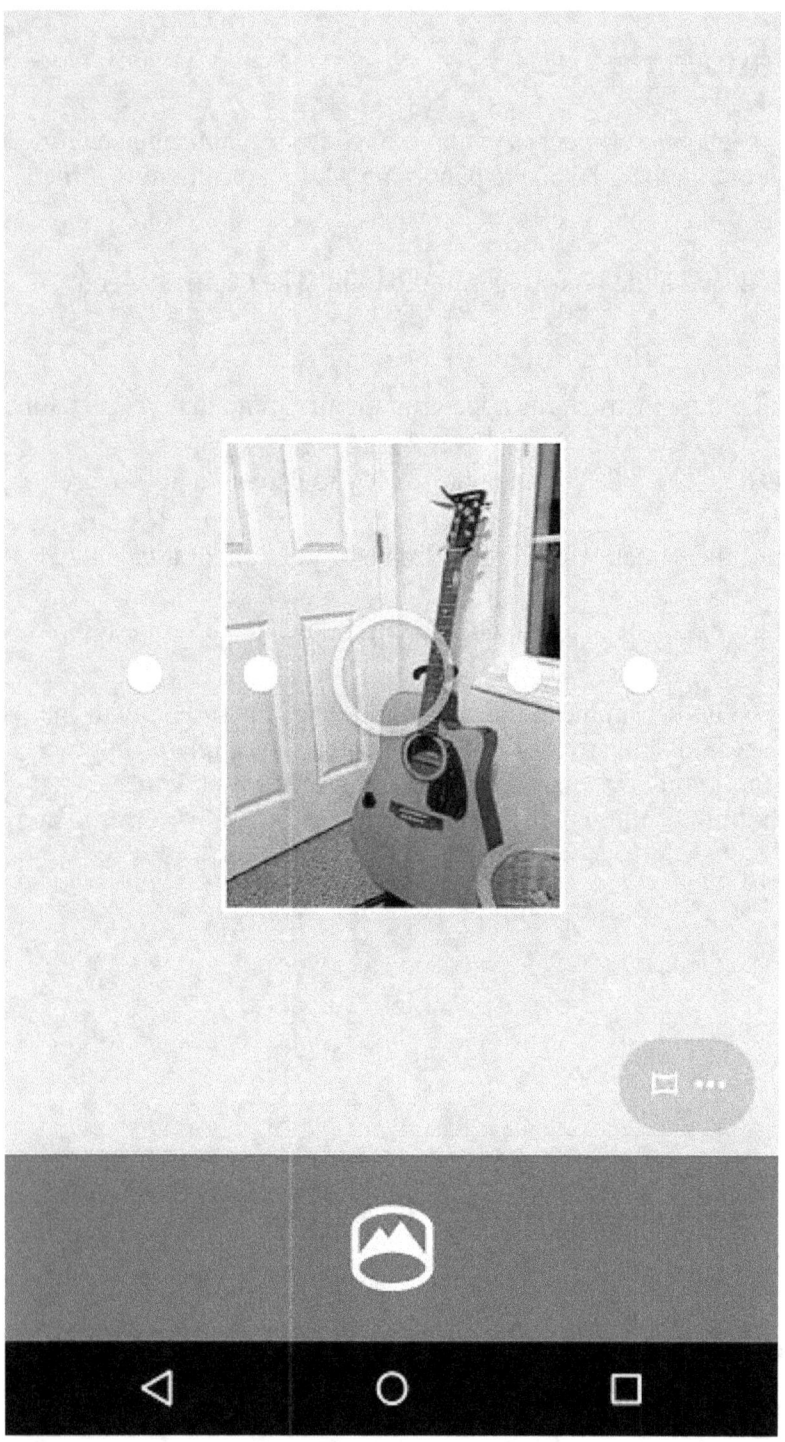

Figure 6: Camera Ready to Capture a 360-Degree Panorama

8. Capturing a Video

The camcorder on the device allows you to capture video. To capture a video:

1. Touch the ⬤ icon. The camera turns on.
2. Touch the left side of the screen, and slide your finger to the right. The Camera Menu appears.
3. Touch the ▭ icon. The camcorder turns on.
4. Touch the ▭ icon at the bottom of the screen. The camcorder begins to record video, as shown in **Figure 8**.
5. Touch the ▪ button. The camcorder stops recording, and the video is stored in photo library.

Figure 7: Camcorder Recording a Video

9. Turning the Flash On or Off (Smartphones Only)

All smartphones that run Android Lollipop have a built-in LED flash, which can be used when taking a picture or capturing a video using the rear-facing camera. To use the flash when taking a picture or capturing a video:

1. Touch the ... icon on the screen. The Camera Options appear. By default, the flash is turned off.

2. Touch the ![icon] icon. The ![icon] icon appears, and the flash is set to Automatic mode. When Automatic mode is turned on, the light sensor on the rear-facing camera determines whether the flash is needed.

3. Touch the ![icon] icon. The ![icon] icon appears, and the flash is turned on. When turned on, the flash goes off every time that a picture is taken or a video is captured.

4. Touch the ![icon] icon. The ![icon] icon appears, and the flash is turned off.

Note: Automatic mode is not available when capturing a video.

Managing Photos and Videos

Table of Contents

1. Browsing Pictures

You can browse captured or saved photos using the Gallery application. To view the images stored on your device:

1. Touch the ![icon] icon on the Home screen, or touch the ![icon] icon and then touch the ![icon] icon. The Gallery opens, as shown in **Figure 1**. By default, the photos are sorted by date.
2. To browse the photos by album, touch the left side of the screen and slide your finger to the right. The Photos menu appears, as shown in **Figure 2**.
3. Touch Albums. The Photo Albums appear, as shown in **Figure 3**.
4. Touch a photo. The image appears in Full-Screen mode. Touch the ![key] key to return to the photo thumbnails.

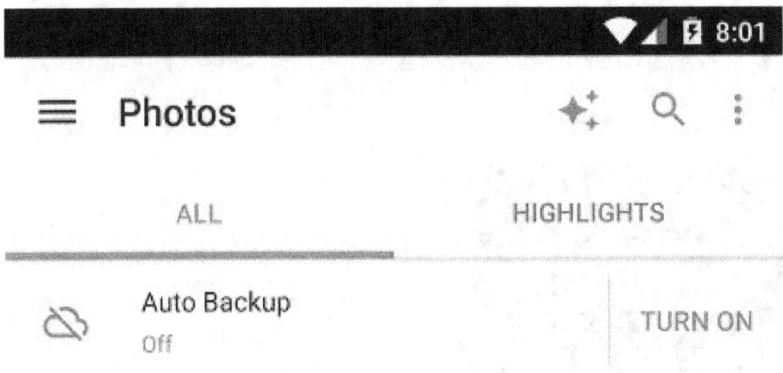

Figure 1: Gallery

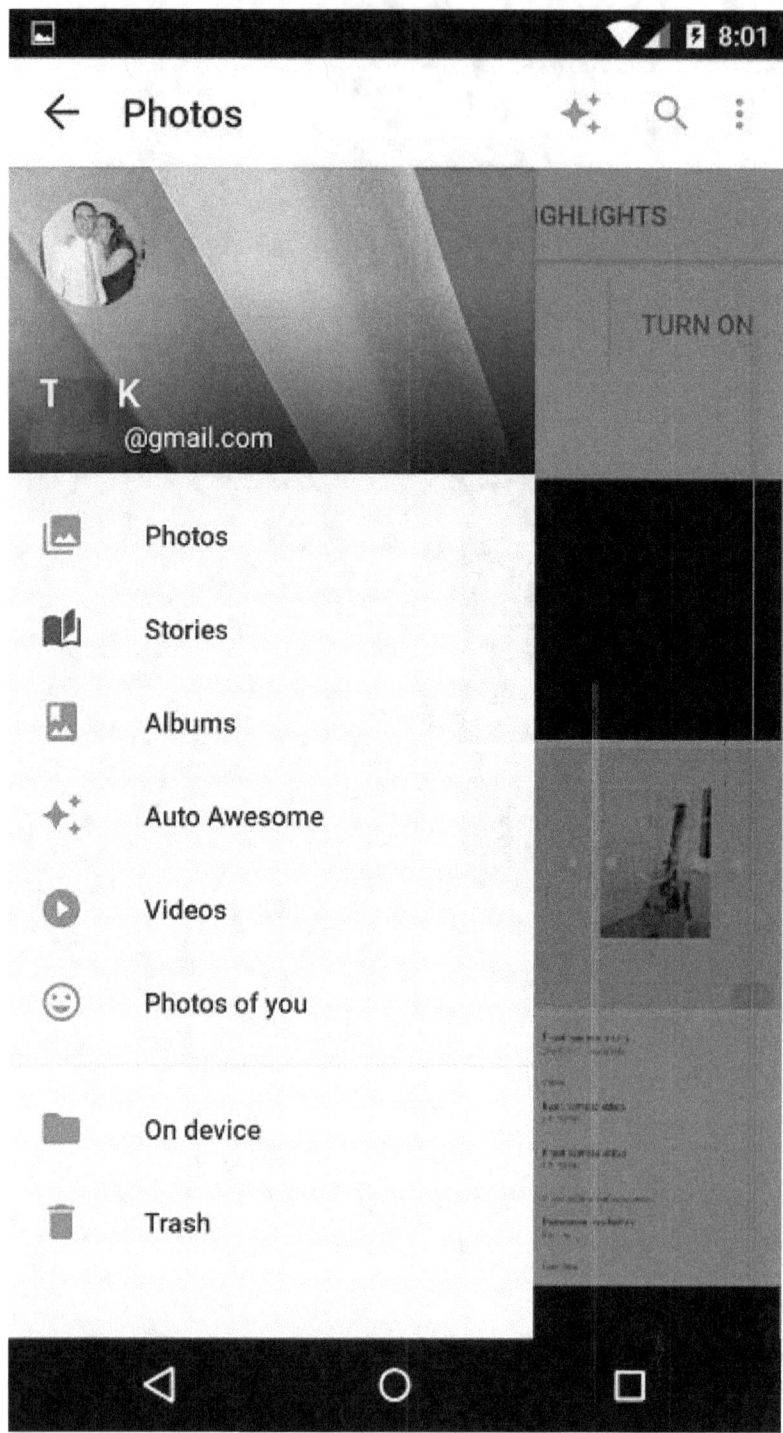

Figure 2: Photos Menu

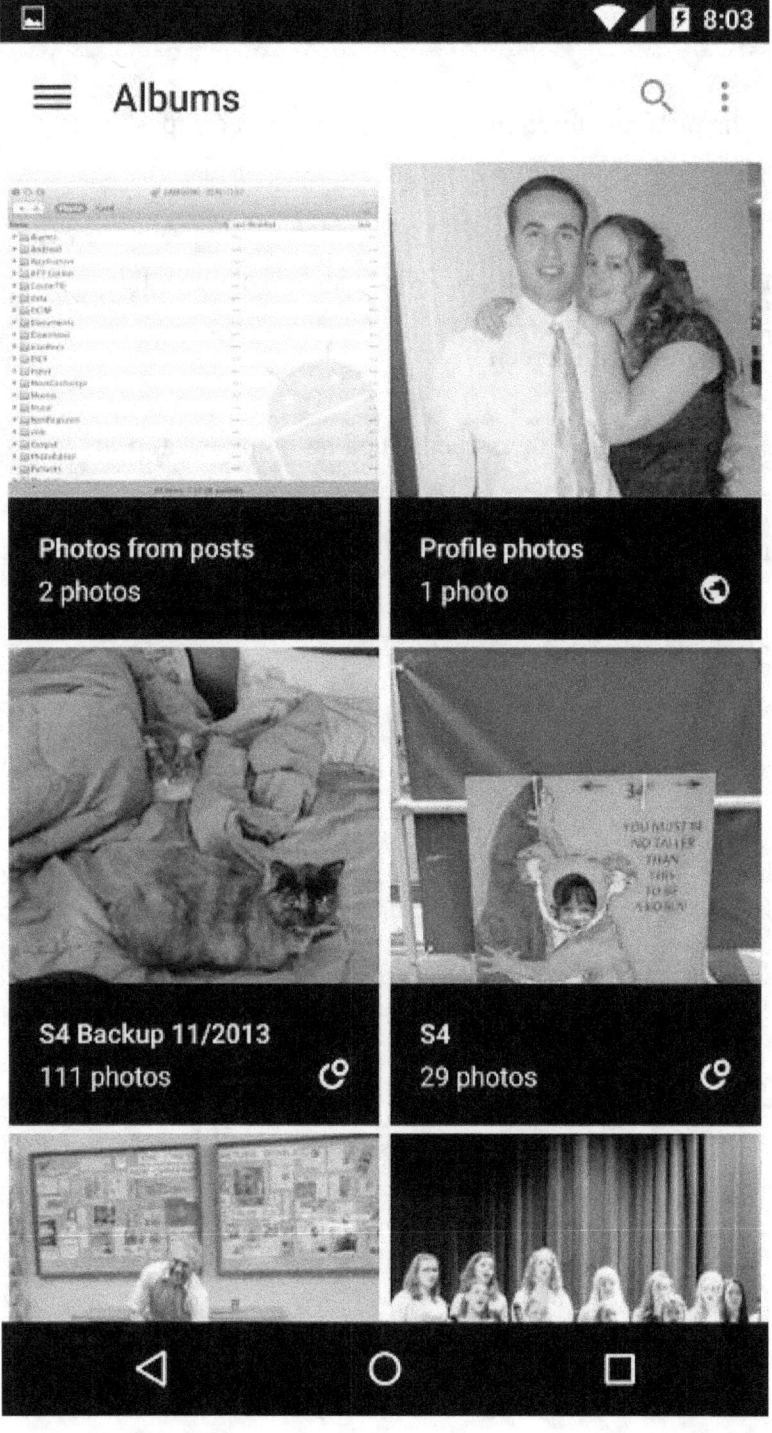

Figure 3: Photo Albums

2. Starting a Slideshow

The device can play slideshows using the pictures stored in the Gallery. To start a slideshow:

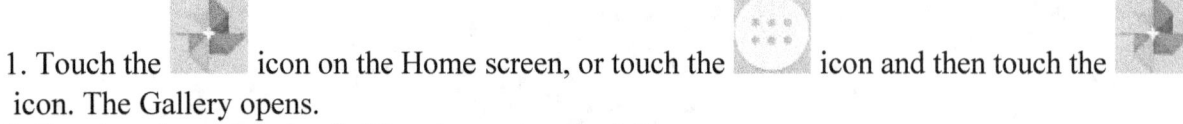

1. Touch the icon on the Home screen, or touch the icon and then touch the icon. The Gallery opens.
2. Touch a photo thumbnail. The photo opens in full screen.

3. Touch the icon in the upper right-hand corner of the screen. The Photo options appear, as shown in **Figure 4**.
4. Touch Slideshow. The slideshow begins.
5. Touch the screen once. The slideshow stops.

Figure 4: Photo Options

3. Applying Special Effects to Pictures

Pictures stored on the device can be cropped, rotated, and enhanced with various effects. To edit a picture:

1. Open a photo. The image appears in full-screen mode. Refer to *"Browsing Pictures"* on page 143 to learn how to open an image.

2. Touch the ![pencil icon] at the bottom of the screen. The Photo is opened for editing, as shown in **Figure 5**.

3. Follow the steps in the appropriate section below to learn how to use the various editing options:

Adjusting the Lighting and Color Settings

There are several options that allow you to adjust the amount of light and color in an image. To adjust the lighting and color settings:

1. Follow the instructions above. Then, touch **Tune Image** at the bottom of the screen. The Image Tuning screen appears, as shown in **Figure 6.**

2. Touch the photo anywhere and slide your finger up or down to select one of the following options:
    - **Brightness** - Adjust the amount of light in the photo.
    - **Contrast** - Adjust the different in the amount of light and color between different parts of the photo. Higher contrast results in a sharper photo.
    - **Saturation** - Adjust the intensity of the colors in the photo.
    - **Shadows** - Adjust the intensity of the shadows in the photo.
    - **Warmth** - Adjust the amount of yellow to red, or blue light. Colder colors are resembled as blue light, while warmer colors are yellow to red.

3. Touch the photo anywhere, and slide your finger to the left to reduce the effect, or to the right to increase the effect.

4. Touch the check mark in the upper right-hand corner of the screen. The change is applied to the photo.

5. Touch **Done** in the upper left-hand corner of the screen. The edited photo is saved.

Applying Color Effects

There are several color effects that may be applied to a photo, such as "Black and White" and "Negative." To add a color effect:

1. Follow the instructions at the beginning of this section. Then, touch the icon at the bottom of the screen. The Color Effects menu appears, as shown in **Figure 7**.
2. Touch an effect in the list. The effect is applied to the photo.

3. Touch the check mark in the upper right-hand corner of the screen. The change is applied to the photo.
4. Touch **Done** in the upper left-hand corner of the screen. The edited photo is saved.

Figure 5: Photo Editing Menu

Figure 6: Image Tuning Screen

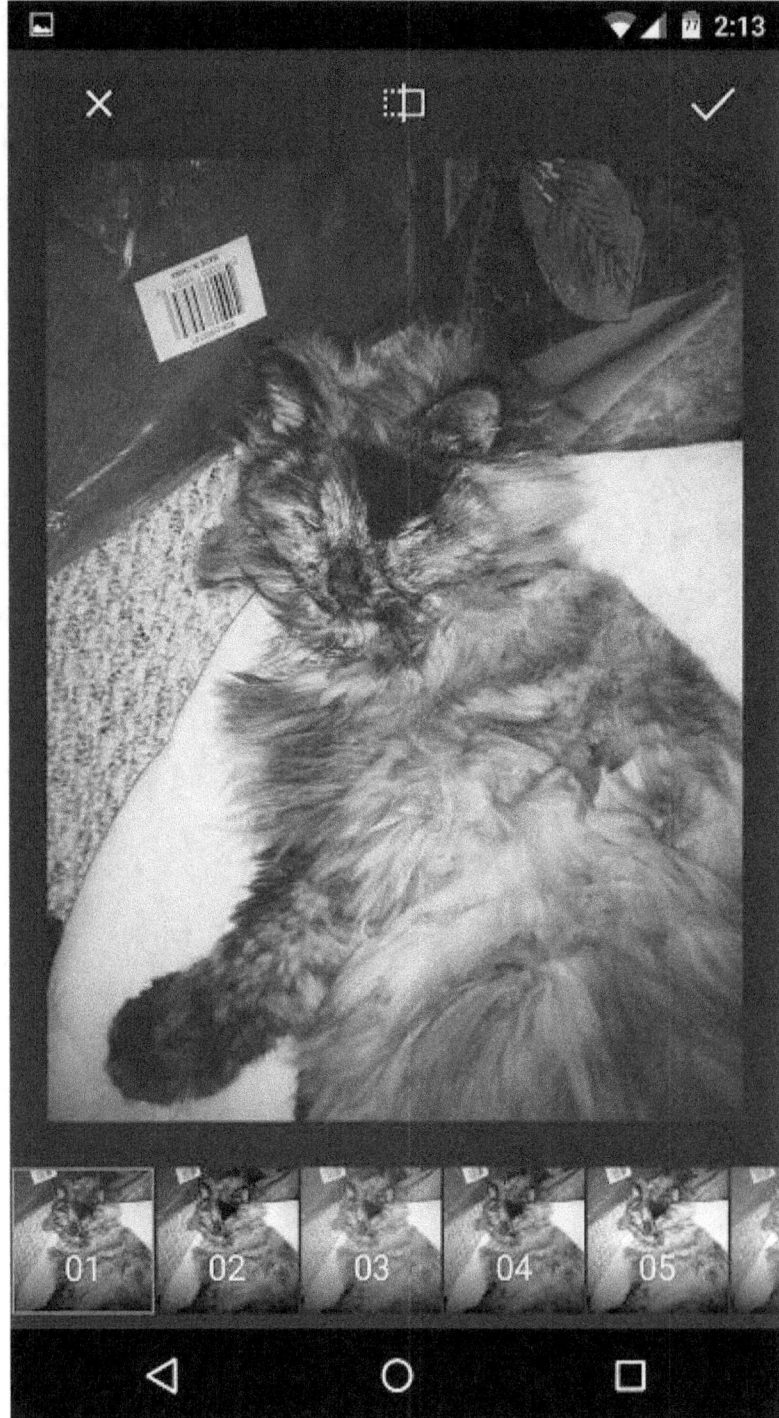

Figure 7: Color Effects Menu

4. Cropping a Picture

You may crop a photo to use a specific piece of it. To crop a photo:

1. Open a photo. Refer to *"Browsing Pictures"* on page 143 to learn how to open an image.
2. Touch the at the bottom of the screen. The Photo is opened for editing.
3. Touch **Crop** at the bottom of the screen. The cropping markers appear on the photo, as shown in **Figure 8**.
4. Touch the corners of the photo, and drag them to resize the crop. The crop is resized.
5. Touch inside the white rectangle, and drag it around to select the portion of the photo that you would like to use. The portion of the photo is selected.
6. Touch the check mark in the upper right-hand corner of the screen. The change is applied to the photo.
7. Touch **Done** in the upper left-hand corner of the screen. The cropped photo is saved.

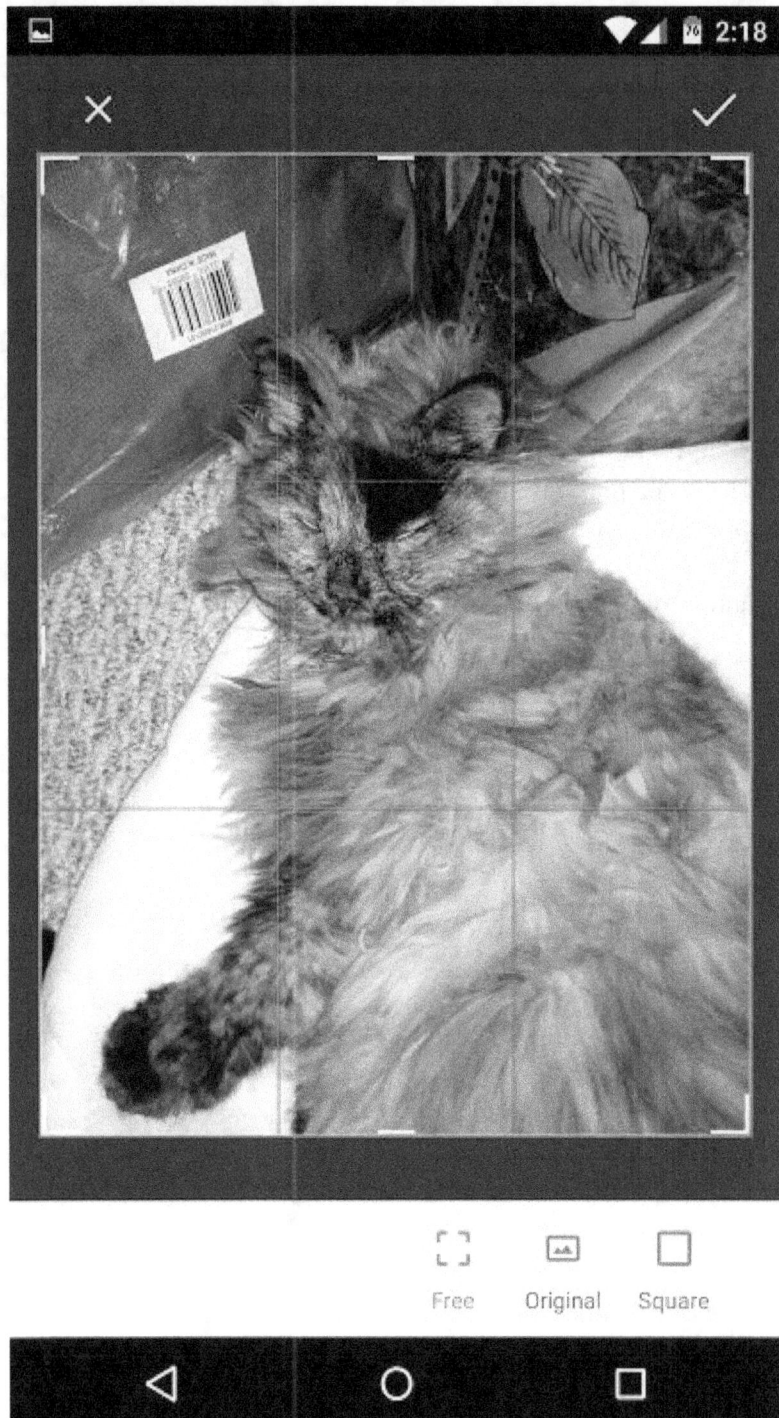

Figure 8: Cropping Markers on a Photo

5. Flipping or Rotating a Picture

You may rotate a photo in 90 degree increments, or flip it to view it upside down or as a mirror image. To flip or rotate a picture:

1. Open a photo. Refer to *"Browsing Pictures"* on page 143 to learn how to open an image.
2. Touch the at the bottom of the screen. The Photo is opened for editing.
3. Touch **Rotate** at the bottom of the screen. The Photo Rotation screen appears, as shown in **Figure 9**.
4. Touch the photo and move your finger in any direction to rotate or flip the photo. The photo is flipped or rotated in the direction indicated. You can also touch **Rotate Left** or **Rotate Right** at the bottom of the screen.
5. Touch the check mark in the upper right-hand corner of the screen. The change is applied to the photo.
6. Touch **Done** in the upper left-hand corner of the screen. The cropped photo is saved.

Figure 9: Photo Rotation Screen

6. Deleting Pictures

Warning: Once a picture is deleted, there is no way to restore it.

To free up some space in the device's memory, try deleting some pictures from the Gallery. To delete a picture:

1. Open a photo album. Refer to *"Browsing Pictures"* on page 143 to learn how to open a photo album.
2. Touch and hold a photo. The photo is selected, and a check mark appears on the thumbnail, as outlined in **Figure 10**. Touch any other photo that you wish to delete.

3. Touch the icon in the upper right-hand corner of the screen. A confirmation dialog appears.
4. Touch **Delete Everywhere**. The Photo is deleted.

Figure 10: Selected Photo

7. Importing and Exporting Pictures Using a PC or Mac

Pictures and other files can be transferred to and from the device. Refer to *"Exporting and Importing Files Using a PC or Mac"* on page 21 to learn how.

8. Sharing a Photo or Video via Email

You may share media by attaching it to an email. This method of transferring photos to your own computer takes much longer than the one discussed in Exporting and Importing Files Using a PC or Mac because the images can be somewhat large in size when taken on the device. To share a photo or video:

1. Open a photo album. Refer to *"Browsing Pictures"* on page 143 to learn how.
2. Touch and hold a photo. The photo is selected, and a check mark appears on the thumbnail. Touch any other photos that you wish to share.

3. Touch the ![share icon] icon at the top of the screen, and then touch the ![gmail icon] icon. A new email appears with the selected photos attached, as shown in **Figure 11**.

4. Touch the ![send button] button. The email with the attached photos is sent.

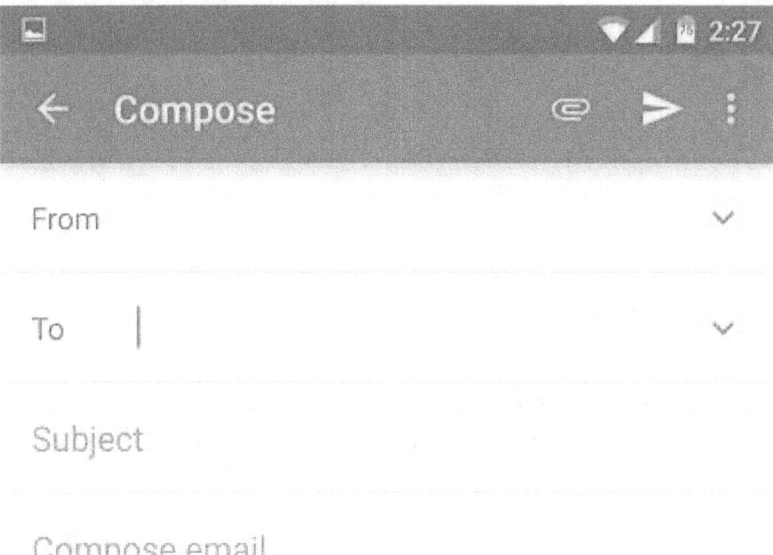

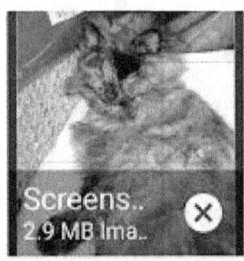

Figure 11: Photos Attached to an Email

9. Creating a Movie Using a Photo Collection

You can create an enhanced slideshow, or movie, using the pictures in your photo library. To create a movie:

1. Touch the 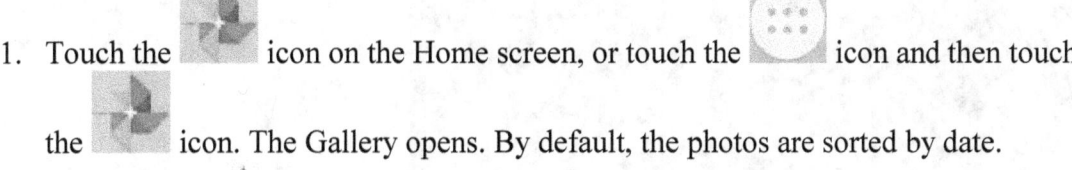 icon on the Home screen, or touch the icon and then touch the icon. The Gallery opens. By default, the photos are sorted by date.

2. Touch the icon at the top of the screen. The New Movie menu appears, as shown in **Figure 12**.
3. Touch **Movie**. The New Movie screen appears, as shown in **Figure 13**.
4. Touch **Select Items**. The photo thumbnails appear.
5. Touch the photos that you would like to use in your movie. Then, touch Select at the top of the screen. The selected photos are added to your movie.
6. Touch **Add a Title** to name your movie. Then, touch Save at the top of the screen. The movie is created and saved in your photos library. Every movie that is created in this

    manner is labeled with a icon.

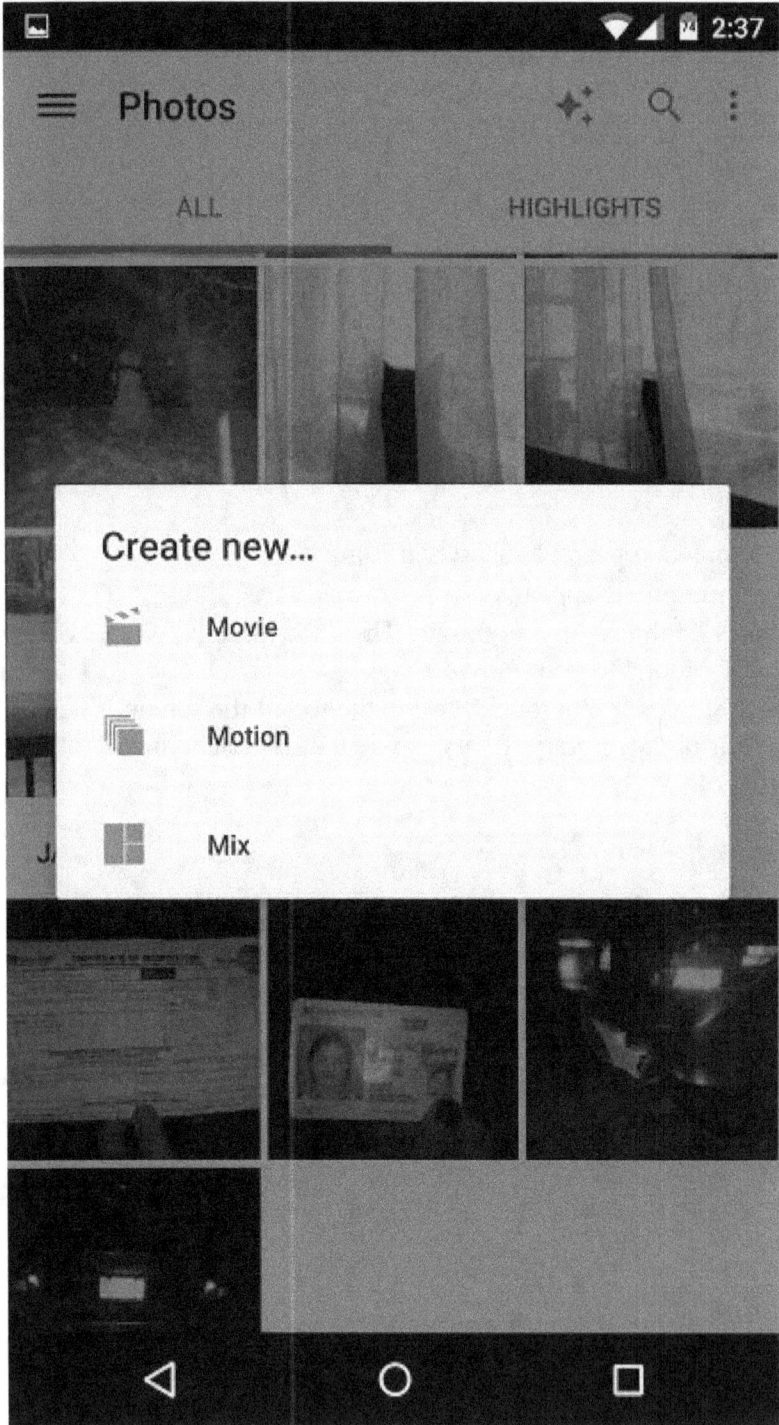

Figure 12: New Movie Menu

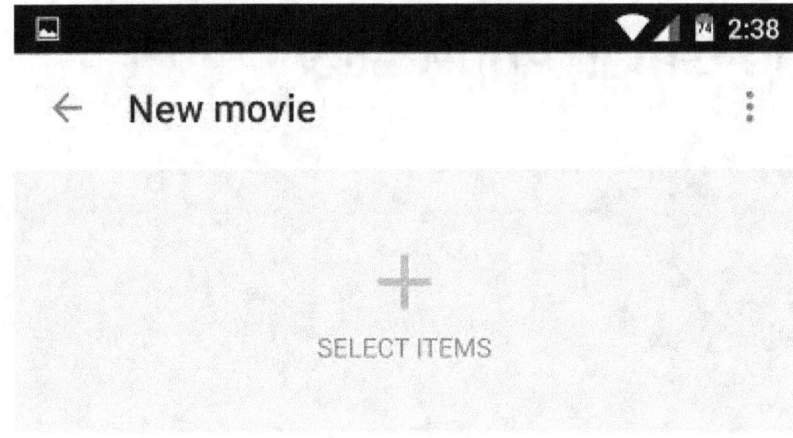

Figure 13: New Movie Screen

Using the Gmail Application

Table of Contents

1. Setting Up the Gmail Application

Before the Gmail application can be used, an email account must be registered to the device. To add your Google account to the device:

1. Touch the icon on the Home screen, or touch the icon and then touch the  icon. The Settings screen appears, as shown in **Figure 1**.
2. Scroll down and touch **Accounts**. The Accounts screen appears, as shown in **Figure 2**.
3. Touch **Add account**. The Add an Account screen appears, as shown in **Figure 3**.
4. Touch **Google**, or touch **Exchange** or **Personal**, if you do not have a Google (Gmail) account. The Google Account screen appears, if you touched Google, as shown in **Figure 4**. The remaining instructions in this section apply only to Google accounts. For other accounts, follow the on-screen instructions, which usually consist of simply entering your email address and password.
5. Touch **Enter your email** if you already have a Google account. Otherwise, touch **Create New Account** to create a new Google account. Once the account is created, it will be added to the device automatically, and you may skip the rest of the steps in this section. If you would like to create your Google account using the Web browser on your computer, navigate to **https://accounts.google.com/SignUp** to do so.
6. Enter your Gmail address, and then touch **Next**. The password screen appears.
7. Enter your password, and touch **Next**. The Sync screen appears, as shown in **Figure 5**.
8. Touch each item that you want Google to sync to your phone, and then touch **Next**. The Google account is added to your device.

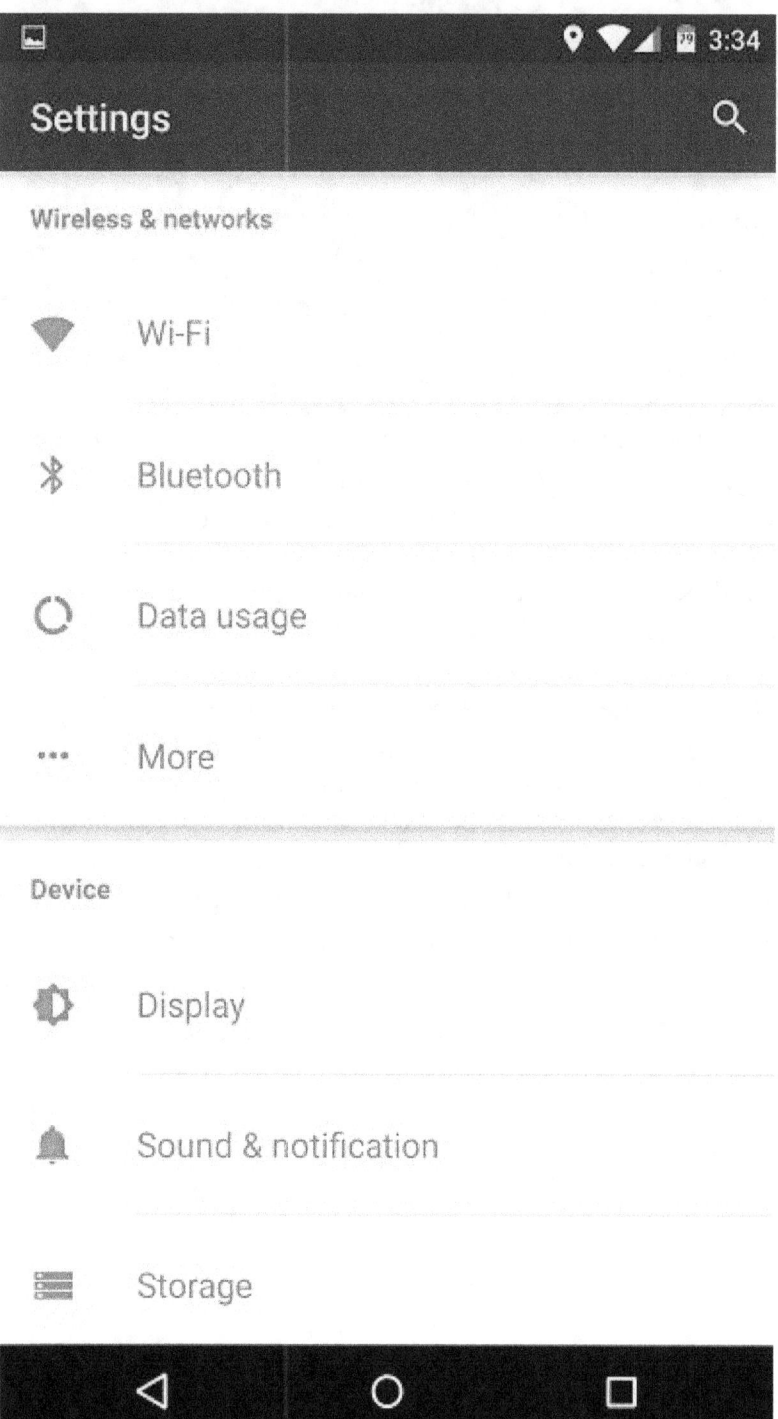

Figure 1: Settings Screen

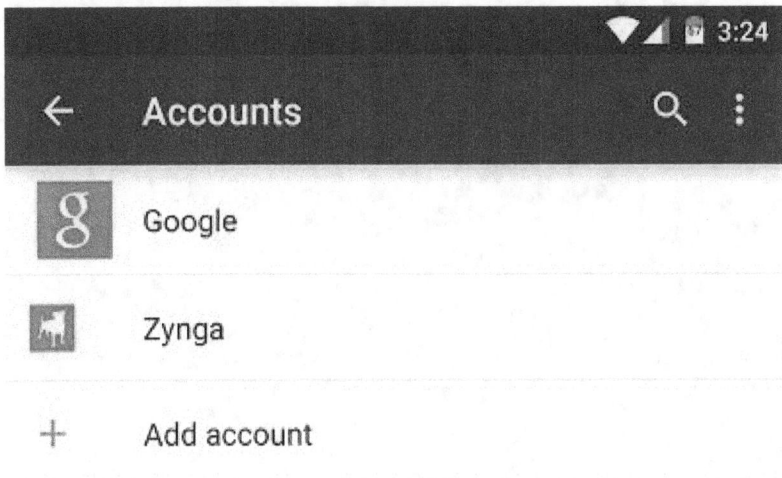

Figure 2: Accounts Screen

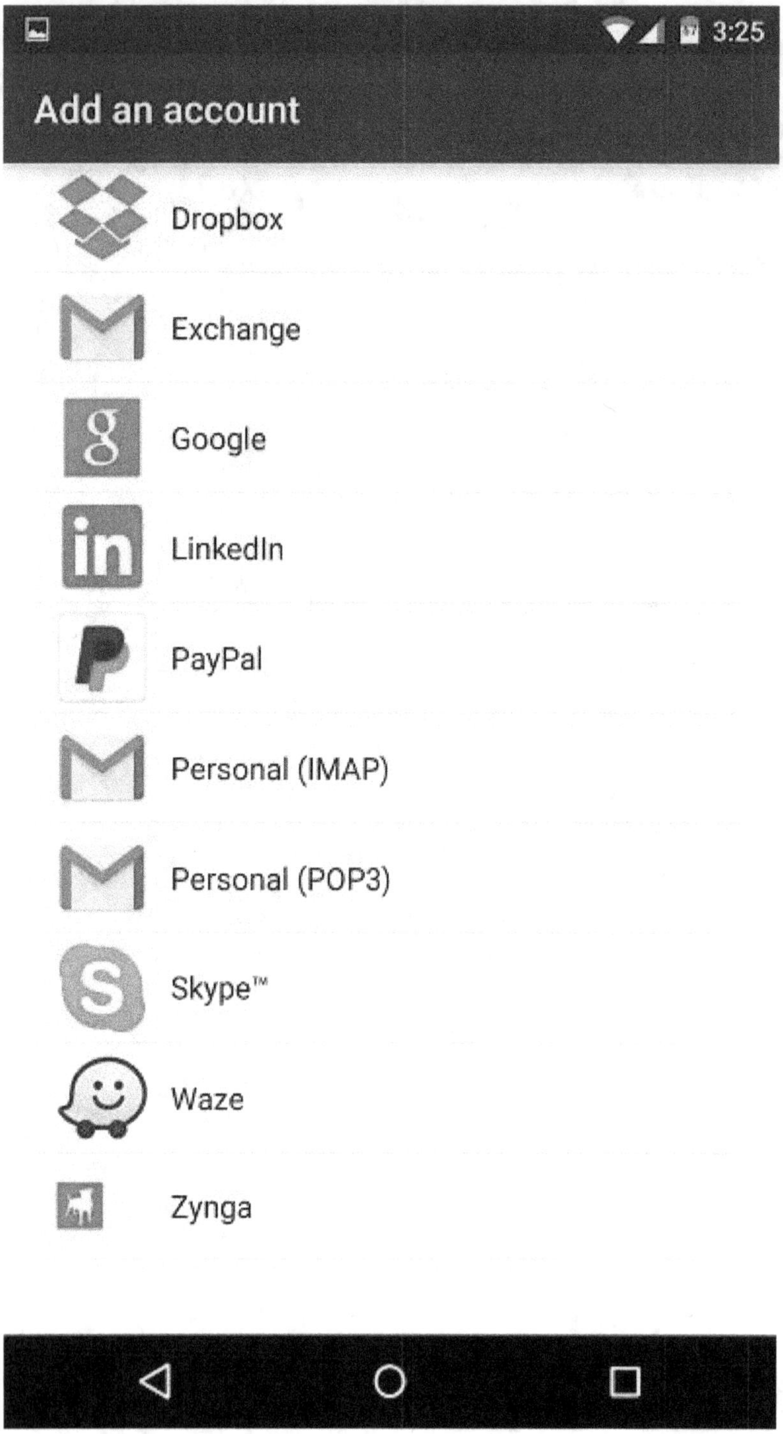

▼◢ 🔋 3:25

Add an account

Dropbox

Exchange

Google

LinkedIn

PayPal

Personal (IMAP)

Personal (POP3)

Skype™

Waze

Zynga

◁　　○　　▢

Figure 3: Add an Account Screen

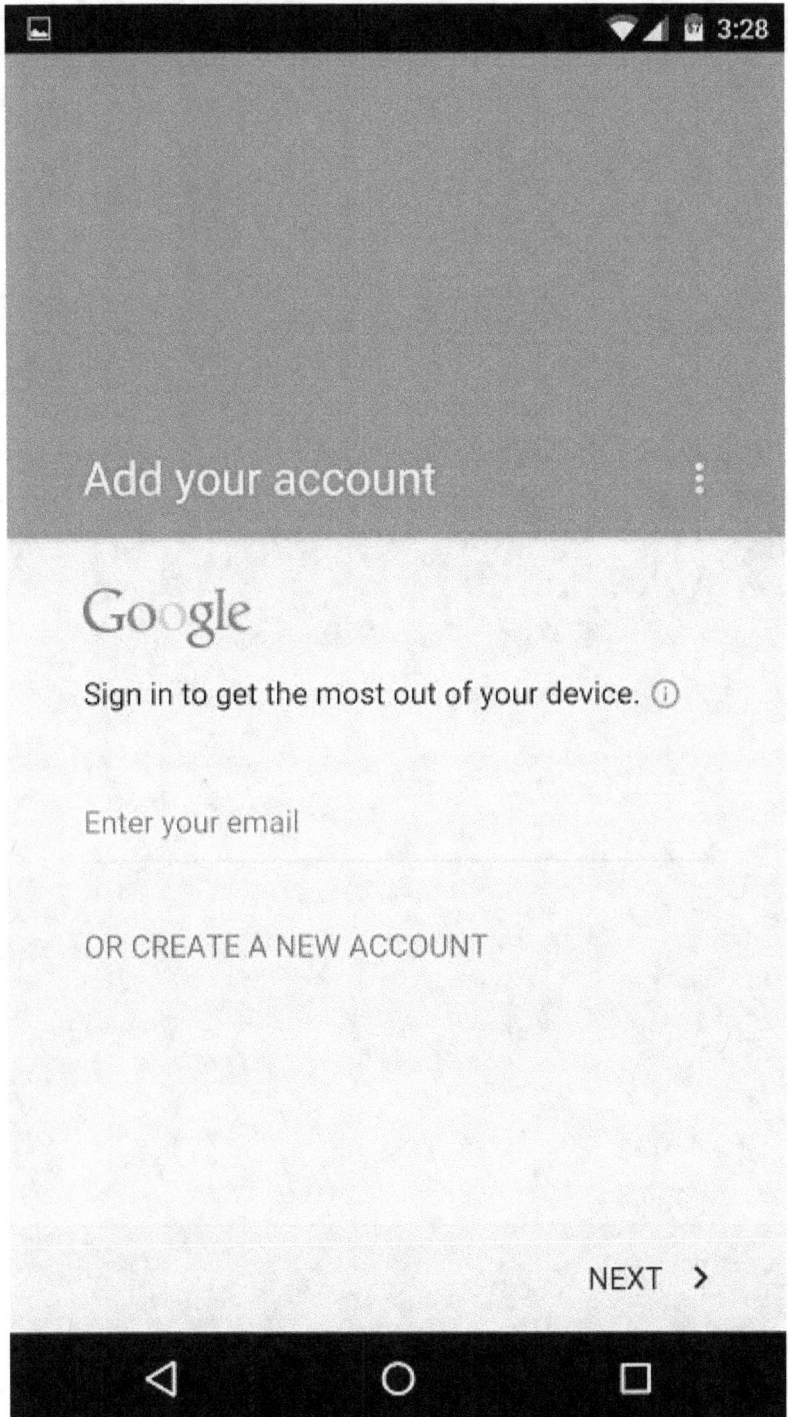

Figure 4: Google Account Screen

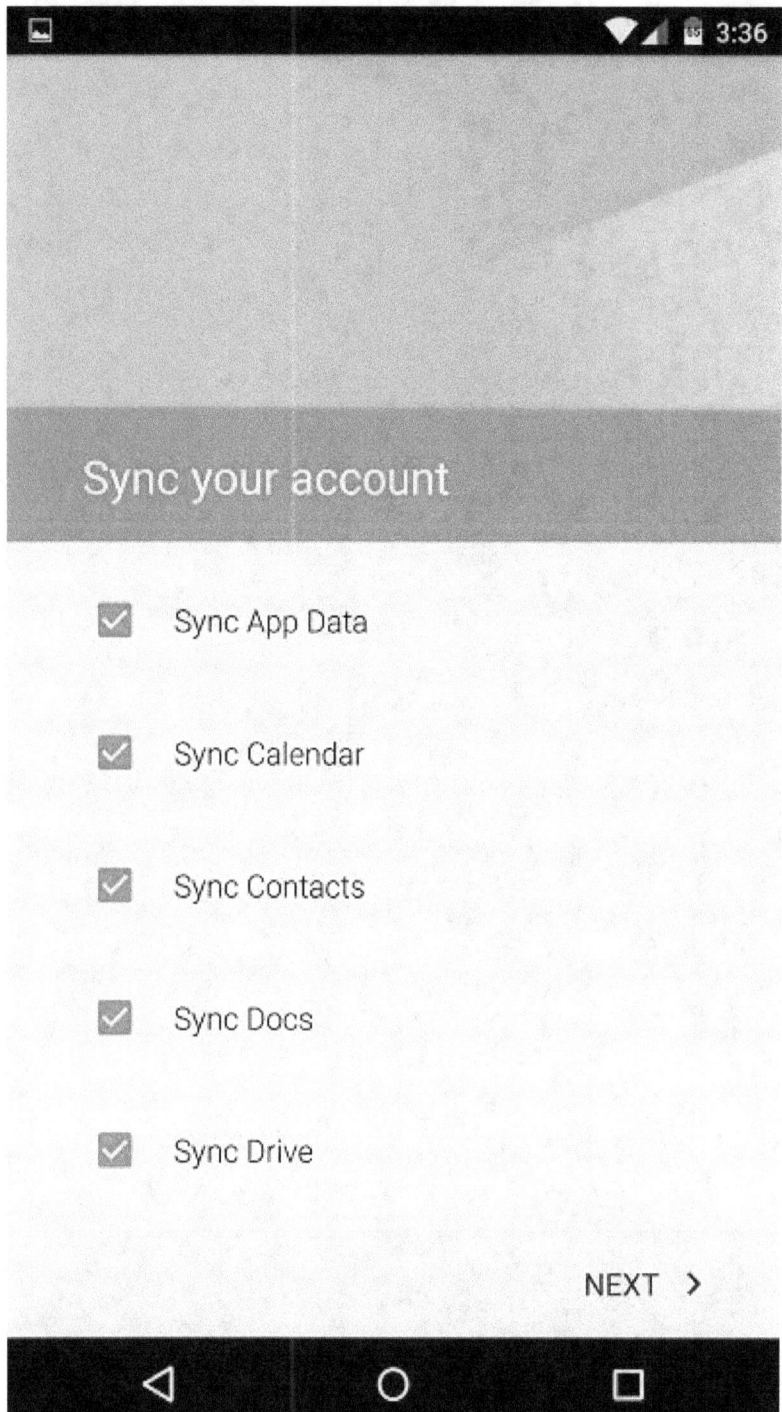

Figure 5: Sync Screen

2. Reading Email

Since the device is completely synced with every Google product, it is highly recommended to use a Gmail account on the device. To read email using your Gmail account:

1. Touch the icon on the Home screen, or touch the icon and then touch the icon. The Gmail application opens and the Inbox appears, as shown in **Figure 6**.
2. Touch an email. The email opens.
3. Touch the screen and move your finger to the left or right to view the previous email or next email, respectively (where "previous" refers to an older email and "next" refers to a newer one).
4. To switch to a different account at any time, touch the left side of the screen, and slide your finger to the right. The Inbox menu appears, as shown in **Figure 7**.
5. Touch your email address at the top of the screen. The email addresses associated with Gmail accounts currently registered to the device appear.
6. Touch an account name. The mailboxes associated with the account appear.

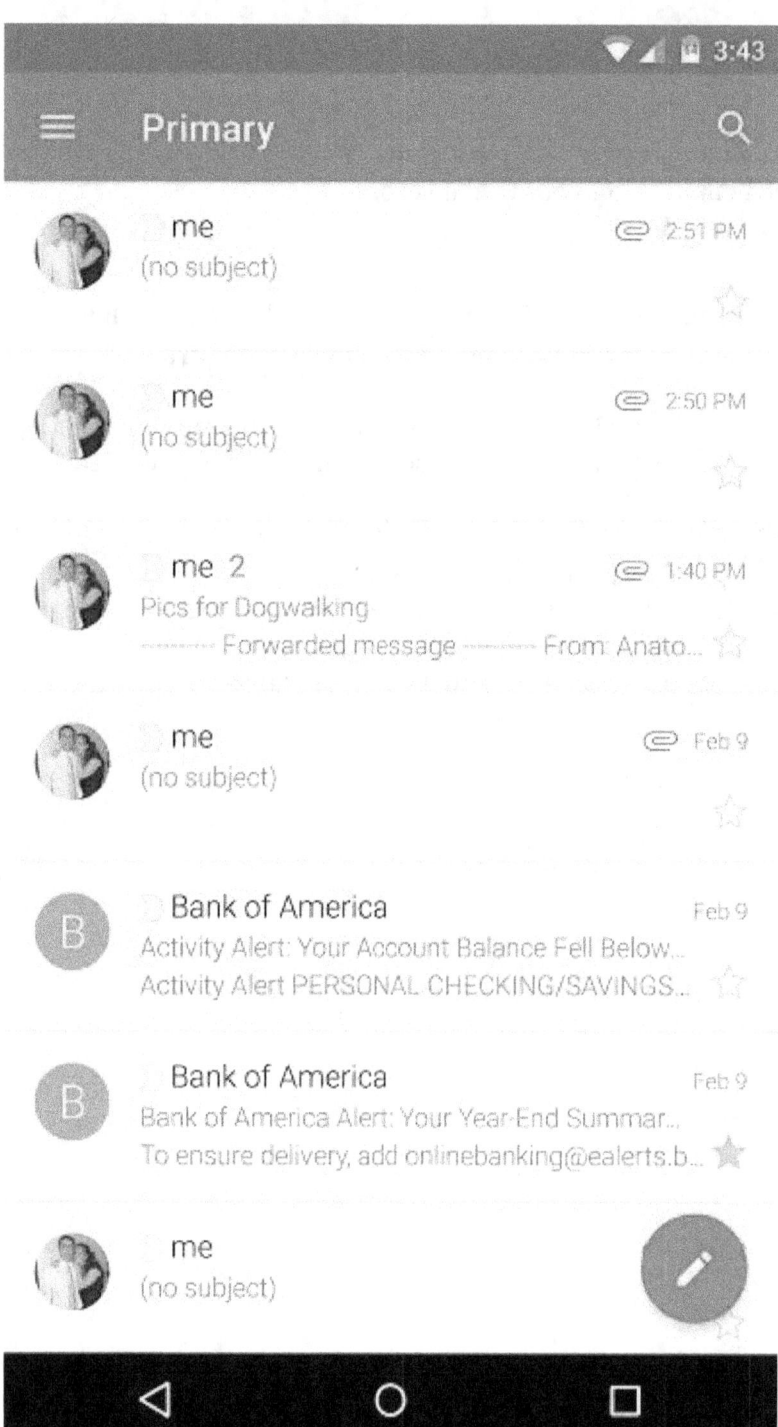

Figure 6: Gmail Inbox

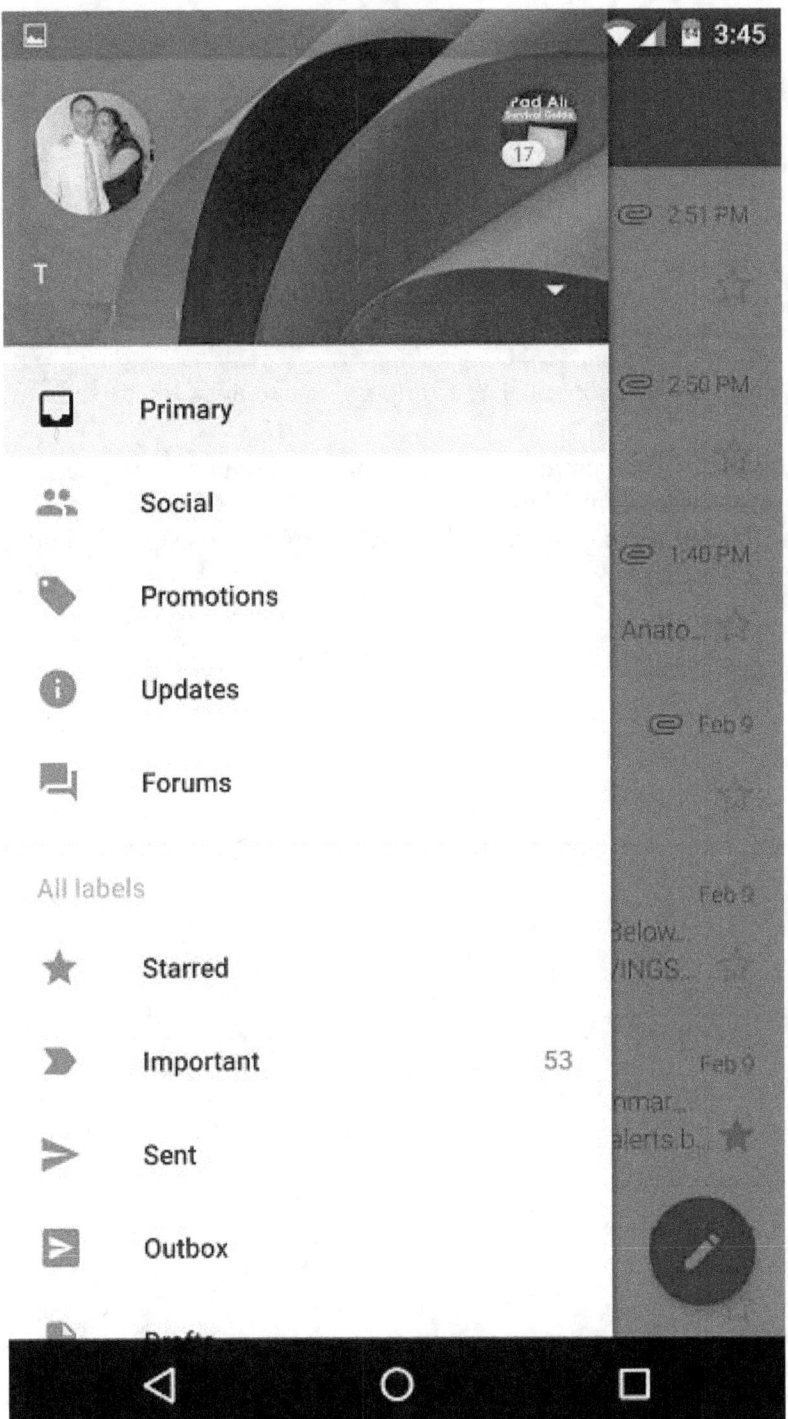

Figure 7: Inbox Menu

3. Writing an Email

Compose email directly from the device using the Gmail application. To write an email:

1. Touch the ![Gmail icon] icon on the Home screen, or touch the ![apps icon] icon and then touch the ![Gmail icon] icon. The Gmail application opens.

2. Touch the ![compose icon] icon at the bottom of the screen. The Compose screen appears, as shown in **Figure 8**.

3. Start typing a name or email address. If the email address is stored in contacts, recipient suggestions appear while typing, as shown in **Figure 9**.

4. Touch the 'Subject' field and enter the topic of the email. Touch the 'Compose email' field and type the message. The message is entered.

5. Touch the ![send icon] button in the upper right-hand corner of the screen, as outlined in **Figure 9**. The email is sent.

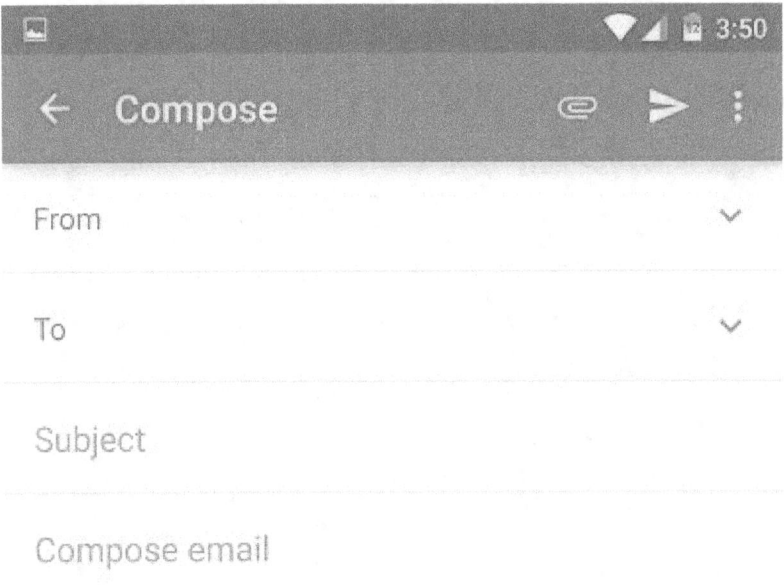

Figure 8: Compose Screen

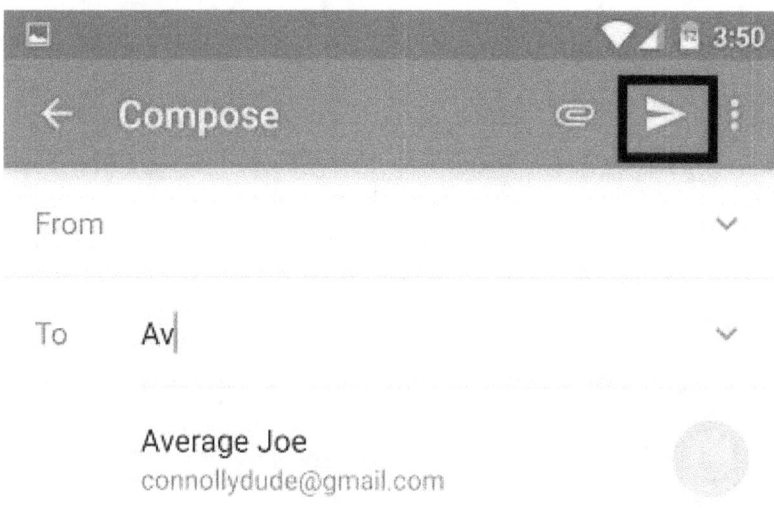

Figure 9: Recipient Suggestions

4. Replying to and Forwarding Emails

After receiving an email in the Gmail application, a direct reply can be sent, or the email can be forwarded. To reply to or forward an email:

1. Touch the M icon on the Home screen, or touch the ⠿ icon and then touch the M icon. The Gmail application opens.
2. Touch an email. The email opens.
3. Touch one of the following icons to perform the associated action, as outlined in

   Figure 10. If you do not see these icons, touch the ⋮ icon next to the ↰ icon, and then touch Reply All or Forward.

    - Send a reply to the sender.

    - Send a reply to all recipients of the original email.

    - Forward the email to a third party.

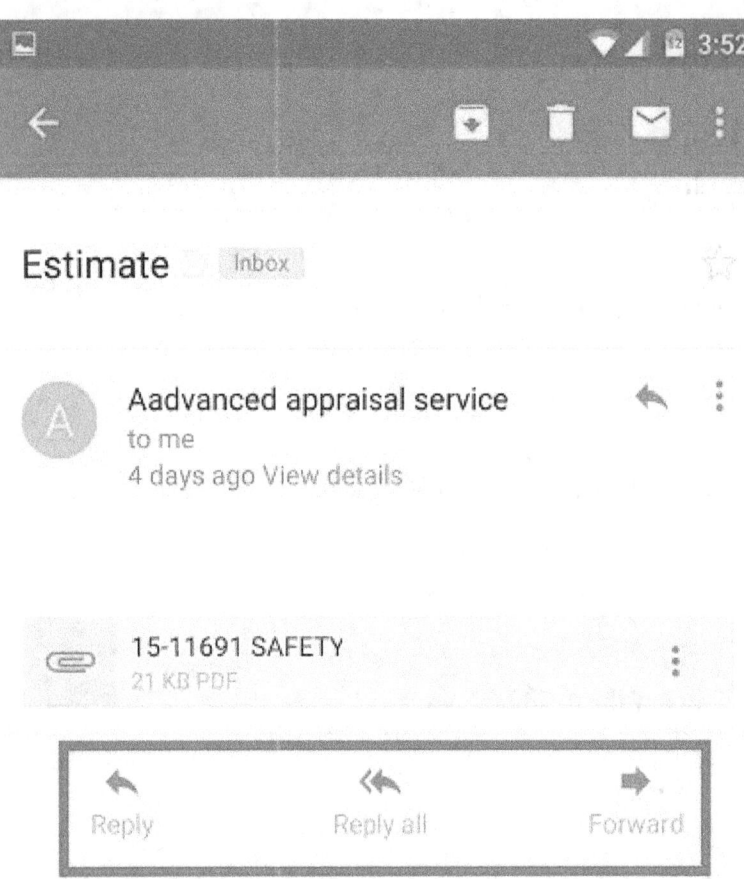

Figure 10: Email Options Outlined

5. Deleting and Archiving Emails

Deleting an email sends it to the Trash folder. To completely delete an email, the Trash folder must then be emptied using a Web browser (not covered in this guide). Otherwise, email will be automatically deleted from the Trash folder after 30 days. To delete an email:

1. Touch the icon on the Home screen, or touch the icon and then touch the icon. The Gmail application opens.
2. Touch the letter or picture to the left of the email that you wish to delete. The letter will always be the first letter of the name or service involved in the email conversation. For

    instance, if it is an email conversation with George, touch the icon. A picture will appear next to an email if the contact is associated with your Google+ account. The email conversation is selected, and a check mark appears next to it. Touch the letter to the left of each email that you wish to delete, as shown in **Figure 11**.

3. Touch the icon at the top of the screen. The selected email is deleted.

To clean up the Inbox without deleting emails, try archiving them. Archiving an email removes it from the Inbox and places it in the All Mail folder. To archive an email, touch the email in the Inbox and slide your finger to the left or right. 'Archived' appears in place of the email in the Inbox. Touch **undo** to return the email to the Inbox.

*Note: To find an archived email, touch the left side of the screen, and slide your finger to the right. Then, touch **All Mail**.*

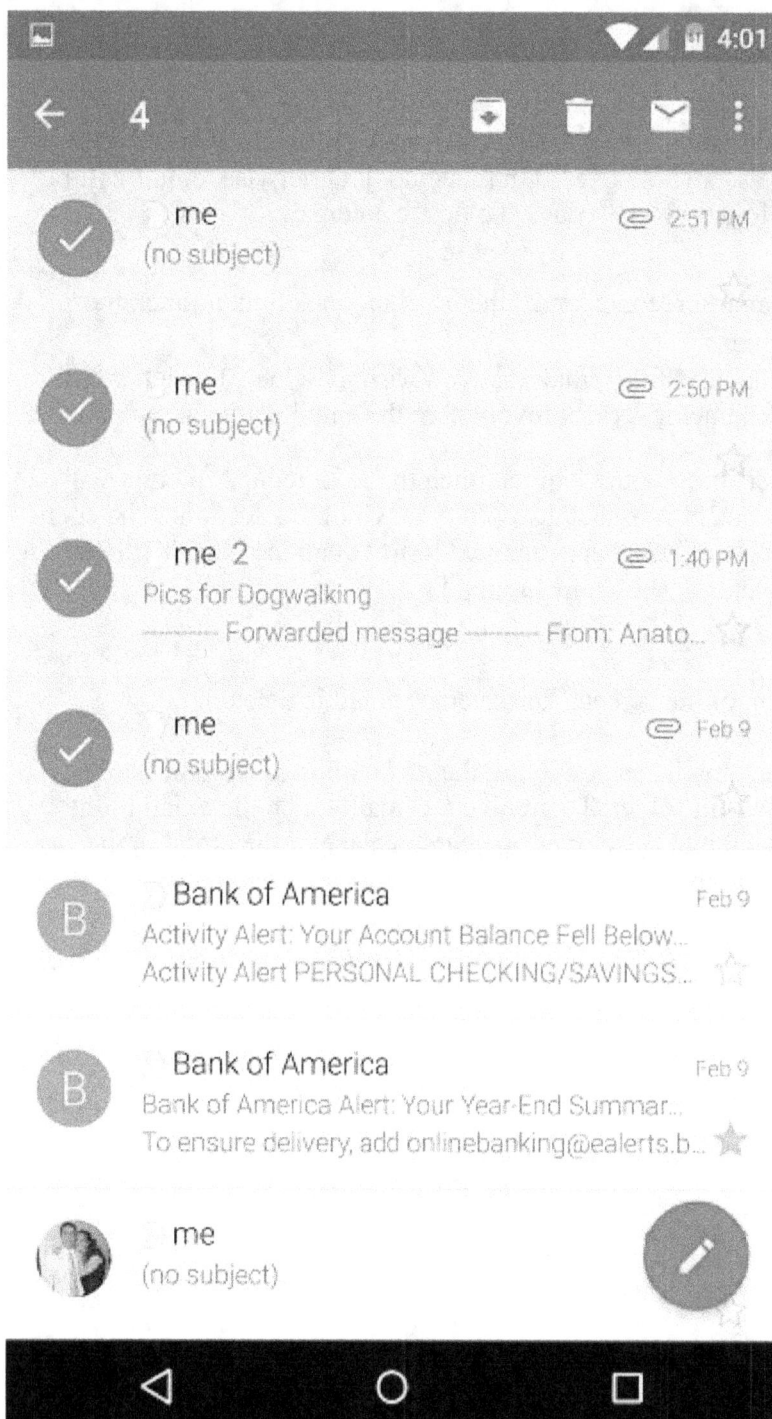

Figure 11: Selected Emails

6. Applying Labels to Emails

Emails can be classified according to the nature of the message, such as 'Work' or 'Personal'. Adding labels can help you to organize your email to find it more quickly. To add a label to an email:

1. Touch the [M] icon on the Home screen, or touch the [::] icon and then touch the [M] icon. The Gmail application opens.
2. Touch the letter or picture to the left of the email to which you wish to apply a label. This letter will always be the first letter of the name or service involved in the email

   conversation. For instance, if it is an email conversation with George, touch the [G] icon. A picture will appear next to an email if the contact is associated with your Google+ account. The email conversation is selected, and a check mark appears. Repeat this step for each email to which you wish to apply the label.

3. Touch the [⋮] icon in the upper right-hand corner of the screen. The Email Conversation menu appears, as shown in **Figure 12**.
4. Touch Change Labels. A list of available labels appears, as shown in **Figure 13**.
5. Touch the labels in the menu that you wish to apply to the selected emails. A [✓] mark appears next to each selected label.\
6. Touch **OK**. The selected labels are applied to the highlighted emails.

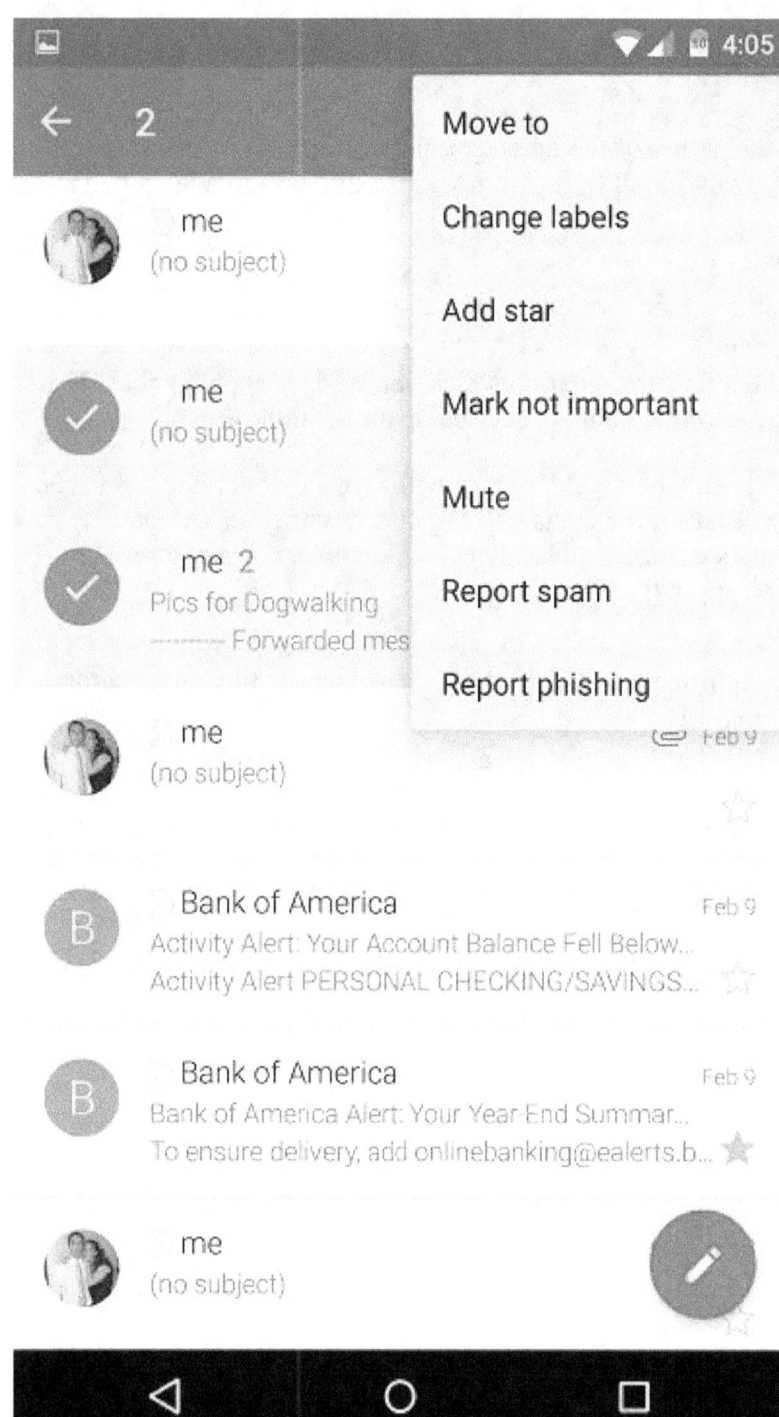

Figure 12: Email Conversation Menu

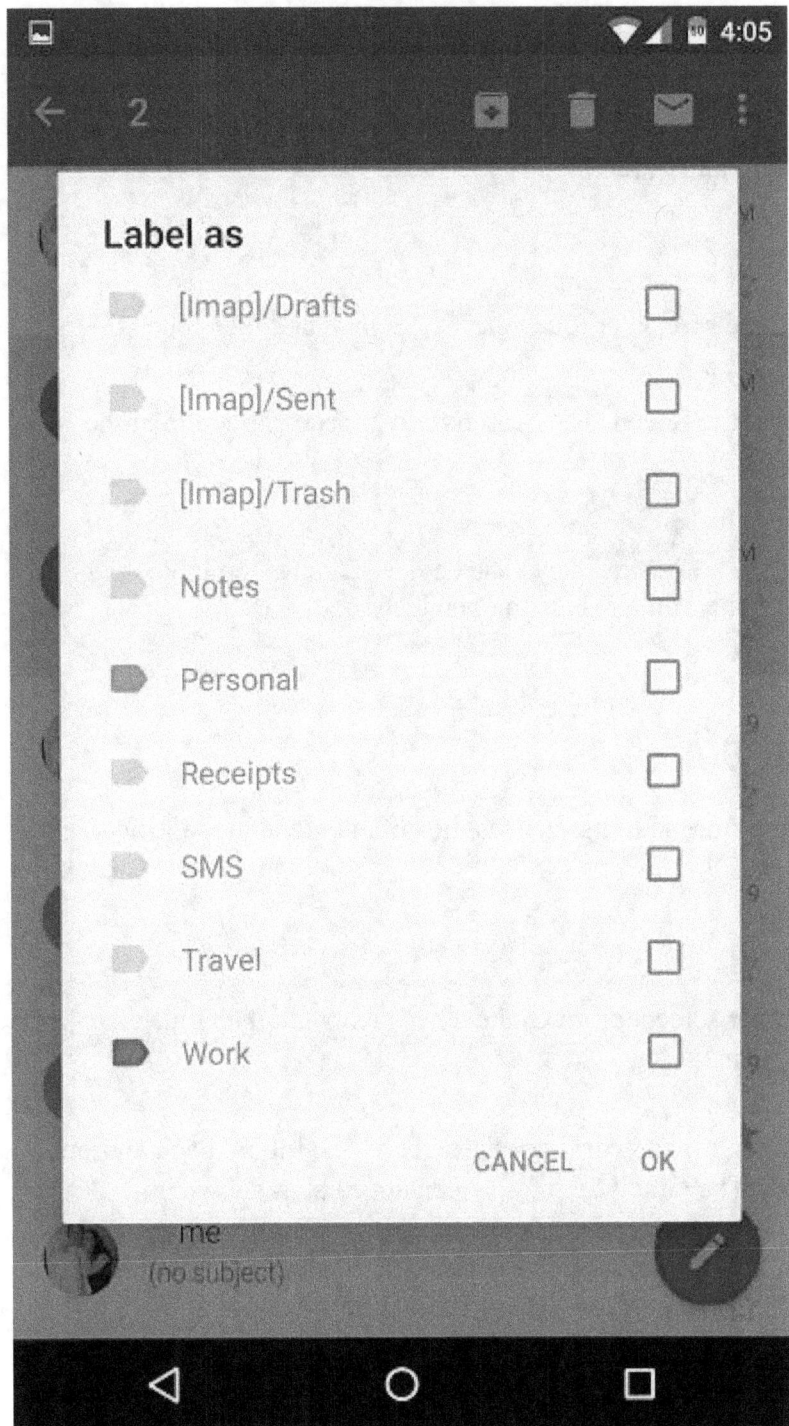

Figure 13: List of Available Labels

7. Searching the Inbox

To find a specific email in the Inbox, use the Search function, which searches email addresses, message text, and subject lines. To search the Inbox:

1. Touch the ![M] icon on the Home screen, or touch the ![grid] icon and then touch the ![M] icon. The Gmail application opens.
2. Touch the ![Q] icon at the top of the screen. The Search field appears at the top of the screen.
3. Enter a search term and touch the ![Q] key. The device searches the Inbox and the matching results appear. Touch one of the results to open the email.

8. Adjusting the Gmail Settings

The Gmail application has several adjustable settings, such as the default signature, notification tones, and text size. To change these settings:

1. Touch the ![M] icon on the Home screen, or touch the ![grid] icon and then touch the ![M] icon. The Gmail application opens.
2. Touch the ![menu] icon in the upper right-hand corner of the screen. The Inbox menu appears.
3. Scroll down and touch Settings. The Gmail Settings screen appears, as shown in **Figure 14**.
4. Touch **General settings**. The General Settings screen appears, as shown in **Figure 15**.
5. Touch one of the following options to perform the corresponding function:

   - **Confirm before deleting** - Display confirmations before deleting emails.
   - **Confirm before archiving** - Display confirmations before archiving emails.
   - **Confirm before sending** - Display confirmations when sending emails.
   - **Auto-advance** - Choose which screen the Gmail application shows after deleting or archiving an email.

- **Clear Search History** (need to touch the ⦿ icon in the upper right-hand corner to access) Clear the email search history to preserve privacy.

- **Clear picture approvals** (need to touch the ⦿ icon in the upper right-hand corner to access) - Pictures embedded in emails won't display automatically unless you allow them.

From the Gmail Settings screen, touch your email address, and then touch one of the following options to perform the corresponding action:

- **Inbox type** - Set whether the Default Inbox or the Priority Inbox is the default. The Priority Inbox will only display priority emails.
- **Inbox categories** - Set the categories that appear in the Inbox, such as 'Social' and 'Updates'. Google automatically sorts your email into these categories and displays them in separate Inboxes.
- **Notifications** - Turn on new Email notifications. The ✉ icon appears in the upper left-hand corner of the screen when a new email arrives. A ✓ mark next to 'Notifications' signifies that the feature is on.
- **Inbox sound** (**Inbox Sound & vibrate** on smartphones) - Display the Manage Labels screen, where you can choose which mailboxes display new email notifications and select the sound that plays when a new email arrives. You can also customize vibrations (smartphones only) on this screen. Touch **Sound** on the Manage Labels screen to select the Notification ringtone.
- **Signature** - Enter a default signature that will be attached to the end of each sent email.
- **Sync Gmail** - Turn automatic email retrieval on or off. A ✓ mark next to 'Sync Gmail' signifies that the feature is turned on.
- **Days of mail to sync** - Choose how many days in the past the Inbox should sync. For instance, if you select '3', the Gmail application will go back three days each time it syncs the email.
- **Manage Labels** - Brings you to the same screen as 'Ringtone & vibrate'.
- **Download attachments** - Turn on to have Gmail automatically download any attached files. A ✓ mark next to 'Sync Gmail' signifies that the feature is on.

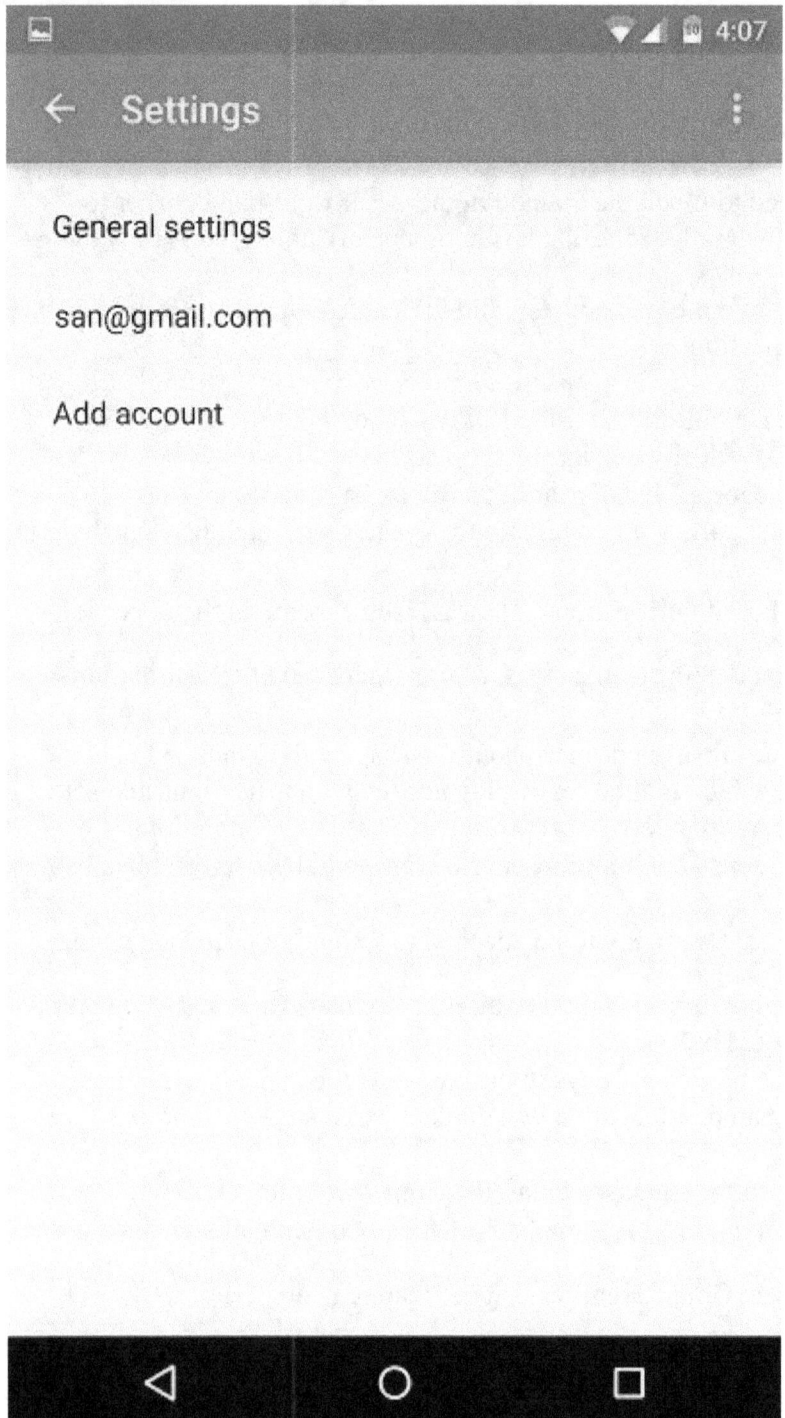

Figure 14: Gmail Settings Screen

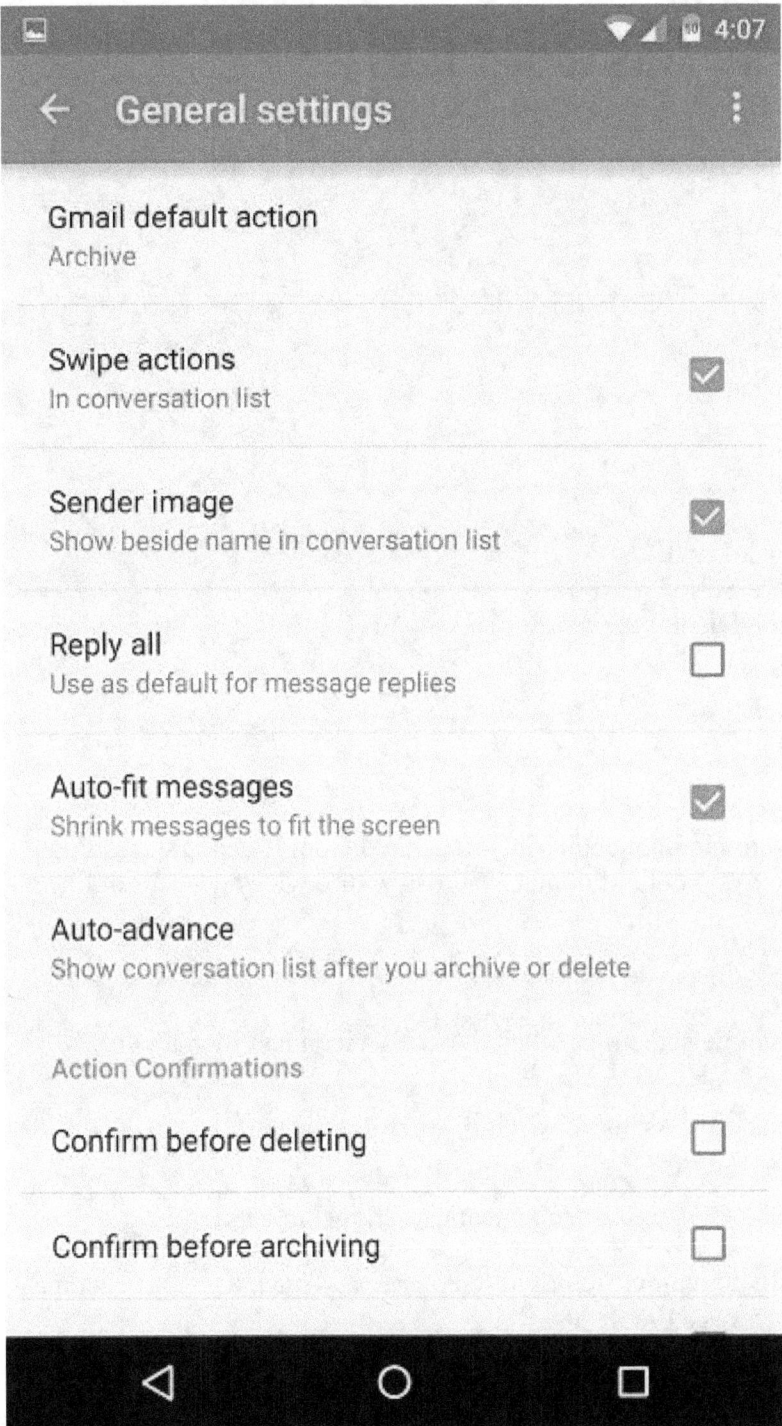

Figure 15: General Settings Screen

Managing Contacts

Table of Contents

1. Adding a New Contact

On the device, a contact can be added to the phonebook in your linked Google account. Adding a contact to a Google account allows total syncing of contacts across your device and your online account. To add a new contact:

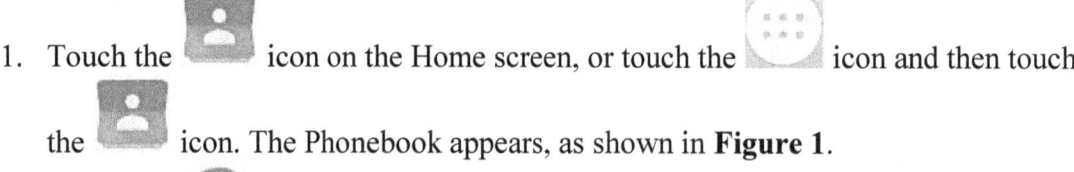

1. Touch the ![icon] icon on the Home screen, or touch the ![icon] icon and then touch the ![icon] icon. The Phonebook appears, as shown in **Figure 1**.

2. Touch the ![icon] icon. The New Contact screen appears, as shown in **Figure 2**.

3. Enter all desired information by touching each field to enter text. Touch the ![icon] icon at the top of the screen. The contact is stored.

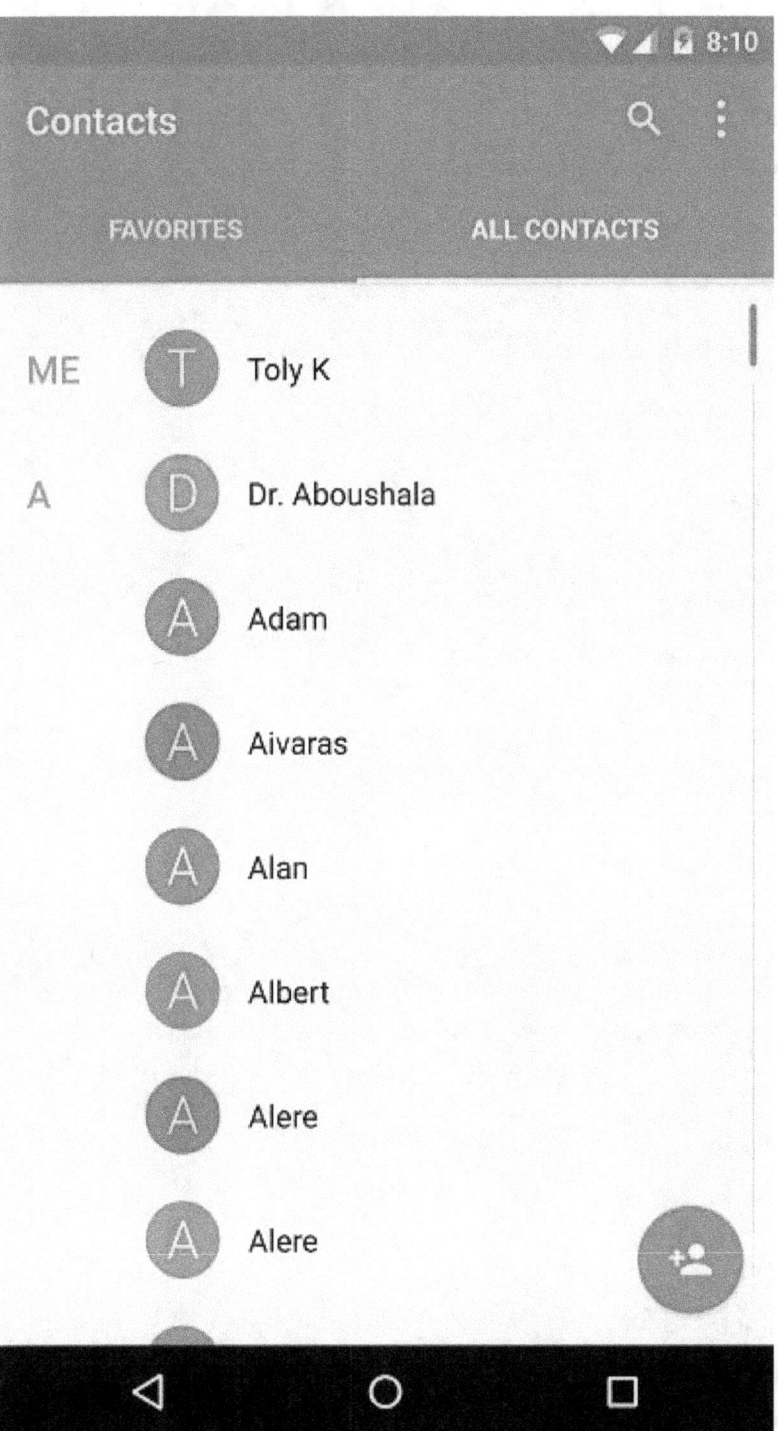

Figure 1: Phonebook

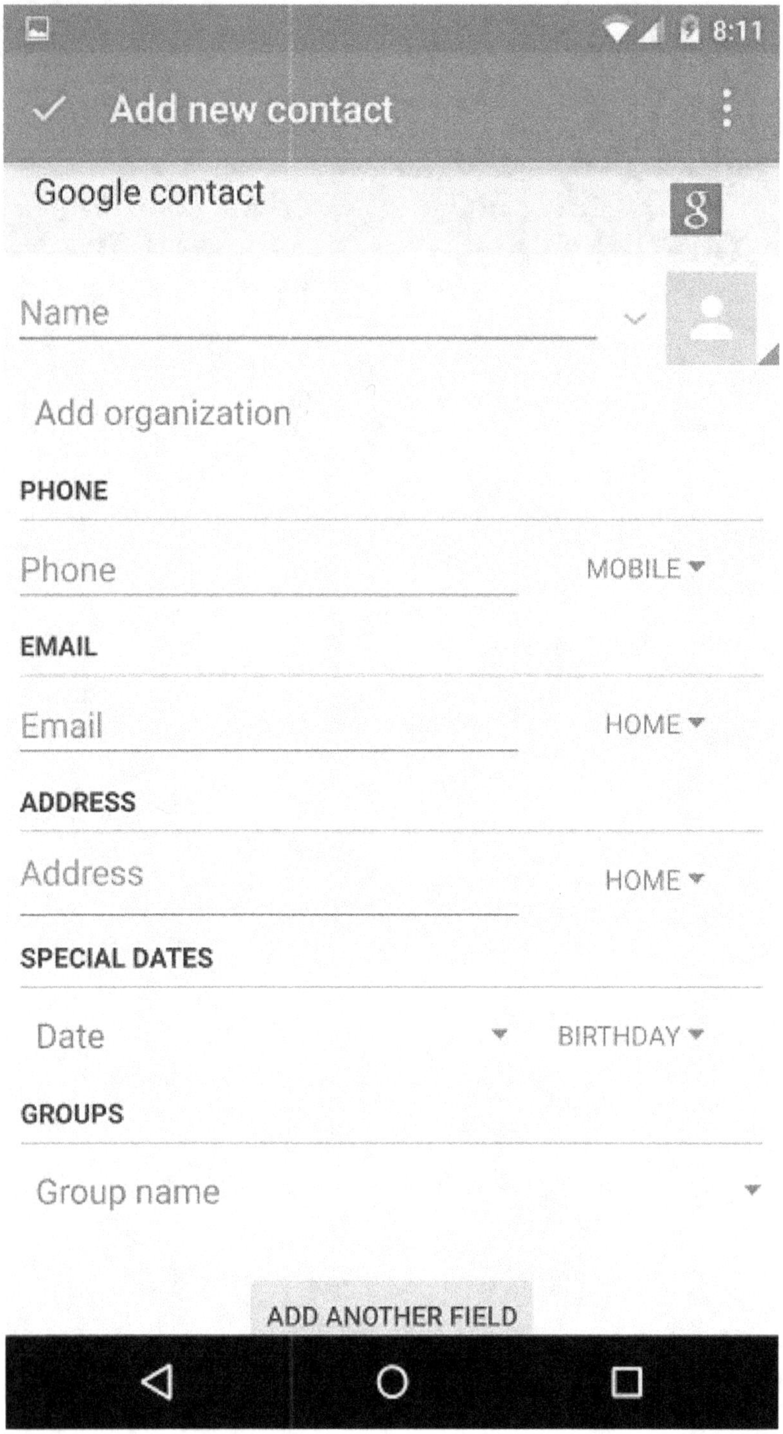

Figure 2: New Contact Screen

2. Creating a Shortcut to a Contact

The fastest way to consistently find a stored contact is to add a shortcut to the contact right from the Home screen. To create a shortcut to a contact:

1. Touch the icon on the Home screen, or touch the icon and then touch the icon. The phonebook appears.
2. Touch the name of the contact that you wish to add to the Home screen. The contact's information appears on the right-hand side of the screen.
3. Touch the icon in the upper right-hand corner of the screen. The Contact menu appears, as outlined in **Figure 3**.
4. Touch **Place on Home screen**. A shortcut to the contact's information is added to the first available Home screen. The Contact shortcut may look similar to the icon outlined in **Figure 4** if there is a picture assigned to the contact. If there is no picture assigned, the first letter of the contact's name is shown. Refer to *"Organizing Home Screen Objects"* on page 19 to learn how to move the new shortcut to another location, or to place it in a folder.

Figure 3: Contact Menu

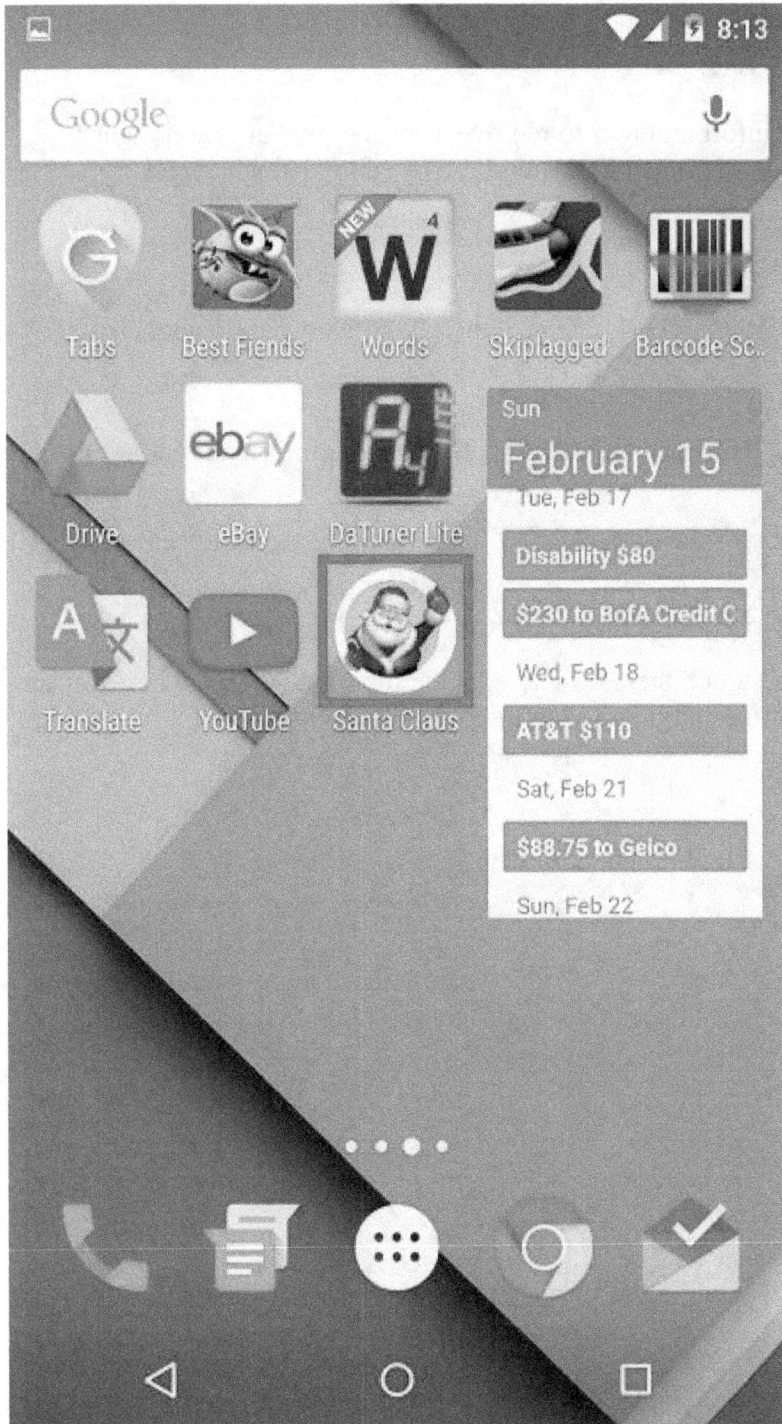

Figure 4: Contact Shortcut on the Home Screen

3. Editing Contact Information

Edit a contact entry to add additional information or to remove information that is no longer applicable, such as an email address or alternate phone number. To edit existing contact information:

1. Touch the ![contact icon] icon on the Home screen, or touch the ![apps icon] icon and then touch the ![contact icon] icon. The phonebook appears.
2. Touch the name of the contact that you wish to edit. The contact's information appears.
3. Touch the ![pencil icon] icon at the top of the screen. The Contact Editing screen appears, as shown in **Figure 5**.
4. Touch a field to edit it. The field is selected.
5. Enter the new information, and touch the ![checkmark icon] icon at the top of the screen when you are finished editing. The new information is stored in the phonebook.

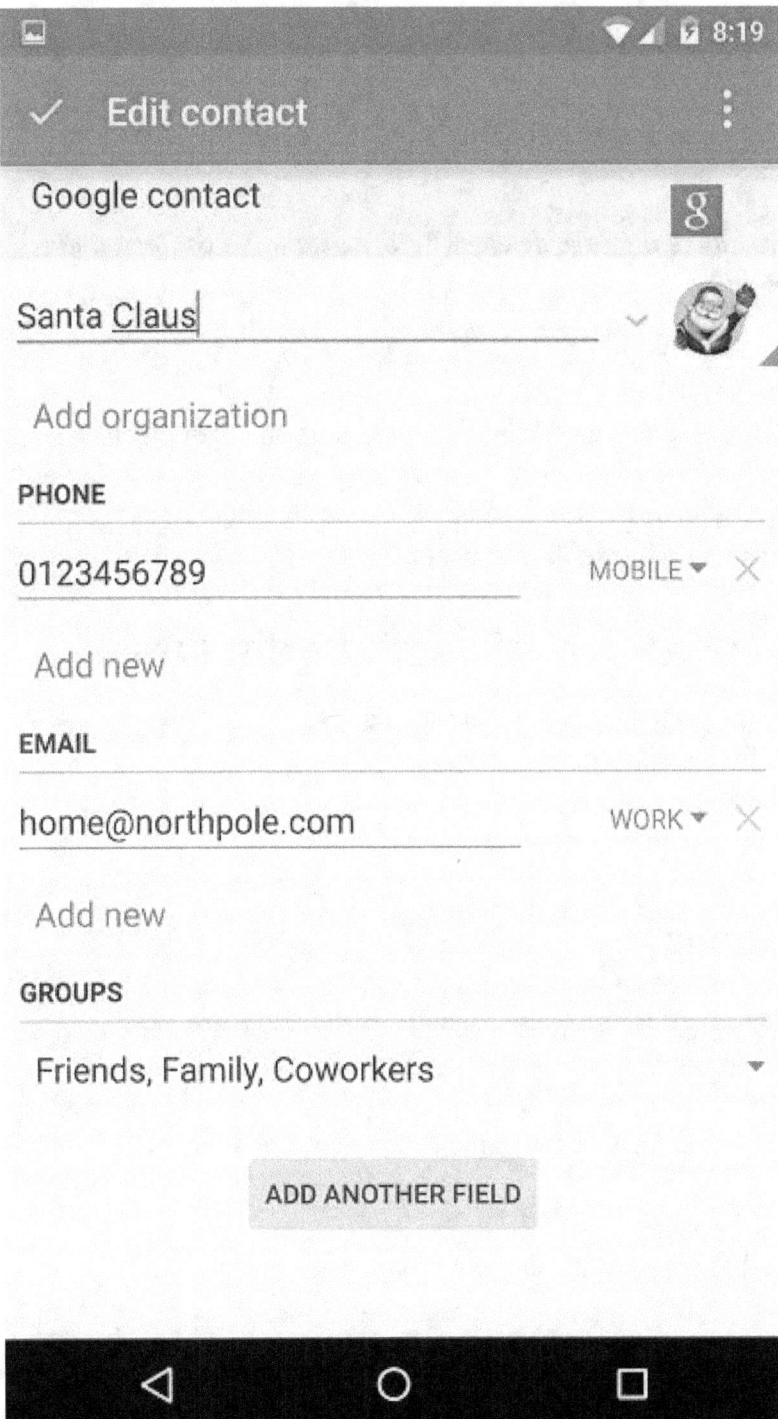

Figure 5: Contact Editing Screen

4. Deleting a Contact

Free up memory on the device by deleting an unneeded contact from the phonebook. To delete a contact:

Warning: Contacts cannot be retrieved once they are deleted. Before deleting a contact, make sure that you do not need the information.

1. Touch the ![icon] icon on the Home screen, or touch the ![icon] icon and then touch the ![icon] icon. The phonebook appears.
2. Touch a contact's name. The contact's information appears.
3. Touch the ![icon] icon at the top of the screen. The Contact Editing screen appears.
4. Touch the ![icon] icon at the top of the screen. The Contact menu appears.
5. Touch **Delete**. A confirmation dialog appears.
6. Touch **OK**. The contact is deleted.

5. Adding a Contact to a Group

Contacts can be organized into groups for easier browsing. To add a contact to a group:

1. Touch the ![icon] icon on the Home screen, or touch the ![icon] icon and then touch the ![icon] icon. The phonebook appears.
2. Touch the name of the contact that you wish to add to a group. The contact's information appears.
3. Touch the ![icon] icon at the top of the screen. The Contact Editing screen appears.
4. Touch list of group names under 'GROUPS', as outlined in **Figure 6**. A list of available groups appears, as shown in **Figure 7**.

5. Touch the names of the groups to which the contact should be assigned. A ✅ mark appears next to each selected group. You may also touch **Create new group** to create your own. After a group has been created, it will appear in the list of available groups.

6. Touch the name of a group in the list that has a ✅ mark next to it. The ✅ mark disappears, and the contact will not be added to the group, or will be removed from the group.

7. Touch the ✅ icon at the top of the screen. The contact is added to, or removed from, the selected groups.

To display only the contacts in a certain group when viewing your phonebook:

1. Touch the ⋮ icon at the top of the phonebook screen. The Phonebook menu appears.
2. Touch Contacts to display. The Contacts to Display screen appears, as shown in **Figure 8**.
3. Touch **Customize**. Your Gmail address appears. If you have not registered your Gmail account with your device, a list of groups appears. In this case, proceed to step 5.
4. Touch your Gmail address. The Define Custom View screen appears, as shown in **Figure 9**.

5. Touch each group that you would like to display in the phonebook. A ✅ mark appears next to each selected group. Any group that is not selected will not be displayed in the phonebook.
6. Touch **OK**. The phonebook now only displays the contacts in the selected groups.
   Touch **Contacts** in Custom View in the phonebook, and then touch **All contacts** to revert back to viewing all contacts in the phonebook.

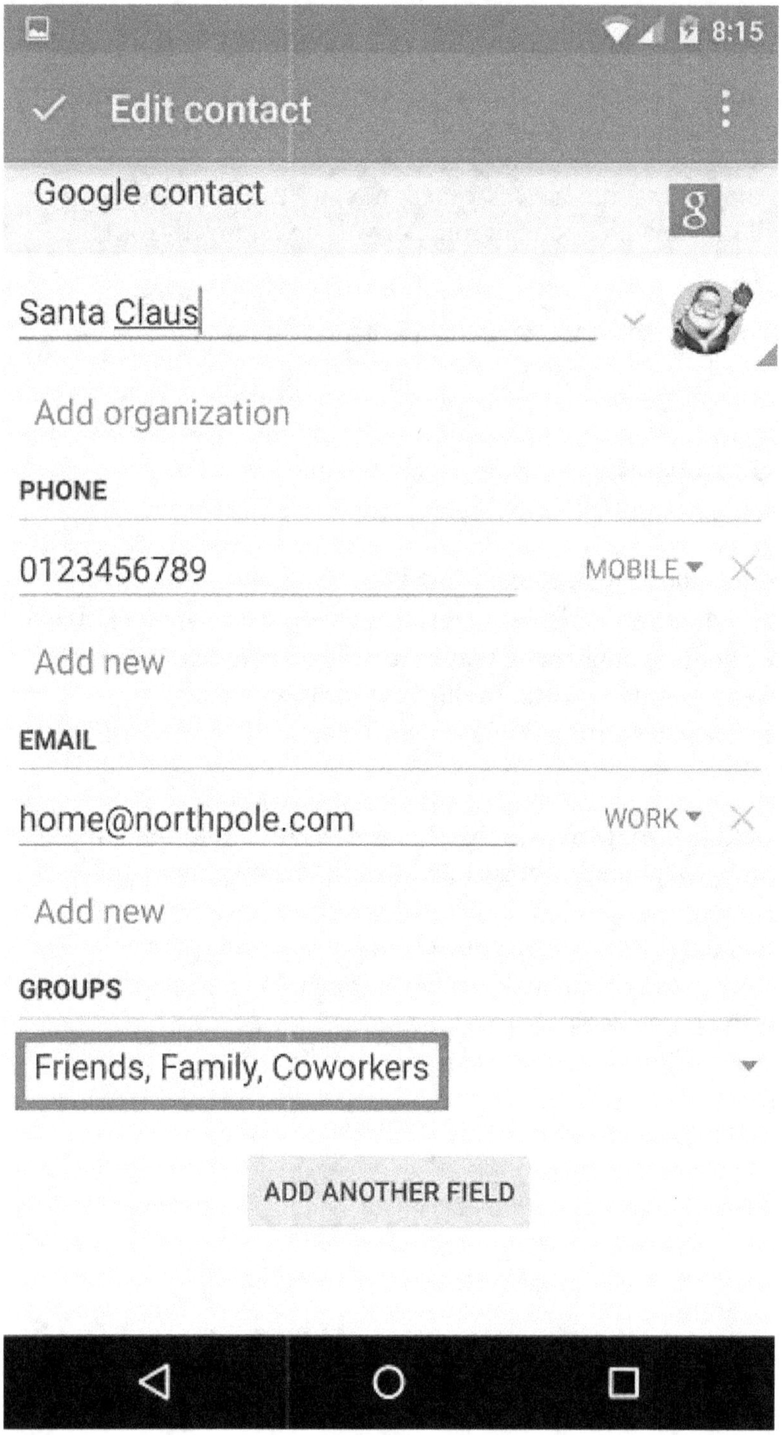

Figure 6: Group Names Outlined

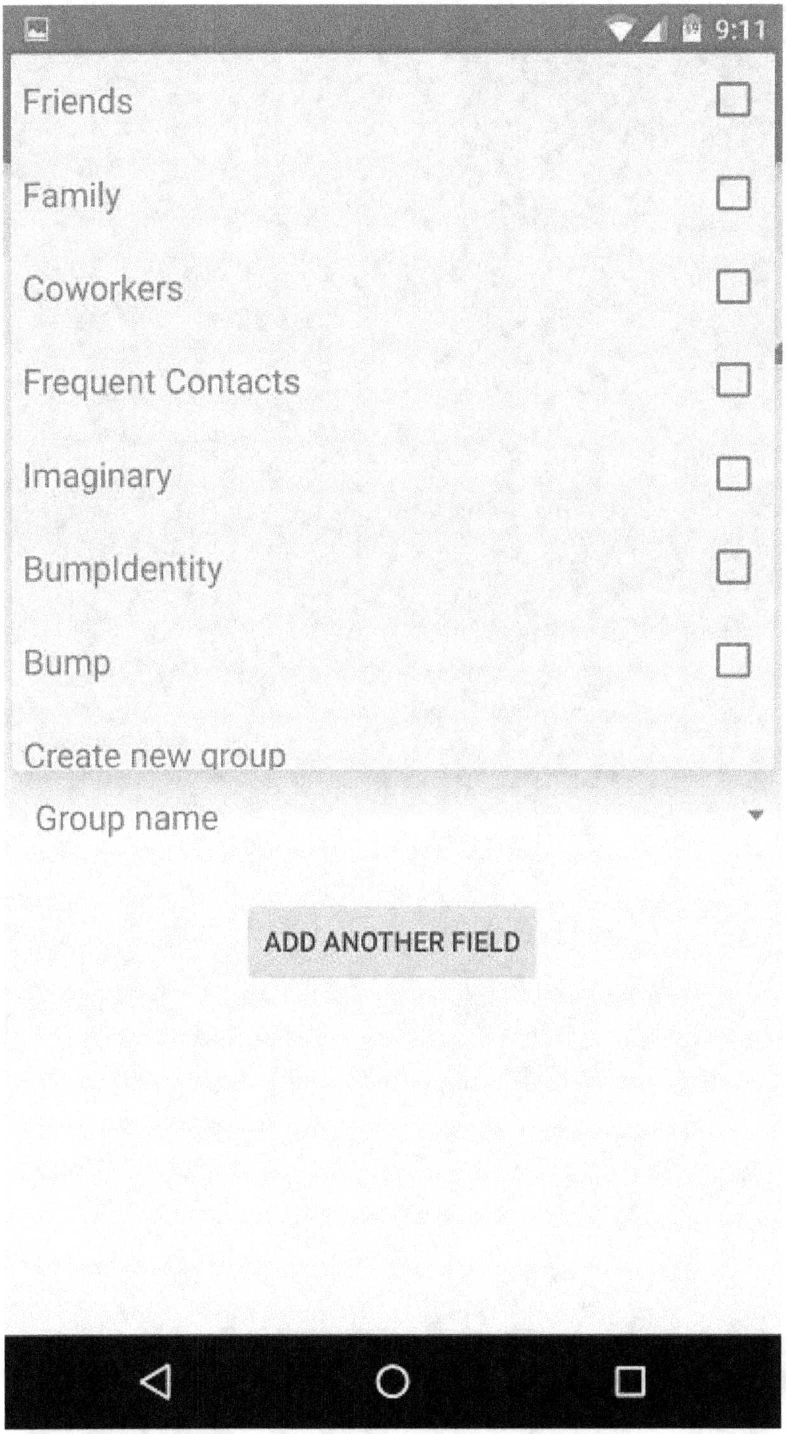

Figure 7: List of Available Groups

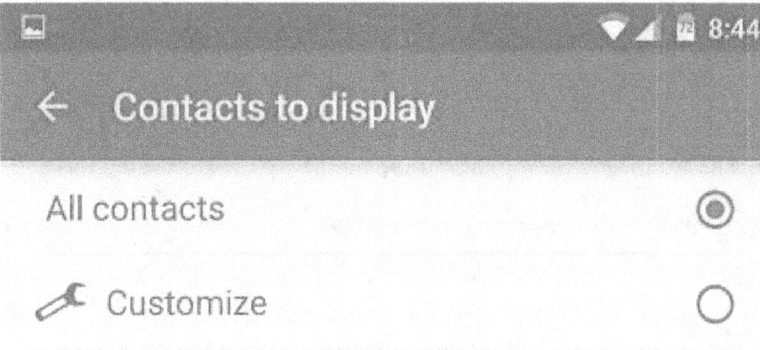

Figure 8: Contacts to Display Screen

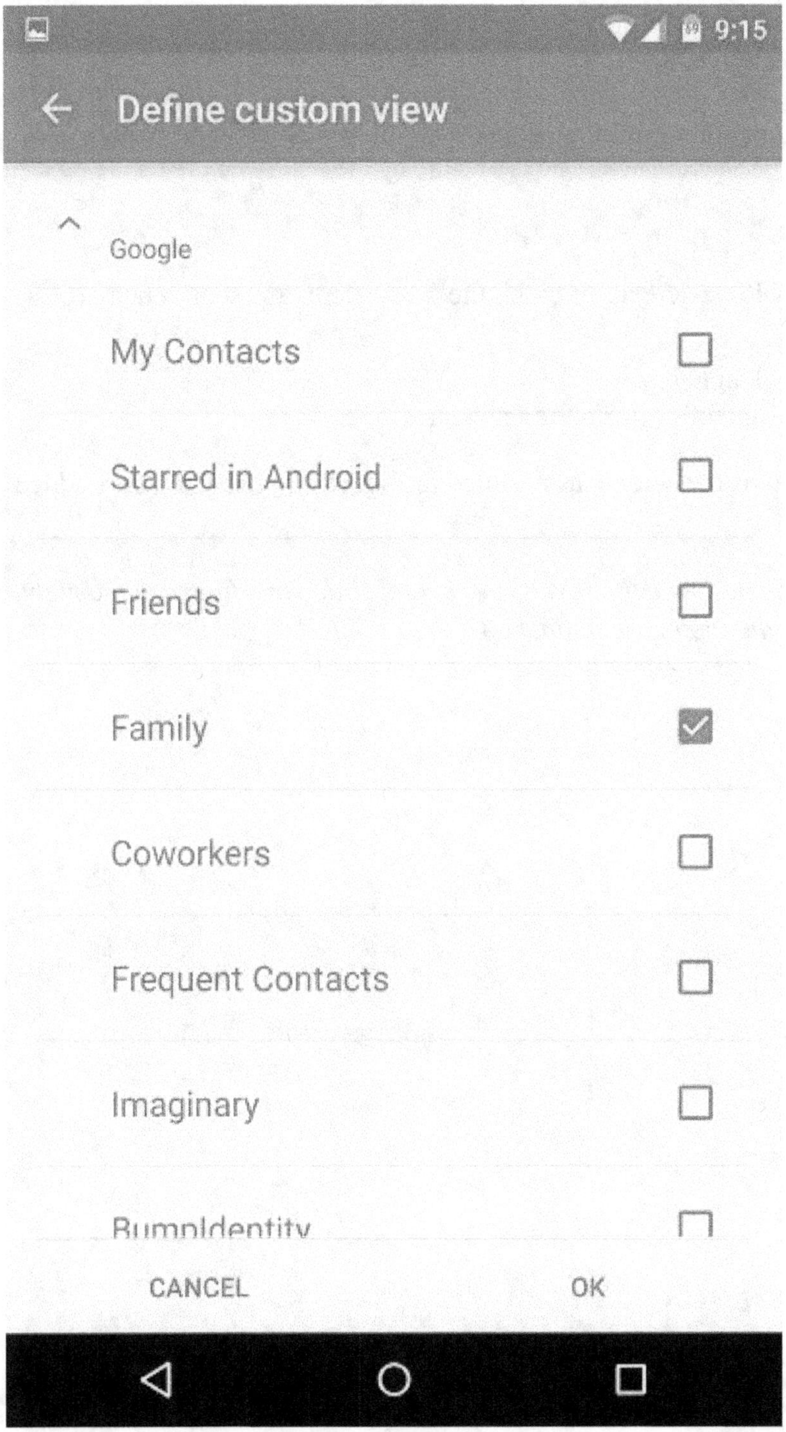

Figure 9: Define Custom View Screen

6. Adding a Contact to Favorites

The Favorites group can be used to quickly access the people that you contact the most often. To add a contact to Favorites:

1. Touch the ![icon] icon on the Home screen, or touch the ![icon] icon and then touch the ![icon] icon. The phonebook appears.
2. Touch a contact's name. The contact's information appears.
3. Touch the ![icon] icon at the top of the screen, as outlined in Figure 10. The contact is added to Favorites.

Note: To access your Favorites, touch the phonebook anywhere, and slide your finger to the right. You can also touch **FAVORITES** *at the top of the phonebook.*

Figure 10: Favorites Icon Outlined

7. Sharing Contact Information via Email

When a contact is stored in the phonebook, all of the information for that contact is available in the form of a Namecard. A Namecard is a VCF file (opened with Outlook or a similar program) that can be shared with others, which conveniently transfers all of the contact's information to other devices. To share contact information:

1. Touch the ![icon] icon on the Home screen, or touch the ![icon] icon and then touch the ![icon] icon. The phonebook appears.
2. Touch a contact's name. The contact's information appears.
3. Touch the ![icon] icon at the top of the screen. The Contact menu appears.
4. Touch **Share**. The Sharing Method menu appears, as shown in **Figure 11**. The sharing methods vary based on the applications that you have installed on your device.
5. Touch **Gmail** (recommended). A new message appears with the Namecard attached, as shown in **Figure 12**.
6. Enter an email address, subject, and optional message by touching each field. The information is entered. Refer to *"Writing an Email"* on page 175 to learn more about composing emails.
7. Touch the ![icon] button in the upper right-hand corner of the screen. The email is sent and the contact information is shared. On a mobile device, the recipient can save the Namecard directly to the phonebook.

Note: Sharing contact information via Bluetooth is not covered in this guide due to its complexity and the fact that devices often fail to communicate with one another properly.

Figure 11: Sharing Method Menu

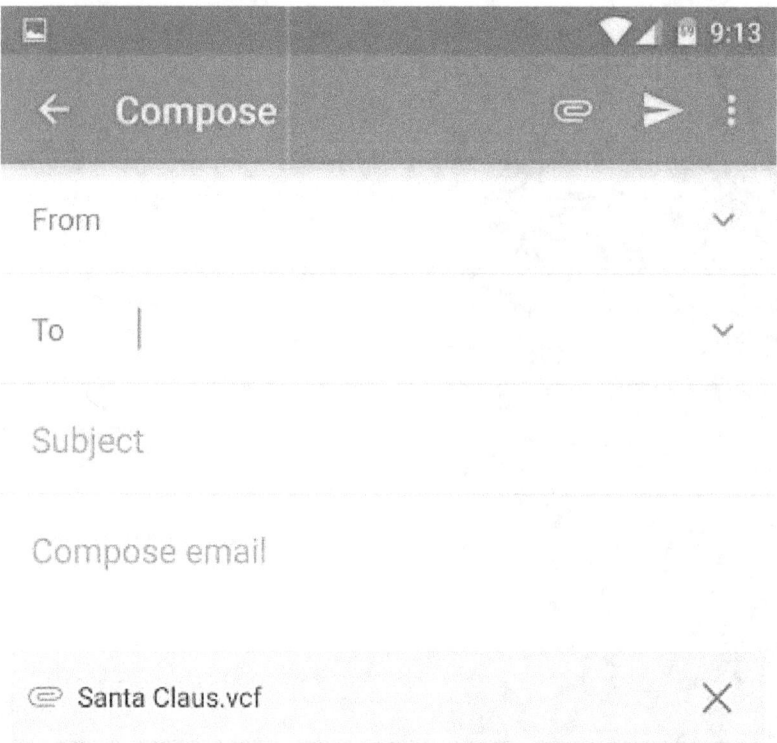

Figure 12: New Message with Attached Namecard

8. Changing the Way Contacts are Sorted

By default, contacts in the phonebook are sorted alphabetically by first name. For example, John Diss is listed before Ray Beeze because John comes before Ray in the alphabet. The last name is disregarded when sorting, unless there is more than one person with the same first name, in which case it is used to determine which name is listed first. To change the way contacts are sorted:

1. Touch the [icon] icon on the Home screen, or touch the [icon] icon and then touch

    the [icon] icon. The phonebook appears.

2. Touch the [icon] icon at the top of the screen. The Contact menu appears.
3. Touch **Settings**. The Phonebook Settings screen appears, as shown in **Figure 13**.
4. Touch **Sort by**. The Sorting window appears.
5. Touch **Last name**. The contacts in the phonebook will now be sorted according to their last name. Using the example in this section, Ray Beeze would now come before John Diss.
6. Touch **First name**. The contacts in the phonebook will now be sorted according to their first name.

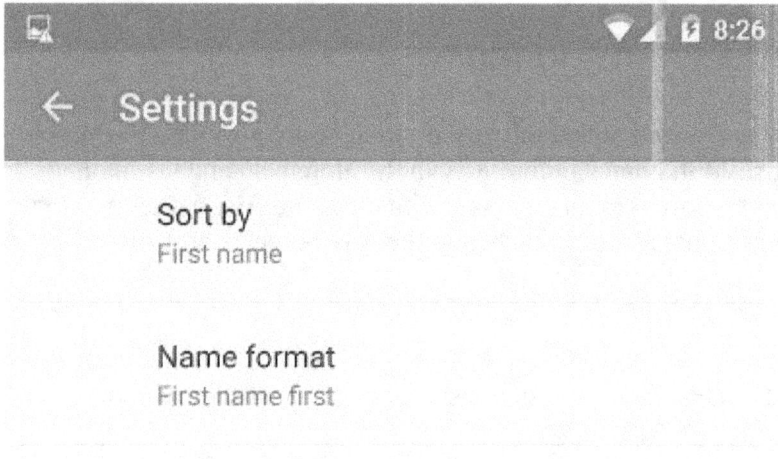

Figure 13: Phonebook Settings Screen

9. Changing the Way Contacts are Displayed

By default, contacts in the phonebook are displayed with the first name appearing first. For example, Sarah Bellum is displayed as "Sarah Bellum." To change the way contacts are displayed:

1. Touch the icon on the Home screen, or touch the icon and then touch the icon. The phonebook appears.

2. Touch the icon at the top of the screen. The Contact menu appears.
3. Touch **Settings**. The phonebook Settings screen appears.
4. Touch **Name format**. The Contact Display window appears.
5. Touch **Last name first**. Contacts will now be displayed with the last name appearing first. Using the example in this section, Sarah Bellum will now be displayed as "Bellum, Sarah."
6. Touch **First name first**. Contacts will now be displayed with the first name appearing first.

Using the Chrome Web Browser

Table of Contents

1. Navigating to a Website

One way to visit a website is to enter its Web address in the Address bar. To navigate to a website using its Web address:

1. Touch the 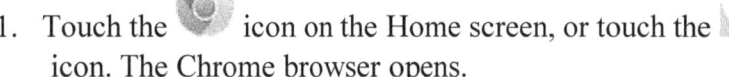 icon on the Home screen, or touch the 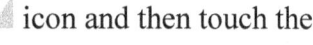 icon and then touch the icon. The Chrome browser opens.
2. Touch Search or type URL in the Address bar at the top of the screen, as outlined in **Figure 1**. The Address bar is selected and the keyboard appears.

3. Enter a Web address and touch the button. Chrome navigates to the website.

Figure 1: Address Bar Outlined

2. Adding and Viewing Bookmarks

The device can store websites as bookmarks to access them faster. These bookmarks will appear on both your mobile devices and the computers that are logged in to your Google account in the Chrome browser. To add a bookmark:

1. Navigate to a website. Refer to *"Navigating to a Website"* on page 211 to learn how.
2. Touch the ⋮ icon in the Address bar. The Chrome menu appears, as shown in **Figure 2**.
3. Touch the ☆ icon. The Bookmark Editing window appears, as shown in **Figure 3**.
4. Enter a name for the bookmark. Touch Mobile Bookmarks to select the locations where the bookmark should be saved. A list of available bookmark locations appears, as shown in **Figure 4**.
5. Touch the folder to which you want to save the bookmark. Then, touch Save. The Web page is saved to your bookmarks.

To view your bookmarks:

1. Touch the ⋮ icon in the upper right-hand corner of the browser. The Chrome menu appears
2. Touch **Bookmarks**. The Bookmarks screen appears, as shown in **Figure 5**.
3. Touch a bookmark. Chrome navigates to the selected Web page.

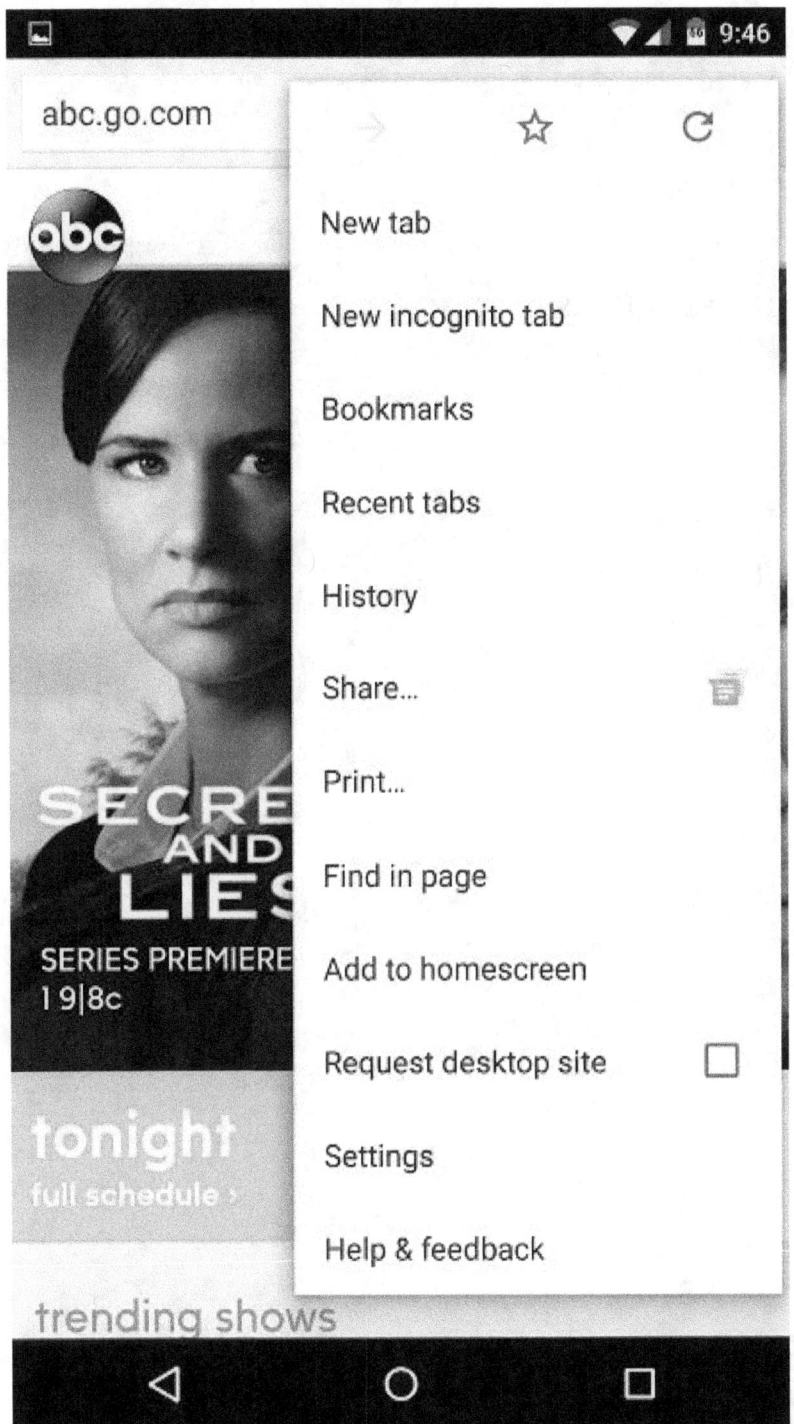

Figure 2: Chrome Menu

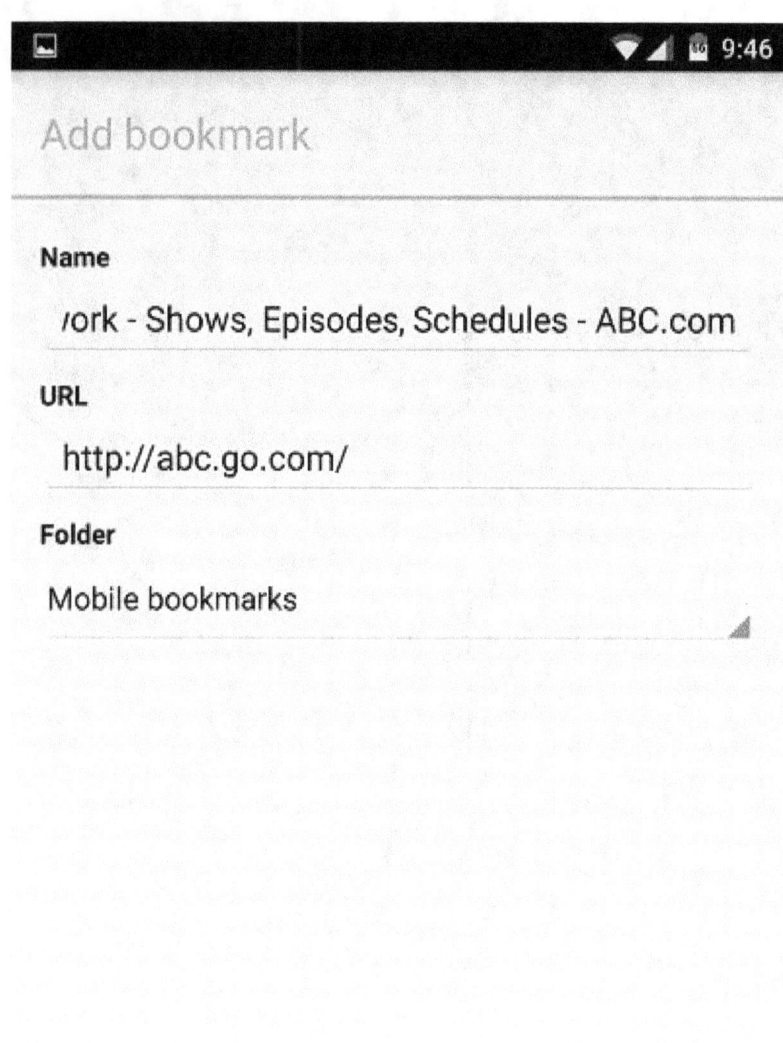

Figure 3: Bookmark Editing Window

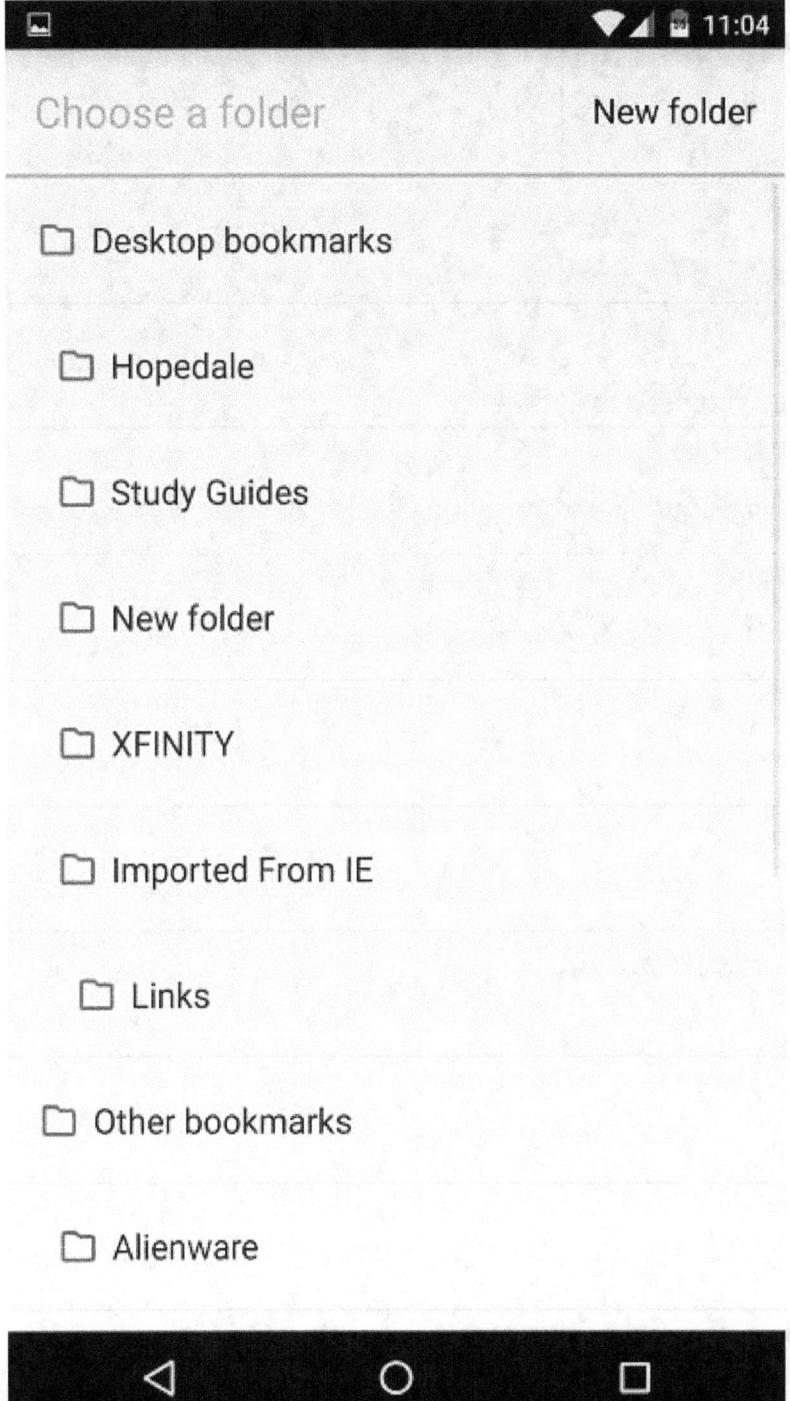

Figure 4: List of Available Bookmark Locations

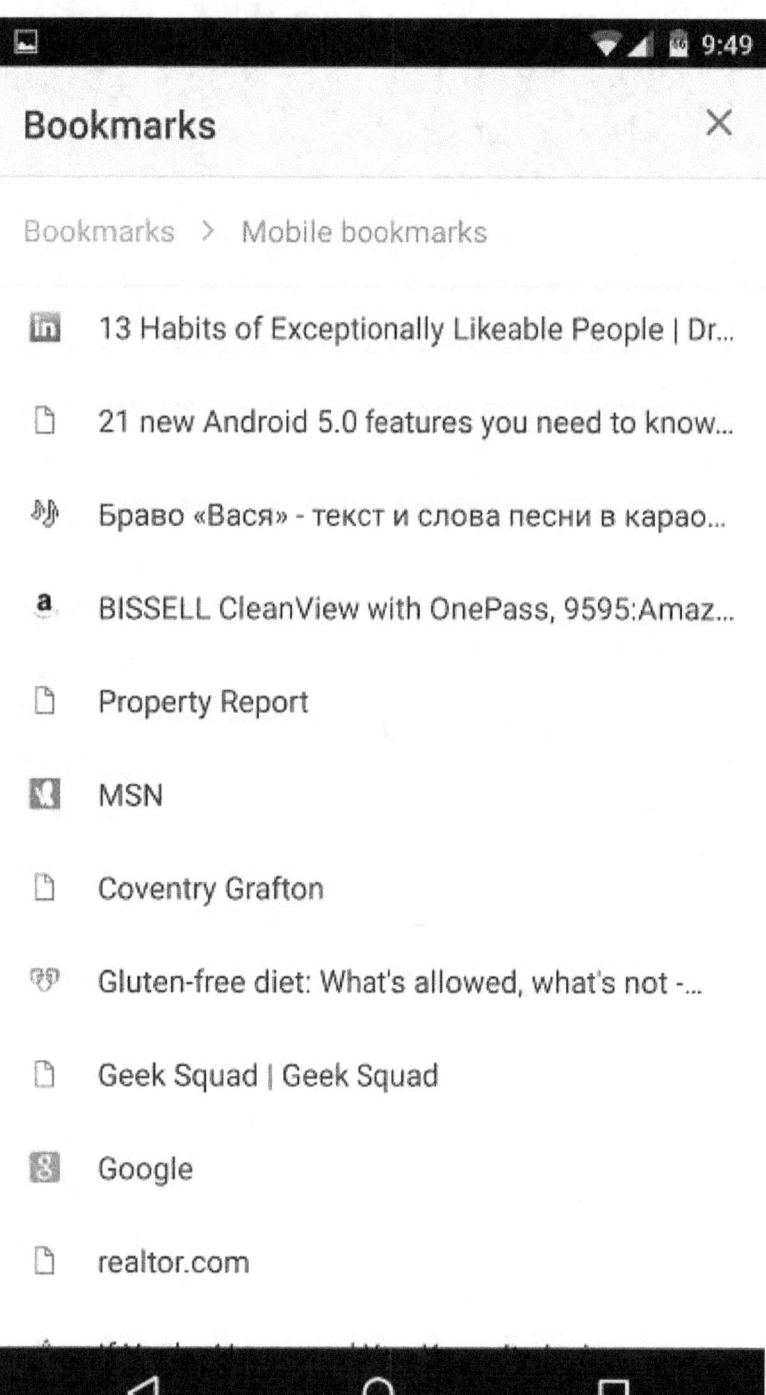

Figure 5: Bookmarks Screen

3. Editing and Deleting Bookmarks

Bookmarks may be edited if a new Web address or label is desired. Bookmarks may also be deleted to free up space.

To edit a bookmark:

1. Touch the ⠿ icon in the upper right-hand corner of the browser. The Chrome menu appears.
2. Touch **Bookmarks**. The Bookmarks screen appears.
3. Touch and hold a bookmark. The Bookmark menu appears, as shown in **Figure 6**.
4. Touch **Edit bookmark**. The Bookmark Editing window appears.
5. Touch a field to change the information. The bookmark is edited.
6. Touch **Save**. The new bookmark information is stored.

To delete a bookmark:

Warning: Once a bookmark is deleted, it is gone forever. There is no confirmation dialog when deleting a bookmark. Make sure that you wish to delete the bookmark before touching Delete Bookmark *in step 4.*

1. Touch the ⠿ icon in the upper right-hand corner of the browser. The Chrome menu appears.
2. Touch **Bookmarks**. The Bookmarks screen appears.
3. Touch and hold a bookmark. The Bookmark menu appears.
4. Touch **Delete bookmark**. The bookmark is deleted.

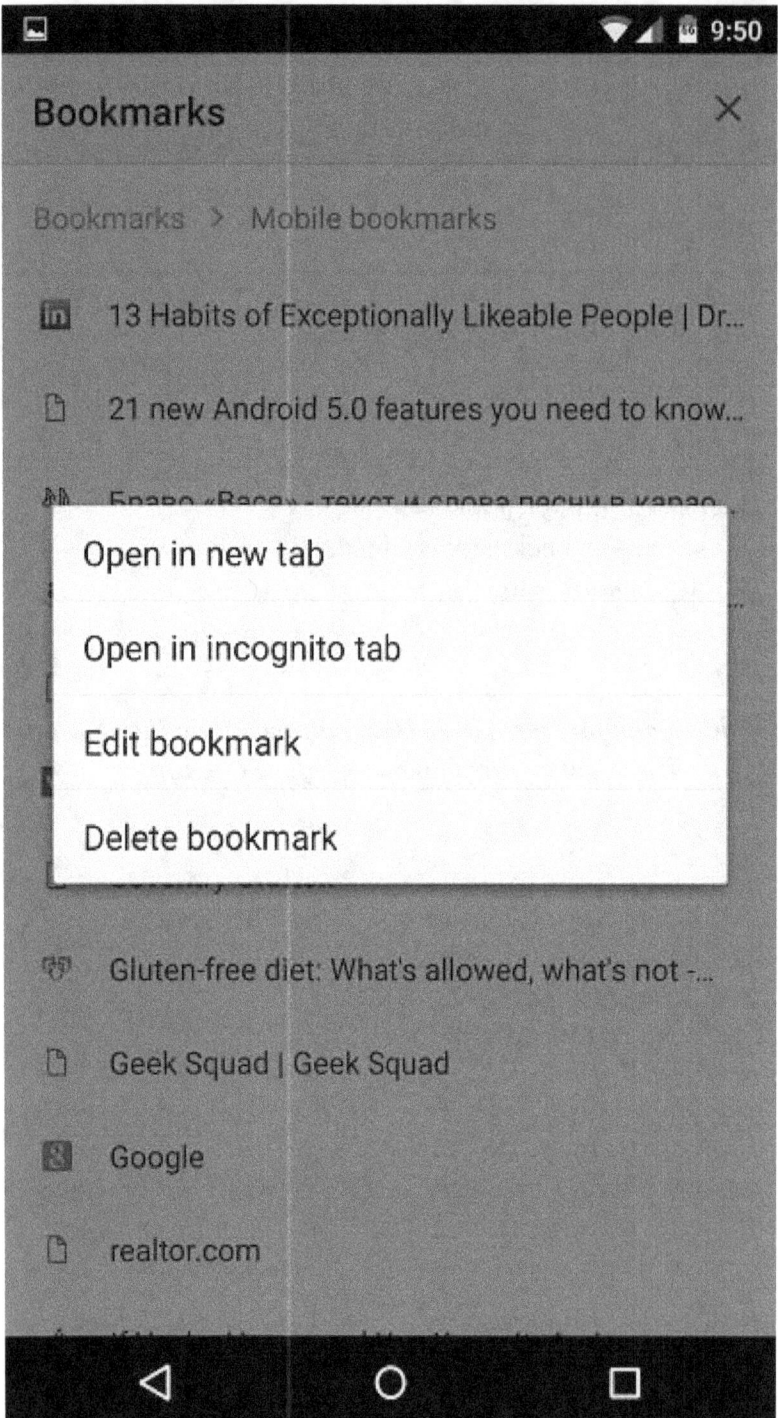

Figure 6: Bookmark Menu

4. Opening More than One Website at a Time

The Chrome browser allows you to have more than one Web page opened at once, using separate tabs. By default, each tab is opened as a separate window in Overview (when you touch the [image] key). Refer to *"Viewing Recently Opened Applications"* on page 116 to learn more about the Overview feature. The number of tabs that may be opened simultaneously is unlimited. Use the following tips to manage Chrome tabs:

- To add a tab, touch the [image] icon, and then touch **New tab**.

- To view an open Web page, touch the [image] key, and then touch the name of the webpage.

- To close a tab, touch the [image] key, and then slide the tab that you want to close to the left or right.

5. Turning Chrome Tabs On or Off

By default, each new tab is opened in a separate window in Overview. Turn on Chrome tabs to make them appear in the Chrome application, as tabs appeared in Android prior to Lollipop. To turn Chrome tabs on or off:

1. Touch the [image] icon in the upper right-hand corner of the browser. The Chrome menu appears.
2. Touch **Settings**. The Chrome Settings screen appears, as shown in **Figure 7**.
3. Touch **Merge tabs and apps**. The Tab Settings screen appears, as shown in **Figure 8**.
4. Touch the [image] switch next to 'Merge tabs and apps'. A confirmation dialog appears.
5. Touch **OK**. The Chrome application closes. When you reopen Chrome, tabs will now appear in the Chrome application, and not in Overview.
6. To merge tabs and apps again, repeat steps 1-3 above, and then touch the [image] switch. A confirmation dialog appears.
7. Touch **OK**. The Chrome application closes. When you reopen Chrome, tabs will now appear in Overview, and not in the Chrome application.

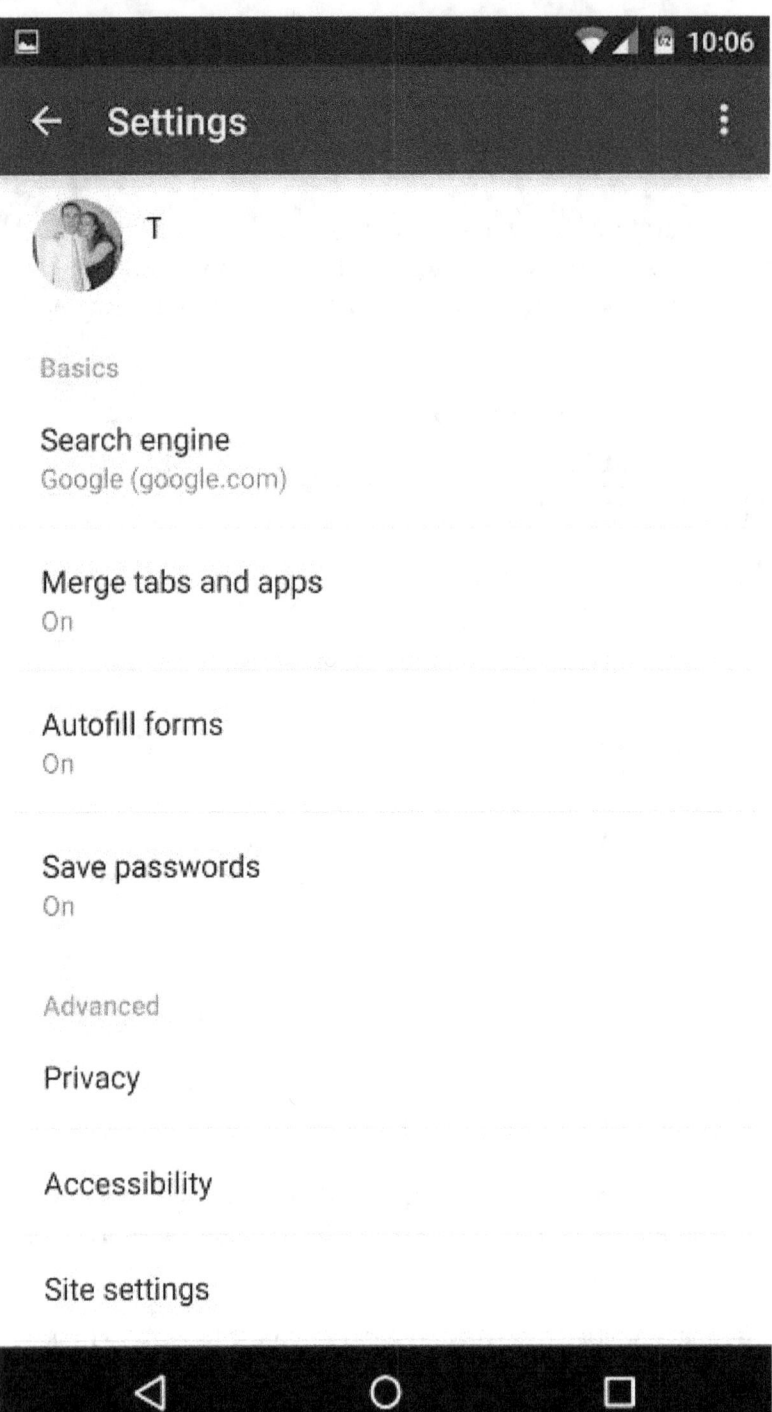

Figure 7: Chrome Settings Screen

Tabs live together with recent apps.

Figure 8: Tab Settings Screen

6. Link Options

In addition to touching a link to navigate to its destination, there are other Link options. Touch and hold a link to see all Link options, as follow:

- **Open in new tab** - Opens the link in a new tab, so as not lose the current Web page. Refer to *"Opening More than One Website at a Time"* on page 220 to learn how to view other open pages.
- **Open in Incognito tab** - Opens the link in a new Incognito tab, which will prevent you from leaving a trail in the form of a Web History while browsing in the tab.
- **Copy link address** - Copies the Web address to the clipboard.
- **Copy link text** - Copies the link as text rather than a hyperlink that can be clicked.
- **Save link** - Downloads the Web page to the device. The Web page can then be accessed by touching the 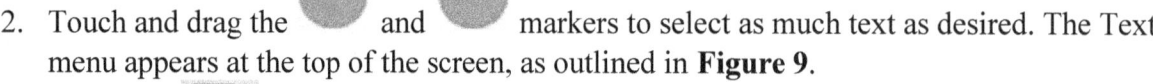 icon and then touching the icon. The device does not need to be connected to a Wi-Fi network to access the saved Web page, but it does need an internet connection if you wish to navigate to any of the links that it contains (if applicable).

7. Copying and Pasting Text

Text on any web page can be selected, copied, and pasted to another location. To copy and paste text:

1. Touch the beginning of the text until a word is highlighted in blue and the and markers appear.

2. Touch and drag the and markers to select as much text as desired. The Text menu appears at the top of the screen, as outlined in **Figure 9**.

3. Touch the icon. The text is copied to the clipboard. You can also touch the icon to select all of the text on the page.

4. To paste the text to another location, such as an application, touch and hold a text field.

5. Touch **Paste**. The text is pasted to the new location.

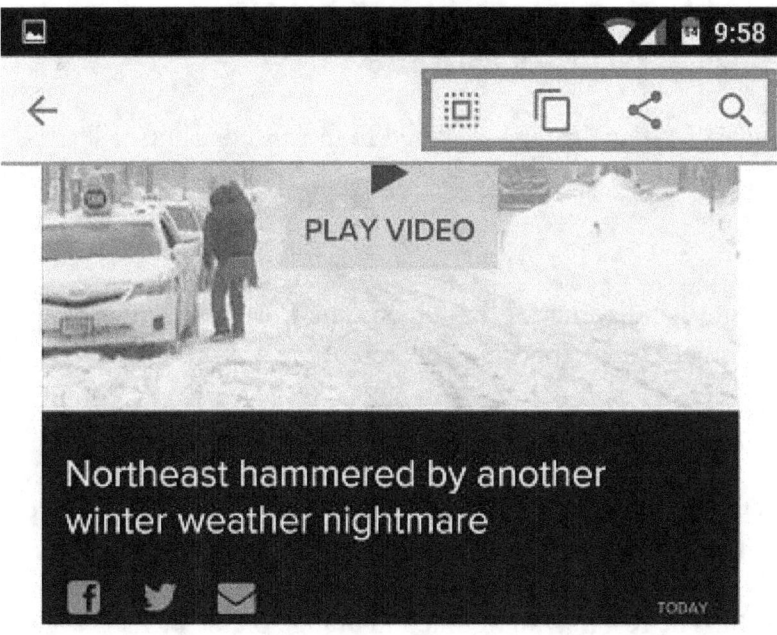

Figure 9: Text Menu

8. Searching a Web Page for a Word or Phrase

While using the Chrome application, any Web page can be searched for a word or phrase. To perform a search of a Web page:

1. Touch the ⋮ icon in the upper right-hand corner of the screen. The Chrome menu appears.
2. Touch **Find in page**. The 'Find in page' field appears at the top of the screen, as shown in **Figure 10**.

3. Enter search keywords and touch the [🔍] button. All matching search results are highlighted on the page, as shown in **Figure 11**.
4. Touch one of the yellow stripes on the right-hand side of the screen, as outlined in **Figure 11**, to navigate to a specific result. The result is highlighted in orange on the page.

Note: You can also touch the ∧ or ∨ icons to the right of the Search field to navigate to the previous or next result, respectively.

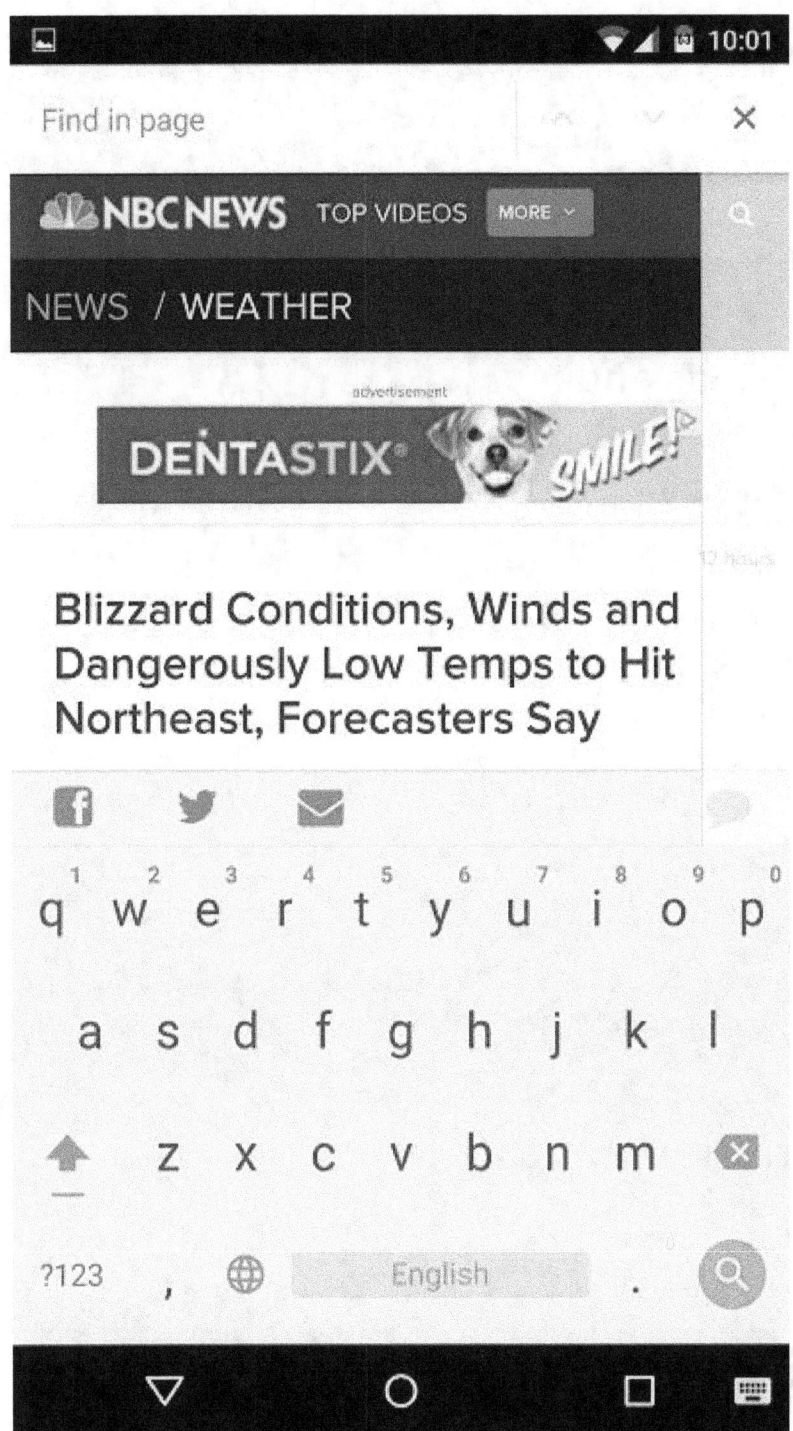

Figure 10: 'Find in Page' Field Outlined

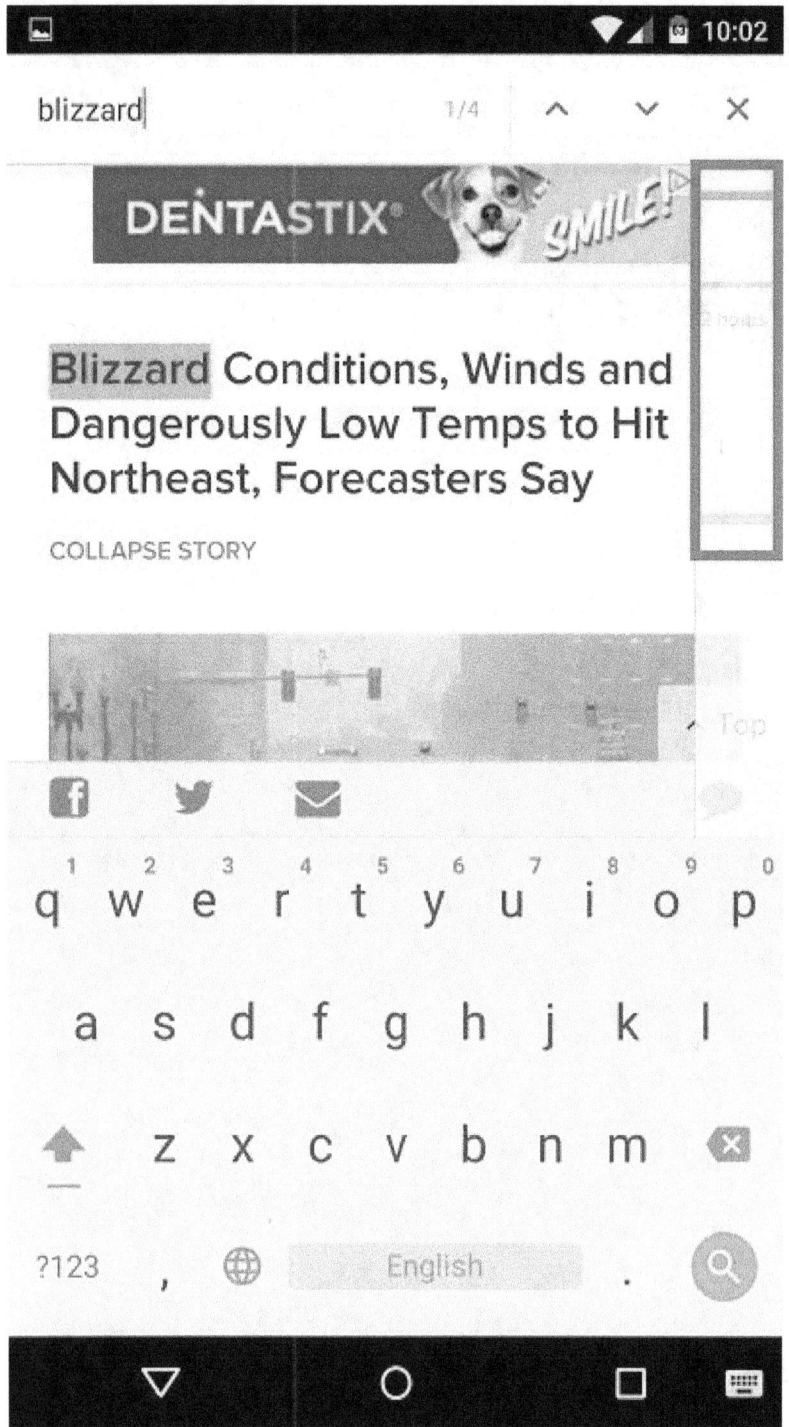

Figure 11: Matching Search Results Highlighted in Yellow

9. Viewing the Most Recently Visited Websites

The device stores all frequently visited websites. To view the most frequently visited sites:

1. Touch the ⋮ icon in the upper right-hand corner of the browser. The Chrome menu appears.
2. Touch **Recent tabs**. The Bookmarks screen appears. The most recently visited sites appear, as shown in **Figure 12**.
3. Touch a site in the list. Chrome navigates to the Web page.

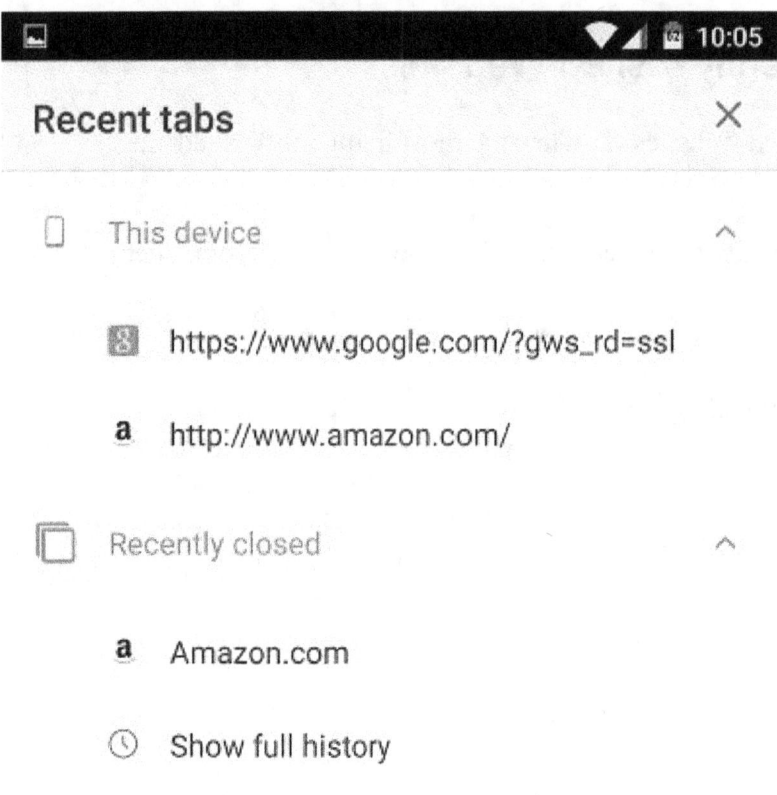

Figure 12: Most Recently Visited Sites

10. Automatically Filling in Online Forms

The Autofill feature can automatically enter your personal information into online forms by using a predefined Autofill profile. To add a new Autofill profile:

1. Touch the ⋮ icon in the upper right-hand corner of the browser. The Chrome menu appears.
2. Touch **Settings**. The Chrome Settings screen appears.
3. Touch **Autofill forms**. The Autofill Profiles screen appears, as shown in **Figure 13**.
4. Touch **Add profile** under 'Autofill Profiles'. The Add Profile screen appears, as shown in **Figure 14**.
5. Touch each field to enter the associated information. Then, touch **Save**. The Autofill profile is saved, and the information that you provided will be automatically entered into online forms.

Note: Refer to "Clearing the Data that is Used to Speed Up Browsing" *on page 241 to learn how to delete all saved forms.*

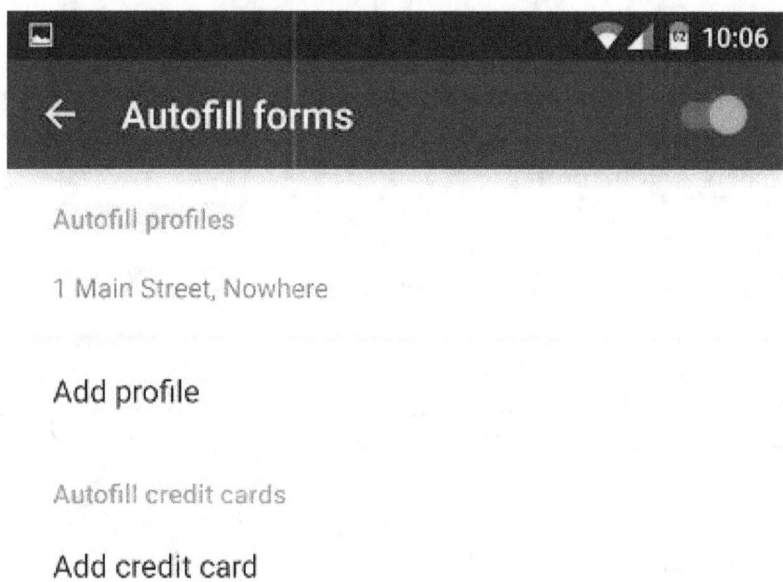

Figure 13: Autofill Profiles Screen

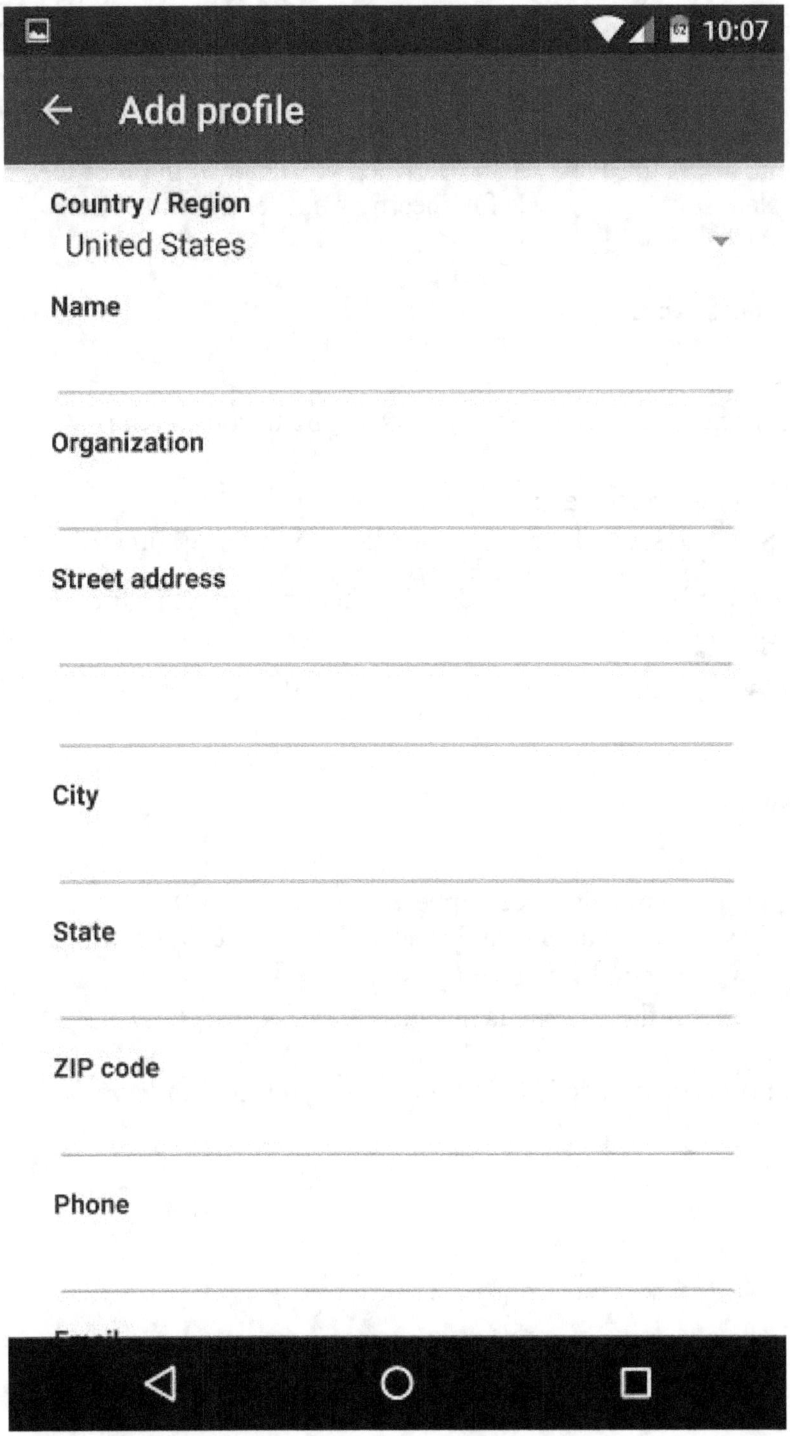

Figure 14: Add Profile Screen

11. Saving and Managing Passwords for Websites

The Chrome browser can save your account credentials for various websites, such as email clients and shopping sites. By default, Chrome offers to save a password when you enter it. In order to protect your privacy, you may also delete saved passwords for specific websites after they have been stored.

To enable the saving of usernames and passwords:

1. Touch the ⋮ icon in the upper right-hand corner of the browser. The Chrome menu appears.
2. Touch **Settings**. The Chrome Settings screen appears.
3. Touch **Save passwords**. The Saved Passwords screen appears, as shown in **Figure 15**.
4. Touch the ⬤ switch at the top of the screen. The ⬤ switch appears and Chrome will no longer offer to save passwords.
5. Touch the ⬤ switch. The ⬤ switch appears and Chrome will offer to save passwords every time that you enter one.

To delete a stored password for a specific website:

1. Follow steps 1-3 above. The Saved Passwords screen appears.
2. Touch a website under 'Saved Passwords'. The Saved Password URL and email to which the account is assigned appear, as shown in **Figure 16**.
3. Touch **Delete**. The saved password for the website is deleted.

Note: Refer to "Clearing the Data that is Used to Speed Up Browsing" *on page 241 to learn how to delete all saved passwords at once.*

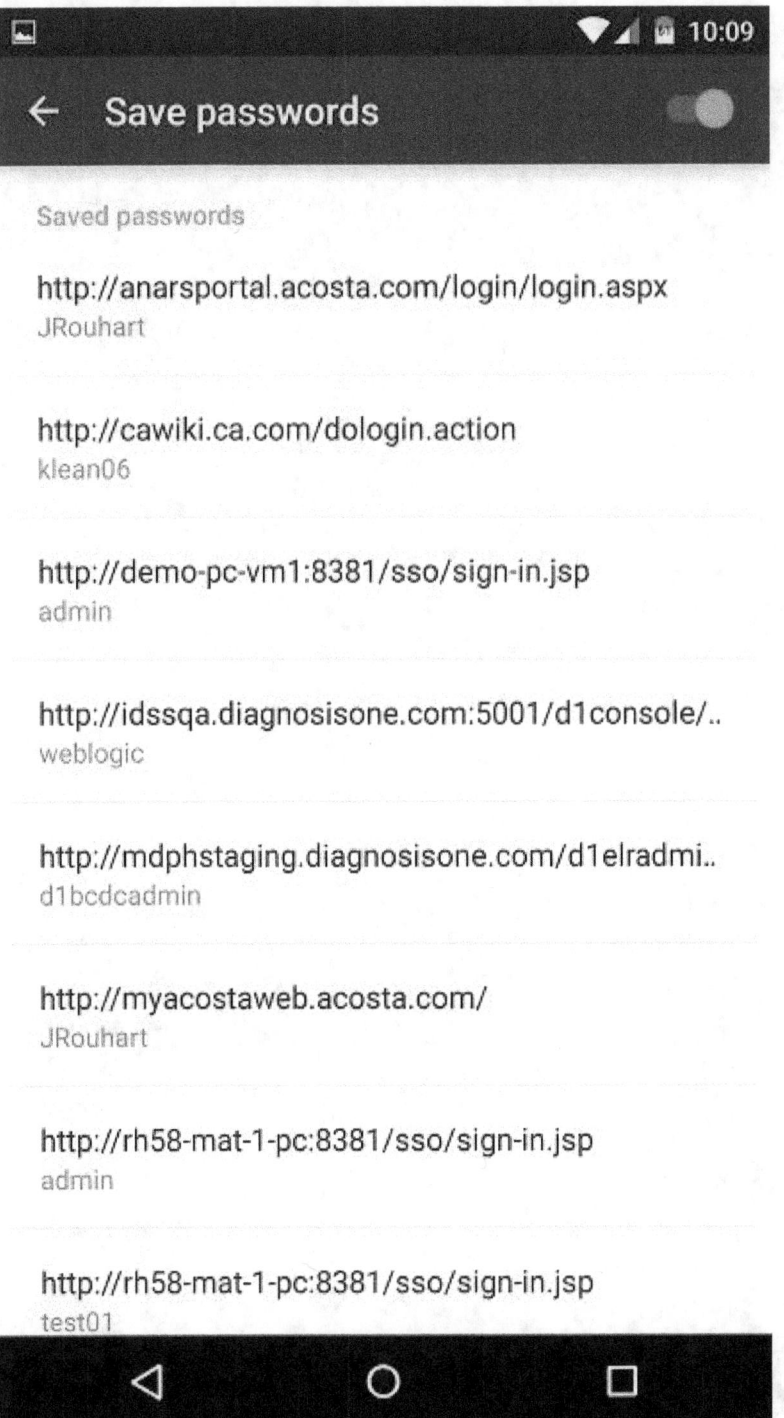

Figure 15: Saved Passwords Screen

admin

http://demo-pc-vm1:8381/sso/sign-in.jsp

Figure 16: Saved Password URL

12. Setting the Search Engine

Google, Yahoo, or Bing may be used as the default search engine in the Chrome browser. To perform a search at any time, enter a search term in the Address bar. Refer to *"Navigating to a Website"* on page 211 to locate the Address bar. To set the search engine:

1. Touch the ⋮ icon in the upper right-hand corner of the browser. The Chrome menu appears.
2. Touch **Settings**. The Chrome Settings screen appears.
3. Touch **Search engine**. A list of available search engines appears.
4. Touch a search engine. The search engine is selected and will be used whenever a search is performed.

13. Setting the Font Size

The text size used in the Chrome browser can be changed. To set the browser's font size:

1. Touch the ⋮ icon in the upper right-hand corner of the browser. The Chrome menu appears.
2. Touch **Settings**. The Chrome Settings screen appears.
3. Touch **Accessibility**. The Chrome Accessibility Settings screen appears, as shown in **Figure 17**.

4. Touch the ⬤ slider and drag it to the left or right to decrease or increase the font size, respectively. The font size is adjusted and will be used on all websites.

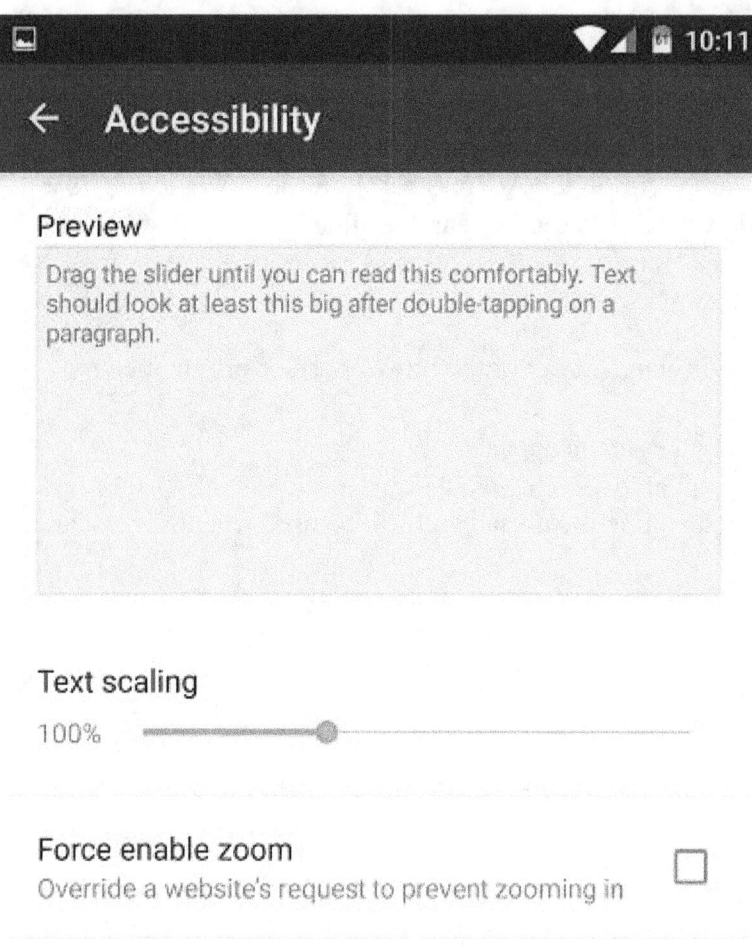

Figure 17: Chrome Accessibility Settings Screen

14. Blocking Pop-Up Windows

Some websites may cause pop-up windows to appear, interfering with your surfing. By default, pop-ups are blocked. To prevent pop-up windows:

1. Touch the ⋮ icon in the upper right-hand corner of the browser. The Chrome menu appears.
2. Touch **Settings**. The Chrome Settings screen appears.
3. Touch **Site settings**. The Site Settings screen appears, as shown in **Figure 18**.
4. Touch **Pop-ups**. The Pop-ups screen appears.
5. Touch **Pop-ups blocked**. 'Pop-ups Allowed' appears, and pop-ups are turned on.
6. Touch **Pop-ups allowed**. 'Pop-ups Blocked' appears, and pop-ups are turned off.

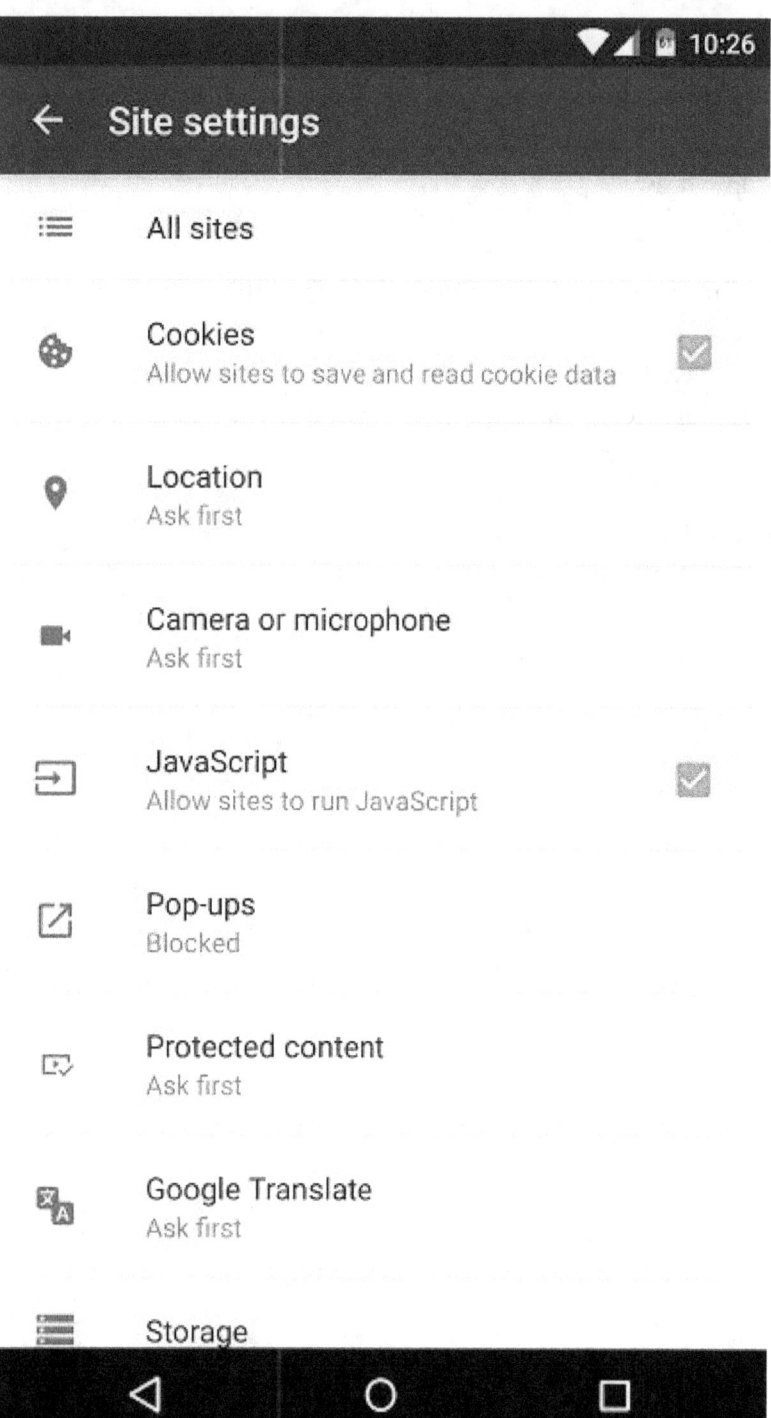

Figure 18: Site Settings Screen

15. Recalling Sites More Quickly on Subsequent Visits

The Chrome browser can store data that is used to quickly recall sites that you have previously visited, called Cookies. This feature provides convenience, but may also take up some space on your device. By default, the Chrome browser stores these data. To recall sites faster on subsequent visits:

1. Touch the ⦙ icon in the upper right-hand corner of the browser. The Chrome menu appears.
2. Touch **Settings**. The Chrome Settings screen appears.
3. Touch **Site settings**. The Content Settings screen appears.
4. Touch **Cookies**. The ✓ mark disappears, and Chrome will not store data that will help to recall sites faster on subsequent visits.
5. Touch **Cookies again**. The ✓ mark appears and Chrome will save data that will help to recall sites faster on subsequent visits.

Note: Refer to "Clearing the Data that is Used to Speed Up Browsing" *on page 241 to learn how to delete Cookies.*

16. Turning JavaScript On or Off

JavaScript is used primarily for animation and interactive elements on websites, as with games, audio, and video. Turning on JavaScript will allow you to view such content, but may slow down the loading process when you visit sites that contain it. By default, JavaScript is turned on. To turn JavaScript on or off:

1. Touch the ⦙ icon in the upper right-hand corner of the browser. The Chrome menu appears.
2. Touch **Settings**. The Chrome Settings screen appears.
3. Touch **Site settings**. The Content Settings screen appears.
4. Touch **JavaScript**. The ✓ mark appears and JavaScript is turned on.
5. Touch JavaScript again. The ✓ mark disappears and JavaScript is turned off.

17. Clearing the Data that is Used to Speed Up Browsing

Chrome stores data, which allows it to load previously visited websites and fill in forms more quickly. In order to protect your privacy, you may wish to delete these data. To clear some or all of the data that is used to speed up browsing:

1. Touch the ⋮ icon in the upper right-hand corner of the browser. The Chrome menu appears.
2. Touch **Settings**. The Chrome Settings screen appears.
3. Touch **Privacy**. The Privacy Settings screen appears, as shown in **Figure 19**.
4. Touch the ⋮ icon at the top of the screen. The Privacy Menu appears.
5. Touch **Clear Browsing Data**. A list of browsing data types appears, as shown in **Figure 20**.
6. Touch one of the following options to select the type of data for deletion:
    - **Clear browsing history** - Deletes all history files, including the addresses of recently visited websites.
    - **Clear the cache** - Deletes all Web page data, such as images and other files that comprise a website.
    - **Clear cookies, site data** - Deletes all text data, such as site preferences, authentication, or shopping cart contents.
    - **Clear saved passwords -** Deletes all stored passwords for various websites, such as email clients, marketplaces, and banking sites.
    - **Clear autofill data -** Deletes all form data, including screen names, addresses, phone numbers, and more.
7. Touch **Clear**. The selected data is deleted.

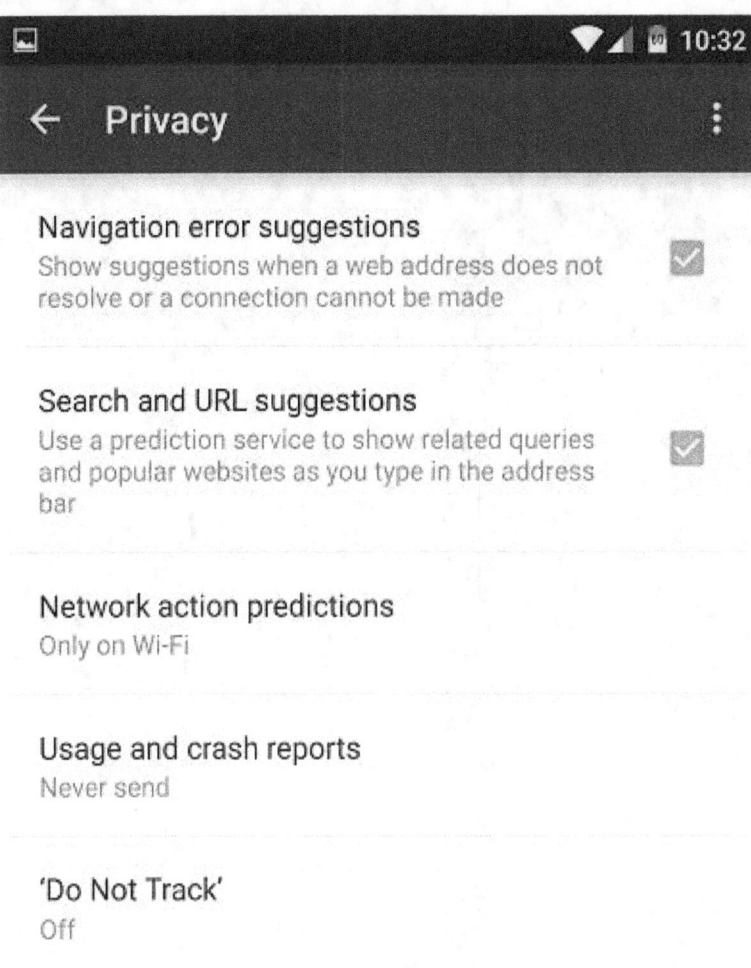

Figure 19: Privacy Settings Screen

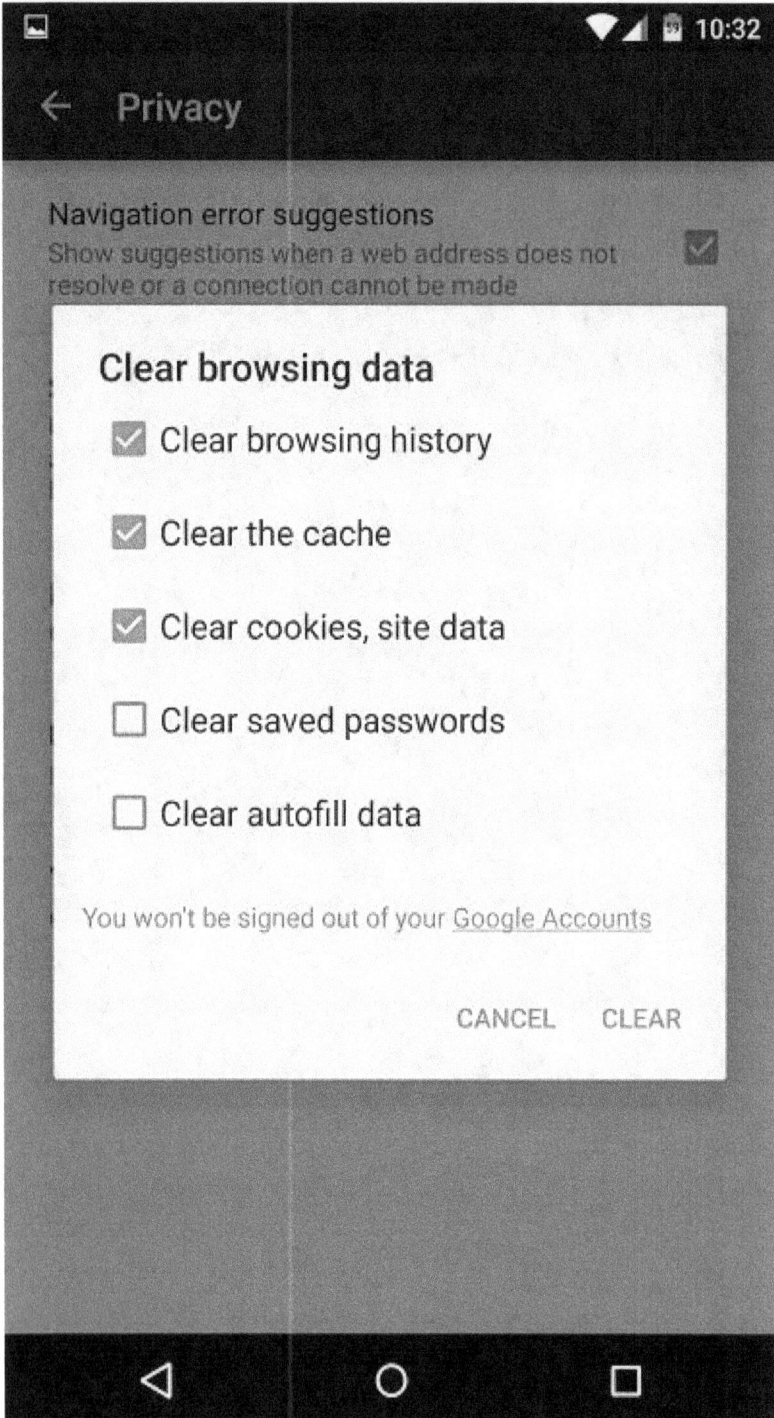

Figure 20: List of Browsing Data Types

18. Turning Suggestions for Searches and Web Addresses On or Off

While you enter a Web address or search query in the Address bar, Chrome can automatically make suggestions based on other popular choices. To set Chrome to show suggestions when you enter a search query:

1. Touch the ⦂ icon in the upper right-hand corner of the browser. The Chrome menu appears.
2. Touch **Settings**. The Chrome Settings screen appears.
3. Touch **Privacy**. The Privacy Settings screen appears.
4. Touch **Search and URL suggestions**. The ✓ mark appears and Chrome will make suggestions when you perform a search or enter a Web address.
5. Touch **Search and URL suggestions again**. The ✓ mark disappears and Chrome will not make suggestions for searches and Web addresses.

Adjusting Wireless Settings

Table of Contents

1. Turning Airplane Mode On or Off

Putting the device in Airplane mode turns off Near Field Communication (NFC), which allows the device to wirelessly send data to other devices. However, Wi-Fi is still available while in Airplane mode and can be used normally. Use Airplane mode to save battery life or while flying. To turn on Airplane mode:

1. Touch the status bar (where the clock and battery meter are located), and slide your finger down. The Quick Notifications appear.
2. Repeat step 1. The Quick Settings appear, as shown in **Figure 1**.

3. Touch the ![airplane icon] icon. Airplane Mode turns on, and all wireless communications are turned off.

4. Touch the ![airplane icon] icon. Airplane Mode turns off, and all wireless communications are turned on.

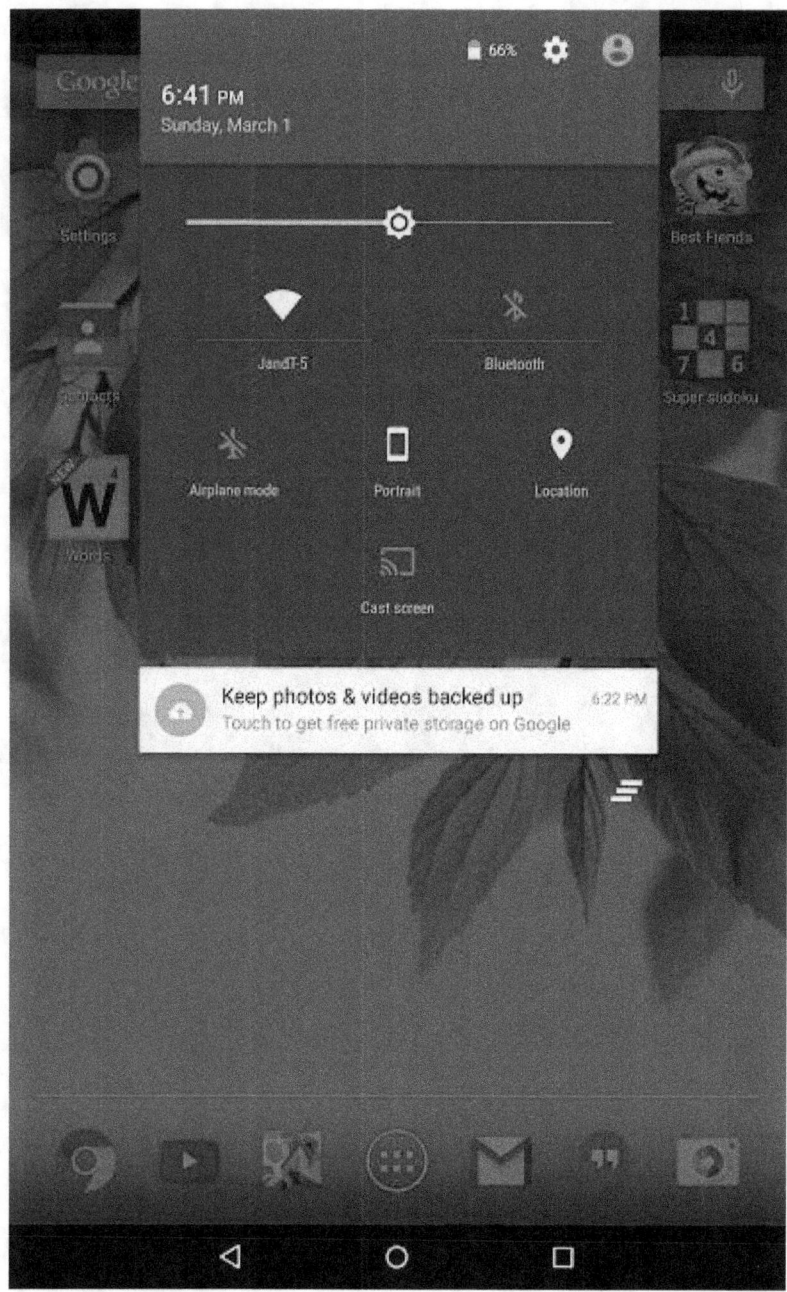

Figure 1: Quick Settings

2. Connecting to a Wi-Fi Network

The device can connect to Wi-Fi when it is near a hotspot. To connect to a Wi-Fi network:

1. Touch the icon. The Apps screen appears.

2. Touch the icon. The Settings screen appears, as shown in **Figure 2**. Refer to *"Tips and Tricks"* on page 312 to learn how to quickly access the Settings screen.

3. Touch **Wi-Fi**. The Wi-Fi screen appears. If Wi-Fi is turned off, touch **Off** under 'Wi-Fi'. A list of available Wi-Fi networks appears, as shown in **Figure 3**.

4. Touch the name of a network. If the network is secured, the Wi-Fi Network Password prompt appears, as shown in **Figure 4**.

5. Enter the network password (usually found on your wireless router) and touch **Connect**. The device connects to the network, provided that the password you entered is correct. If the password is incorrect, 'Authenticating' will appear next to the name of the network indefinitely.

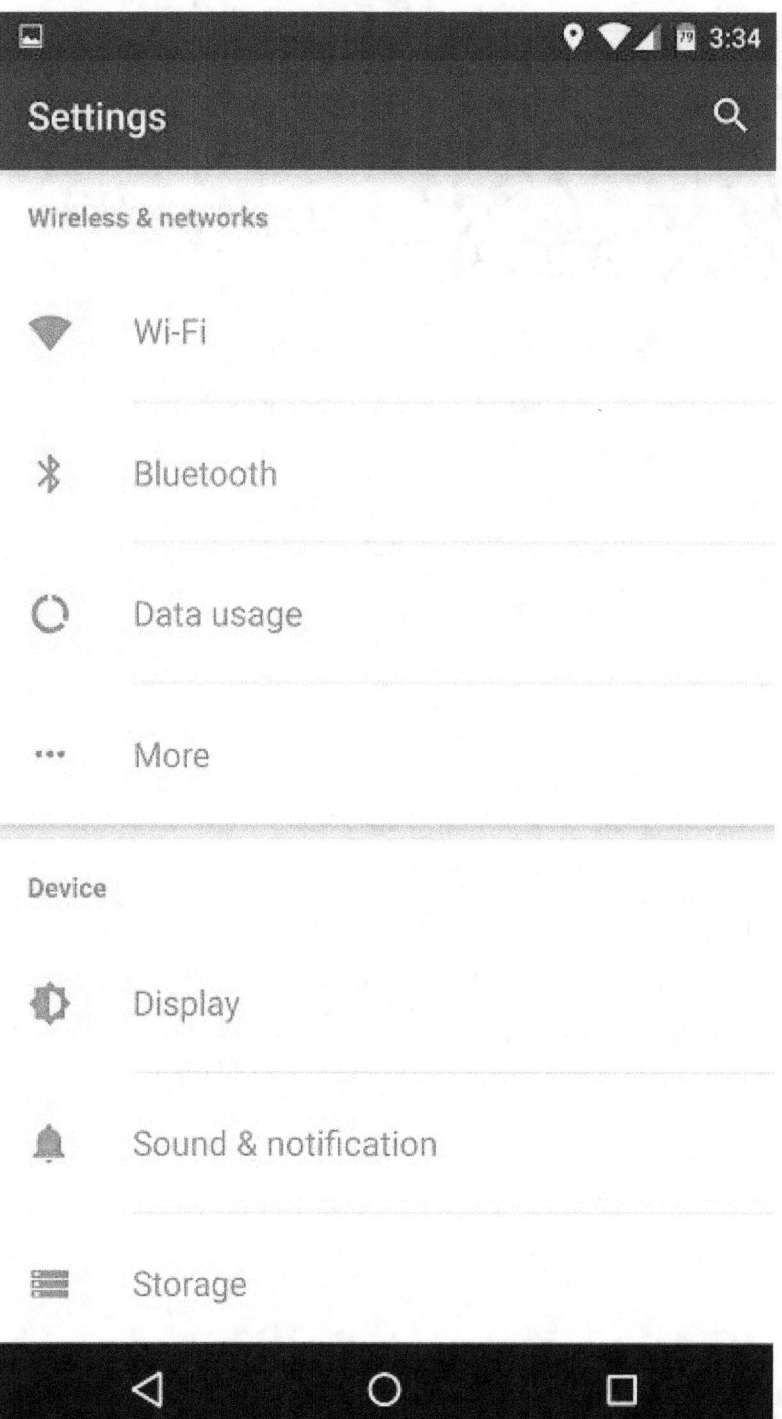

Figure 2: Settings Screen

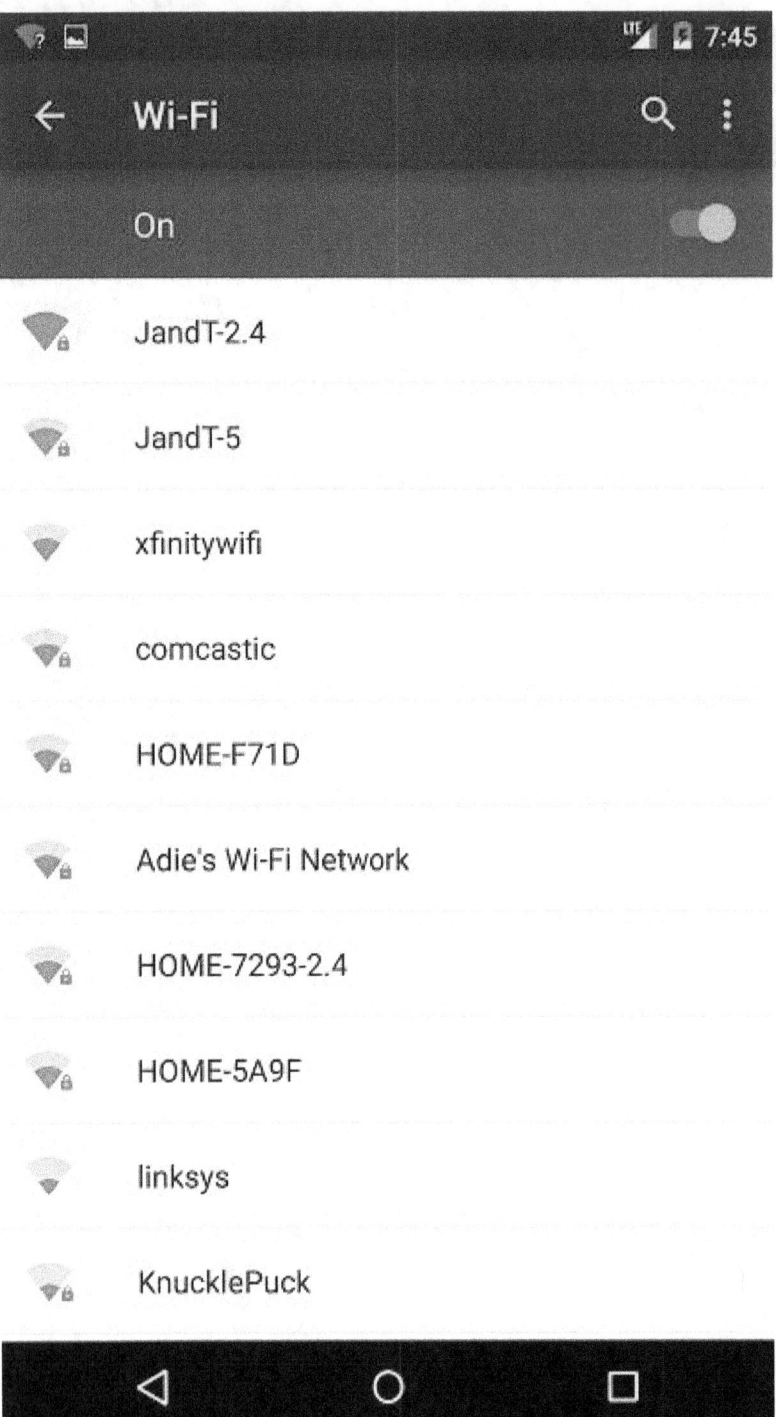

Figure 3: List of Available Wi-Fi Networks

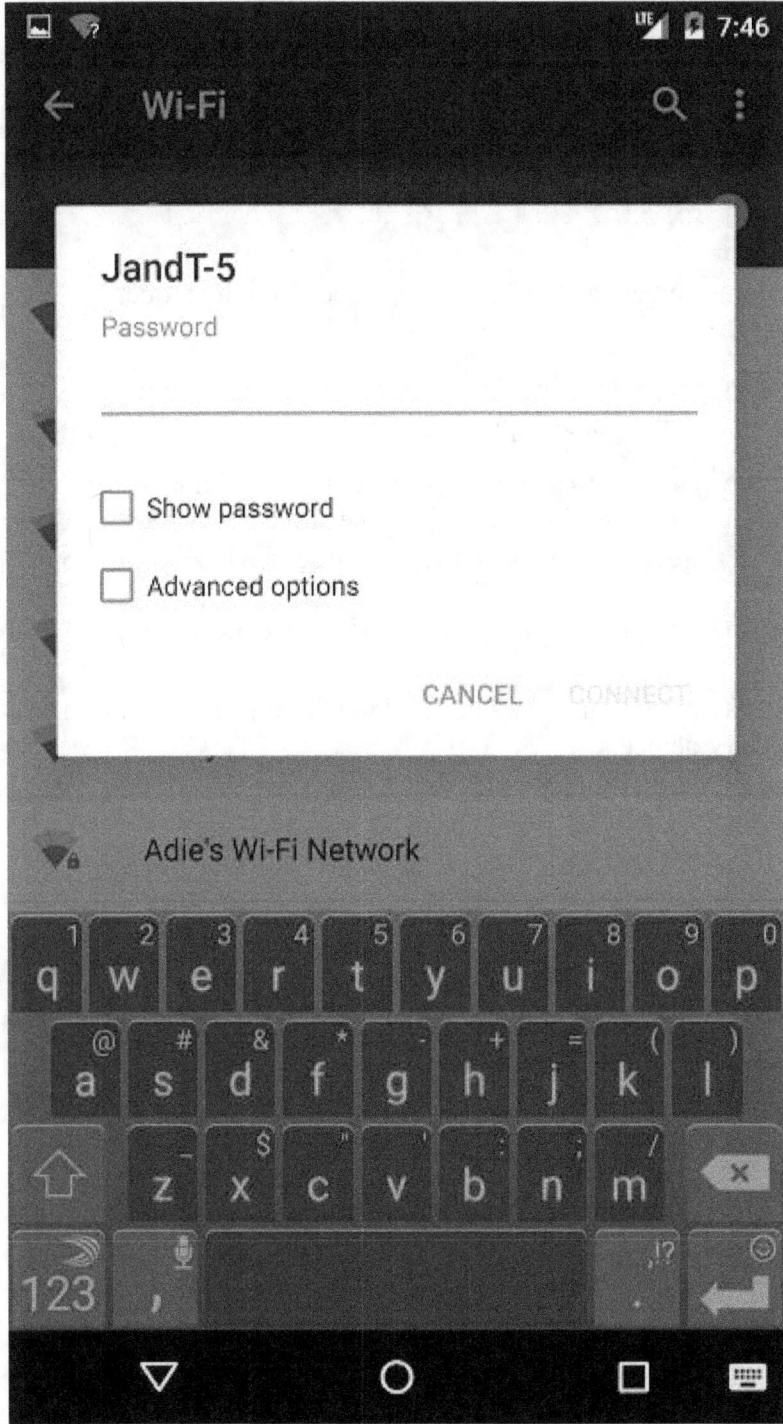

Figure 4: Wi-Fi Network Password Prompt

3. Using Bluetooth

Bluetooth allows the device to communicate with other mobile devices. To turn on Bluetooth and pair with another device:

1. Touch the icon on the Home screen, or touch the icon and then touch the icon. The Settings screen appears.
2. Touch **Bluetooth**. The Bluetooth Settings screen appears.
3. Touch **Off** at the top of the screen. The switch appears and Bluetooth is turned on. A list of devices appears that are in close proximity to the device and also have their Bluetooth turned on, as shown in **Figure 5**. Make sure the secondary device is ready to pair.
4. Touch a device in the list. The Bluetooth Pairing Request window appears, as shown in **Figure 6**.
5. Make sure both devices are displaying the same pass key and touch Pair on each one. The device is paired with the secondary device.
6. Touch **On** at the top of the screen. Bluetooth is turned off.

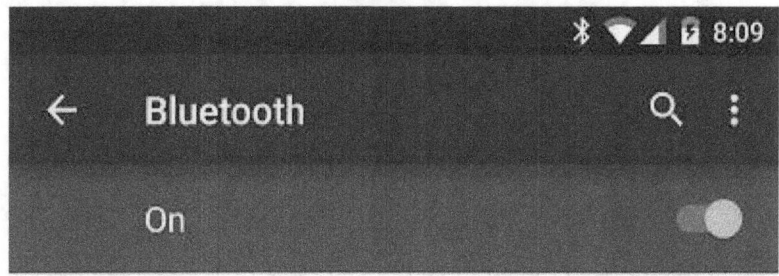

Available devices

SAMSUNG-SGH-I337

Nexus 6 is visible to nearby devices while Bluetooth Settings is open.

Figure 5: List of Devices

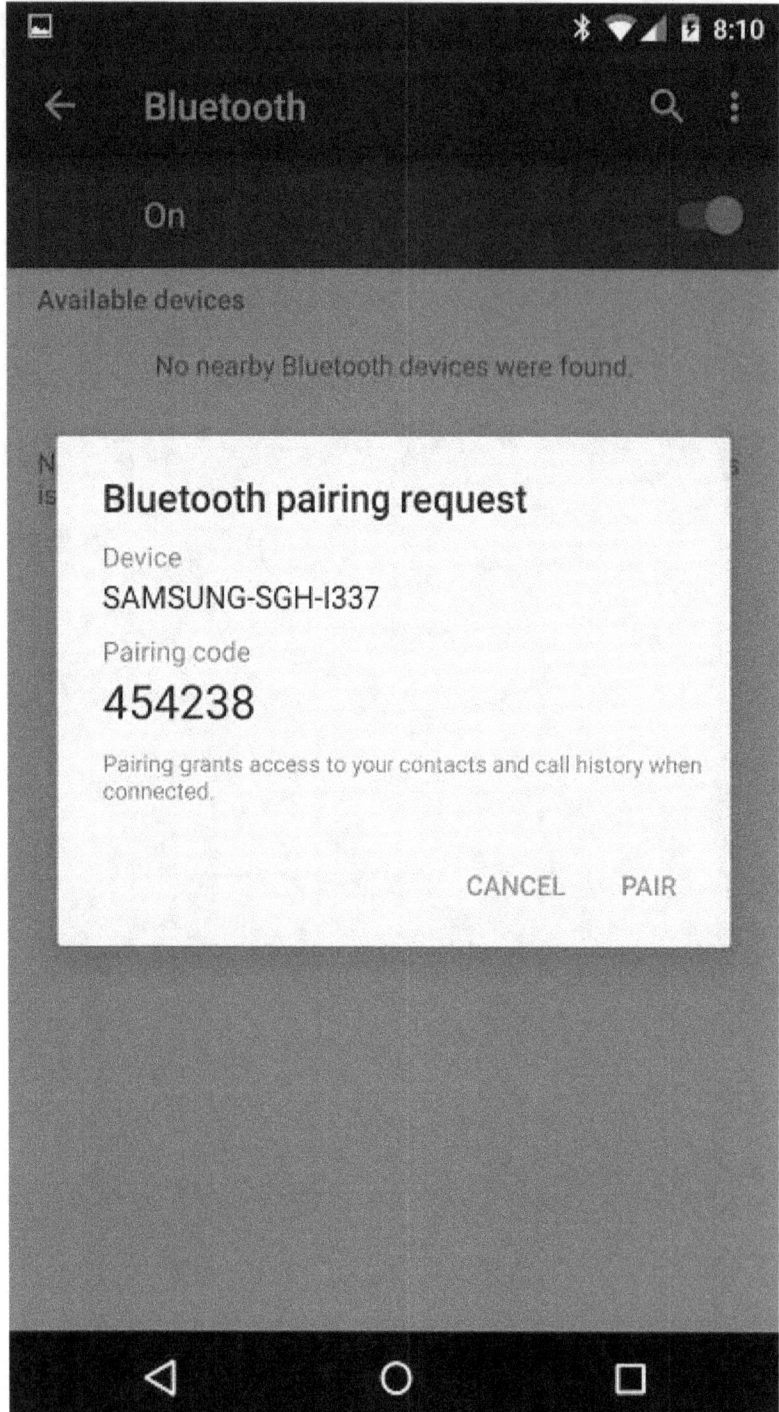

Figure 6: Bluetooth Pairing Request

4. Wirelessly Transferring Data to Another Device

The device can transfer data to another mobile device without the use of Bluetooth or email. By using the Android Beam feature, you can transfer data by holding your device back to back with another Android Beam-enabled device. To wirelessly transfer data using the Android Beam feature:

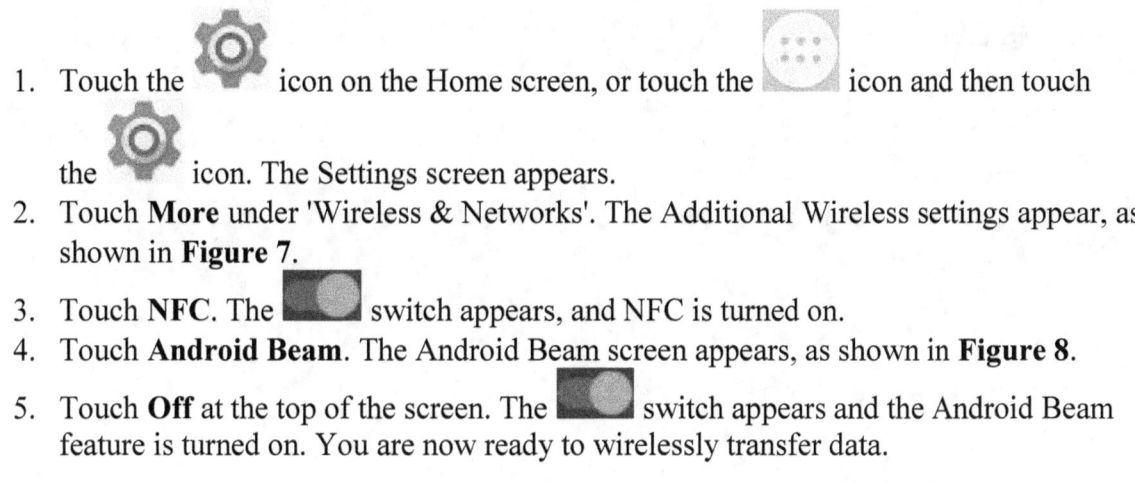

1. Touch the ⚙ icon on the Home screen, or touch the ⊞ icon and then touch the ⚙ icon. The Settings screen appears.
2. Touch **More** under 'Wireless & Networks'. The Additional Wireless settings appear, as shown in **Figure 7**.
3. Touch **NFC**. The ⬤ switch appears, and NFC is turned on.
4. Touch **Android Beam**. The Android Beam screen appears, as shown in **Figure 8**.
5. Touch **Off** at the top of the screen. The ⬤ switch appears and the Android Beam feature is turned on. You are now ready to wirelessly transfer data.

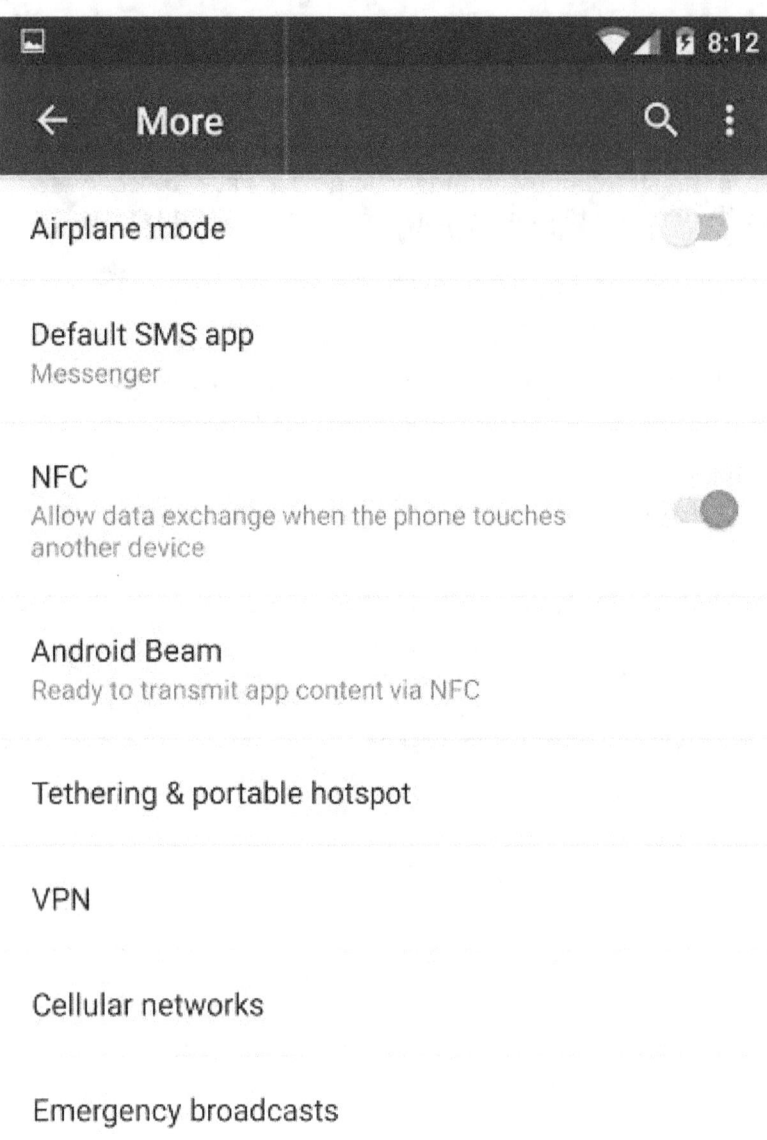

Figure 7: Additional Wireless Settings

When this feature is turned on, you can beam app content to another NFC-capable device by holding the devices close together. For example, you can beam Browser pages, YouTube videos, People contacts, and more.

Just bring the devices together (typically back to back) and then touch your screen. The app determines what gets beamed.

Figure 8: Android Beam Screen

5. Turning Cellular Data On or Off (Smartphones Only)

In an area where there is little to no reception, you may want to turn off cellular data and connect to a wireless network. When you are connected to a Wi-Fi network, cellular data is not used to download applications or stream media. However, the phone will keep searching for a signal, which drains the battery very quickly. To turn cellular data on or off:

1. Touch the status bar (where the clock and battery meter are located), and slide your finger down. The Quick Notifications appear.
2. Repeat step 1. The Quick Settings appear.
3. Touch the  icon. The Cellular Data window appears, as shown in **Figure 9**.
4. Touch **Cellular data** at the top of the screen. The 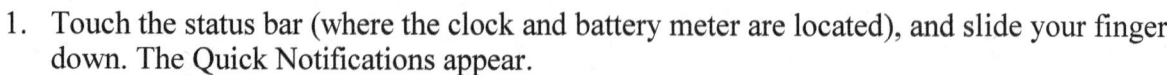 switch appears, and cellular data is turned off.
5. Touch **Cellular data** again. The 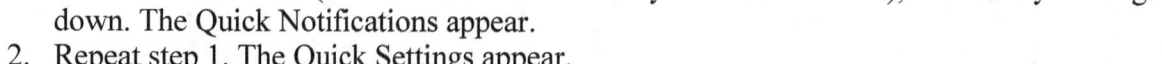 switch appears, and cellular data is turned on.

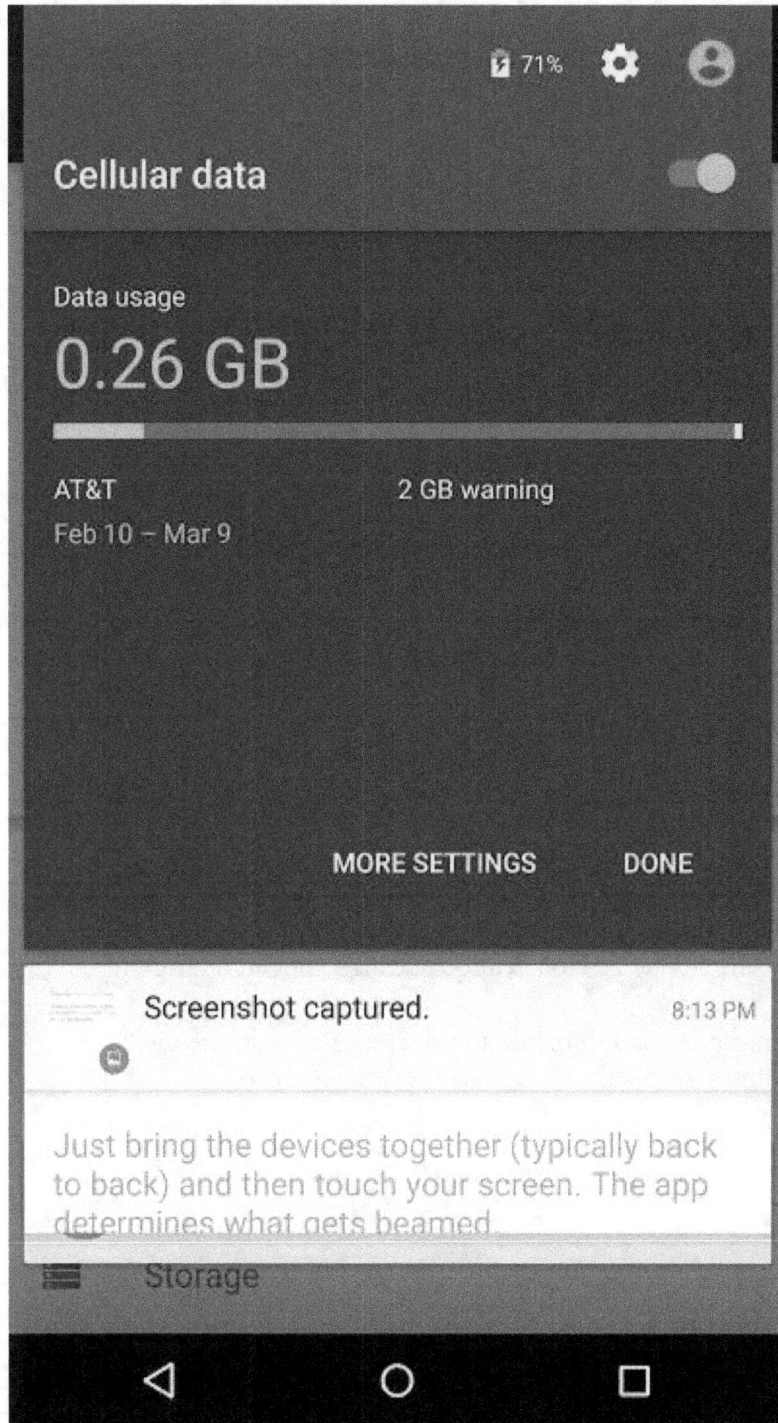

Figure 9: Cellular Data Window

Adjusting Sound Settings

Table of Contents

1. Adjusting the Notification, Media, and Alarm Volume

The volumes for various notifications can be set separately. To set the various Notification volumes:

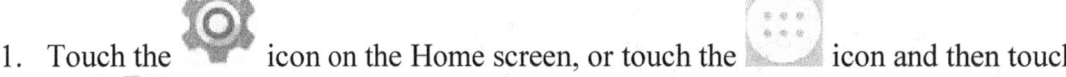

1. Touch the ⚙ icon on the Home screen, or touch the ⊞ icon and then touch
   the ⚙ icon. The Settings screen appears, as shown in **Figure 1**. Refer to *"Tips and Tricks"* on page 312 to learn how to quickly access the Settings screen.
2. Touch **Sound & notification**. The Sound & Notification settings appear, as shown in **Figure 2**.
3. Touch one of the sliders and drag it to the left or right to decrease or increase the corresponding Notification volume, respectively. The volume is adjusted.

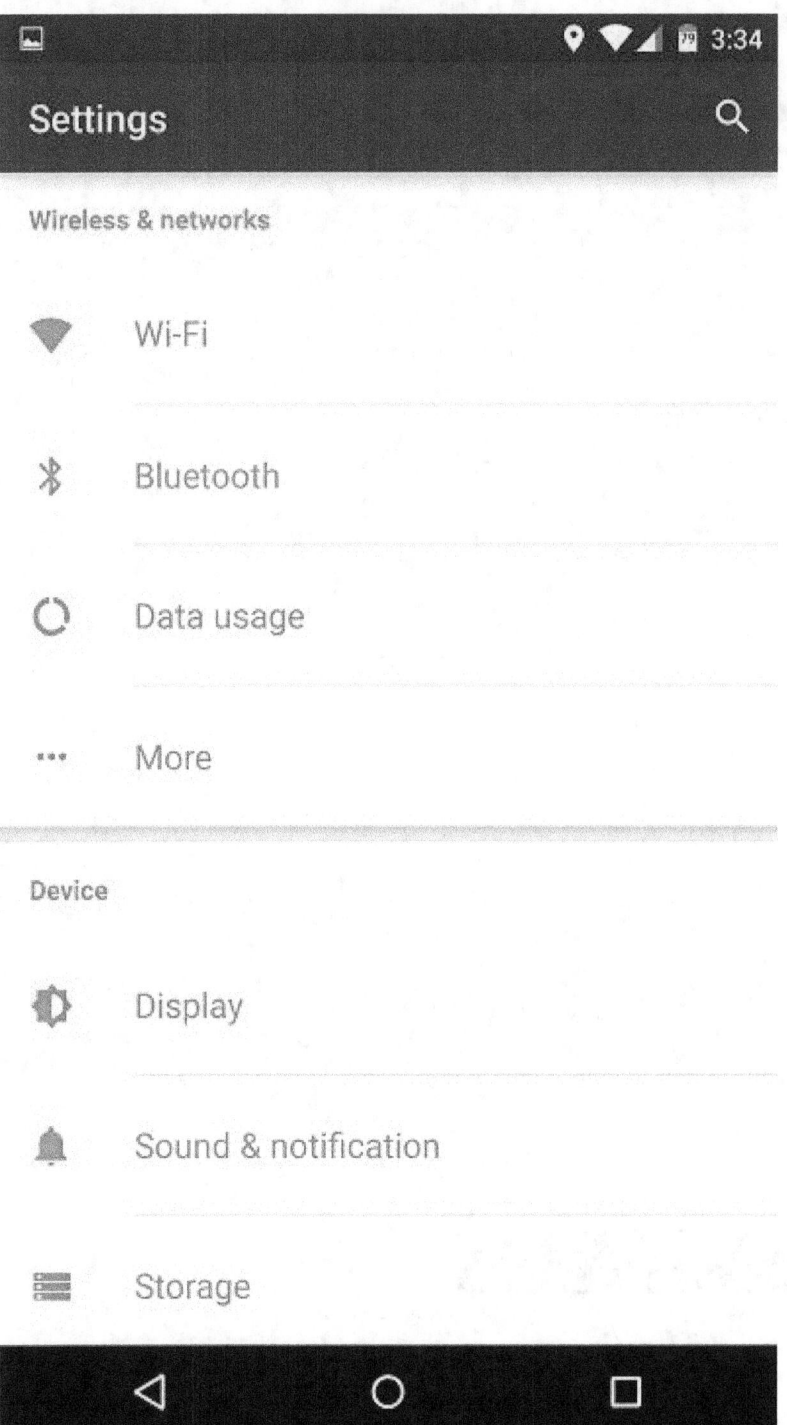

Figure 1: Settings Screen

Figure 2: Sound & Notifications Settings

2. Changing the Notification Ringtone

The default ringtone that is used for all notifications can be changed. To set the Notification ringtone:

1. Touch the 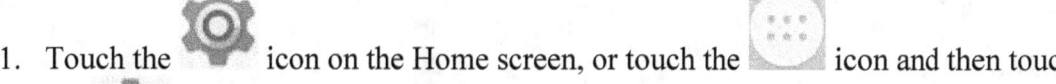 icon on the Home screen, or touch the icon and then touch the icon. The Settings screen appears.
2. Touch **Sound & notification**. The Sound Settings screen appears.
3. Touch **Default notification ringtone**. A list of Notification ringtones appears, as shown in **Figure 3**.
4. Touch a ringtone. A preview of the ringtone plays.
5. Touch **OK**. The new Notification ringtone is set. Alternatively, touch **Cancel** to return to using the previously set ringtone.

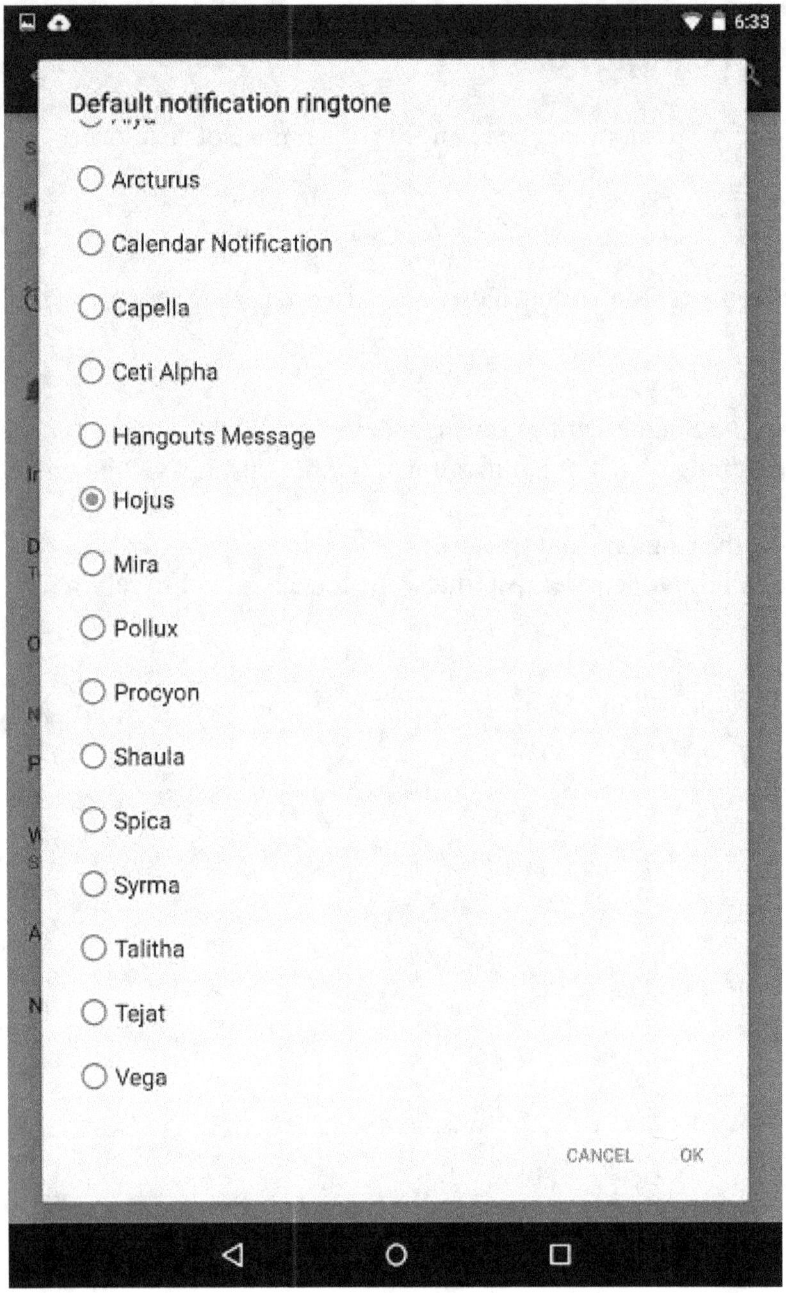

Figure 3: List of Notification Ringtones

3. Turning System Sounds On or Off

When any selection is made on the touchscreen, the device can play a confirmation sound. To turn Touch Sounds on or off:

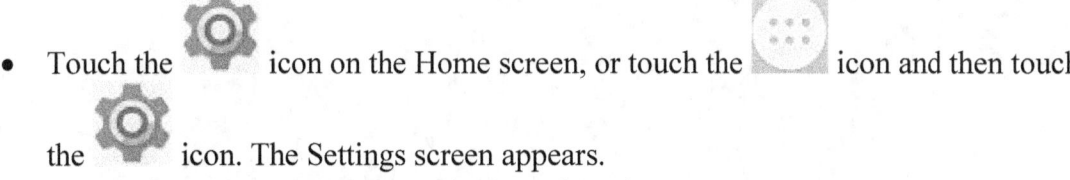

- Touch the ⚙ icon on the Home screen, or touch the ⦙⦙ icon and then touch the ⚙ icon. The Settings screen appears.
- Touch **Sound & notification**. The Sound Settings screen appears.
- Touch **Other sounds**. The Other Sounds settings appear, as shown in **Figure 4**.
- Touch one of the following options in the list. The switch appears next to any sound that is turned on. The switch appears next to any sound that is turned off.

  - **Dial pad tones** (smartphones only) - Sounds that are made when you touch the keys on the phone keypad.
  - **Screen locking sounds** - Sounds that are made every time that you lock or unlock the device.
  - **Touch sounds** - Sounds that are made every time that you touch a selection in a menu.
  - **Vibrate on touch** (smartphones only) - Vibrations that are made every time that you touch the ◁, ○, or □ key.

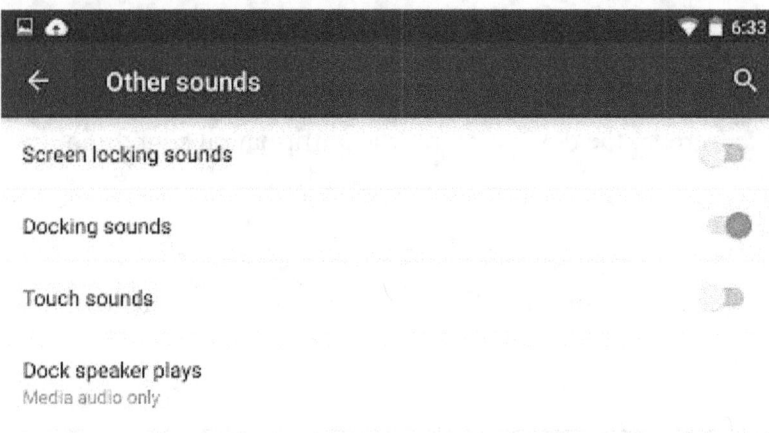

Figure 4: Other Sounds Settings

Adjusting Screen Settings

Table of Contents

1. Adjusting the Brightness

The device can be set to automatically detect light conditions by using the built-in light sensor, and then set the brightness accordingly. When Adaptive Brightness is turned off, you may manually adjust the brightness. To customize the brightness:

1. Touch the icon on the Home screen, or touch the icon and then touch the 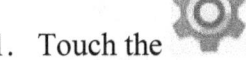 icon. The Settings screen appears, as shown in **Figure 1**.
2. Touch Display. The Display Settings screen appears, as shown in **Figure 2**.
3. Touch **Brightness level**. The Brightness window appears.
4. Touch and drag the slider to the left or right. The brightness is decreased or increased, respectively.
5. You can also touch Adaptive brightness to turn the feature on or off.

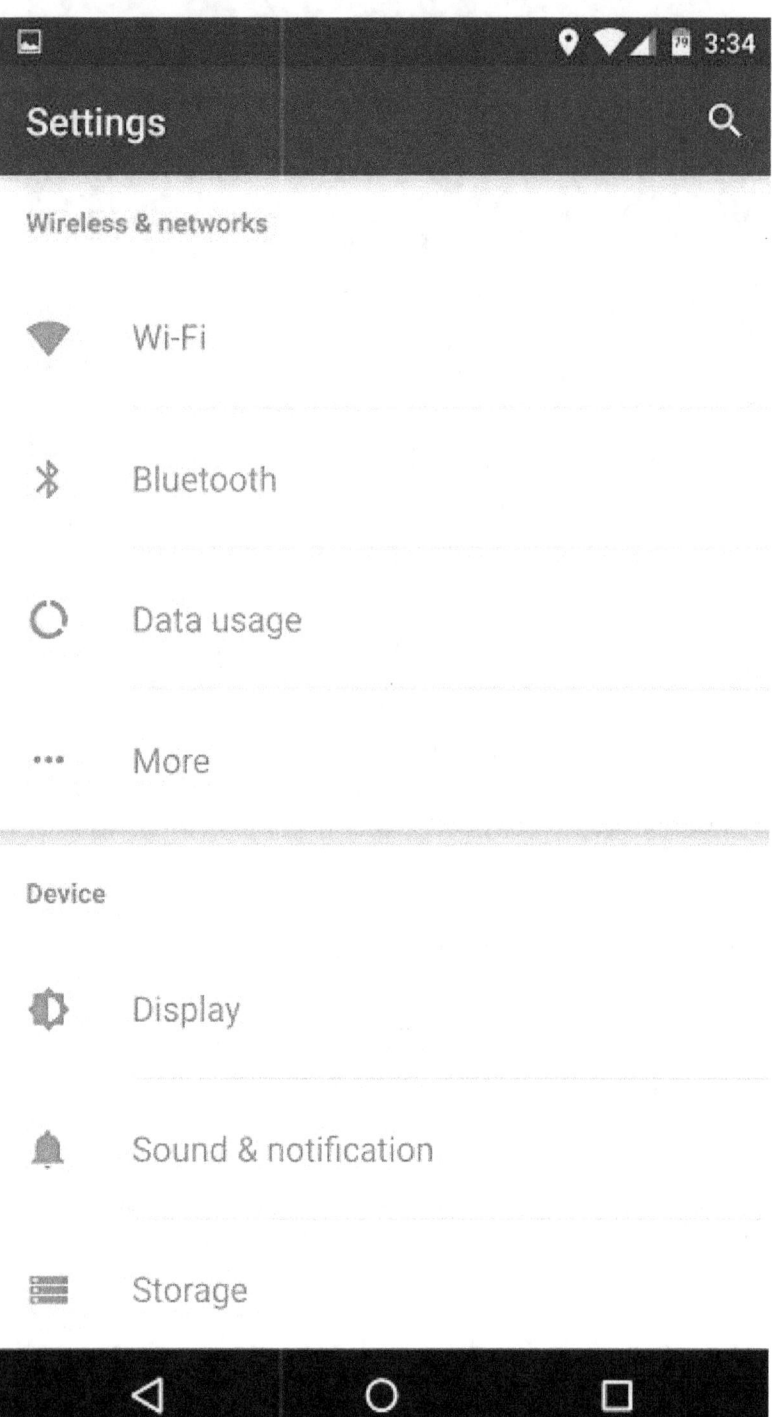

Figure 1: Settings Screen

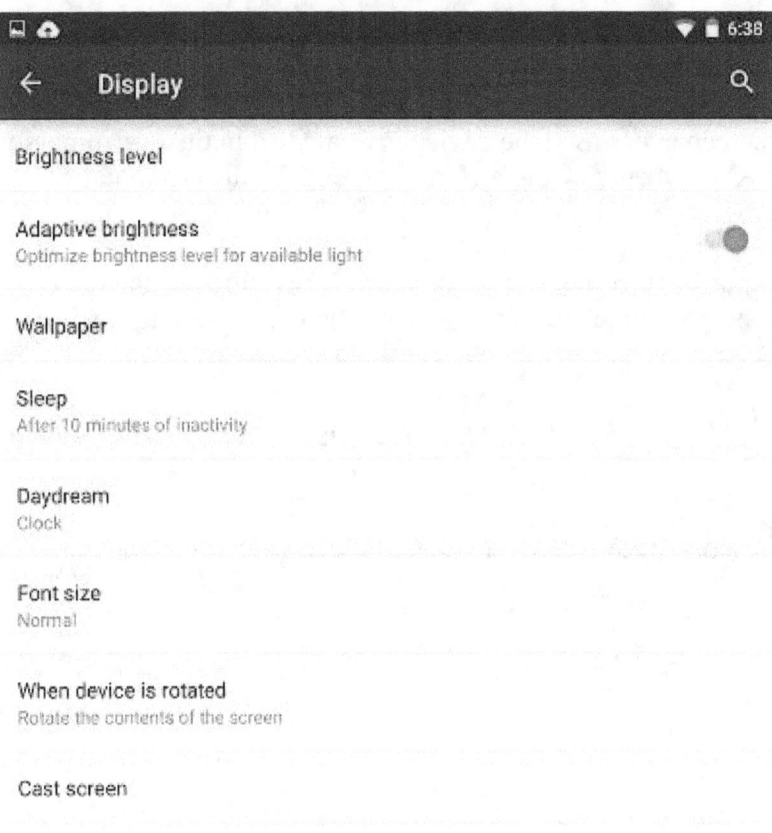

Figure 2: Display Settings Screen

2. Turning Automatic Screen Rotation On or Off

By default, the device will rotate the screen every time the device is rotated from the horizontal to the vertical position and vice versa (except when viewing a Home screen). To turn Automatic Screen Rotation on or off:

1. Touch the clock in the upper right-hand corner of the screen with two fingers, and drag down the Status bar, which is located at the top of the screen. The Quick Settings menu appears, as shown in **Figure 3**.

2. Touch the 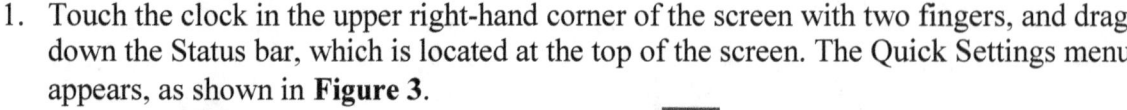 icon at the top of the screen. The icon appears and Automatic Screen Rotation is turned off.

3. Touch the 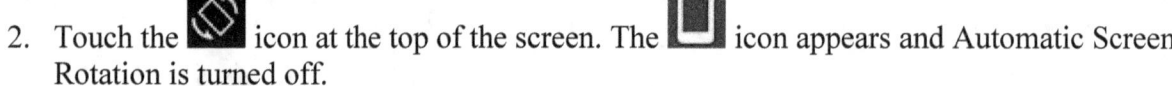 icon. The icon appears and Automatic Screen Rotation is turned on.

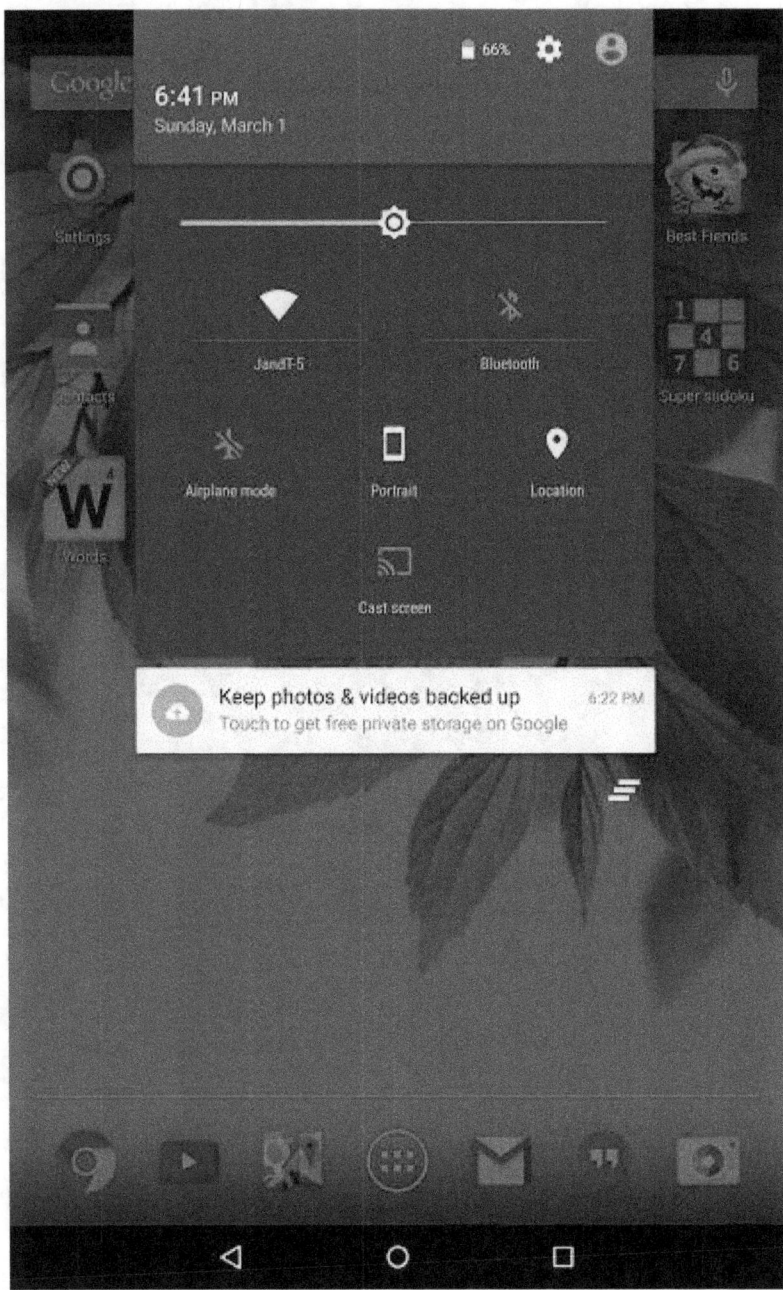

Figure 3: Quick Settings Menu

3. Changing the Wallpaper

The wallpaper is the image that is displayed in the background on the Lock and Home screens. To change the wallpaper:

1. Touch and hold an empty spot on any Home screen. The Home Screen menu appears, as shown in **Figure 4**.
2. Touch **Wallpapers**. Thumbnails for images in the corresponding source appear.
3. Touch the desired image and then touch **Set wallpaper** if you are choosing from the 'Wallpapers' or 'Live Wallpapers' source. If choosing from the Gallery, touch **Pick image**. You may need to crop the image before setting it as the wallpaper. Refer to *"Cropping a Picture"* on page 154 to learn how.

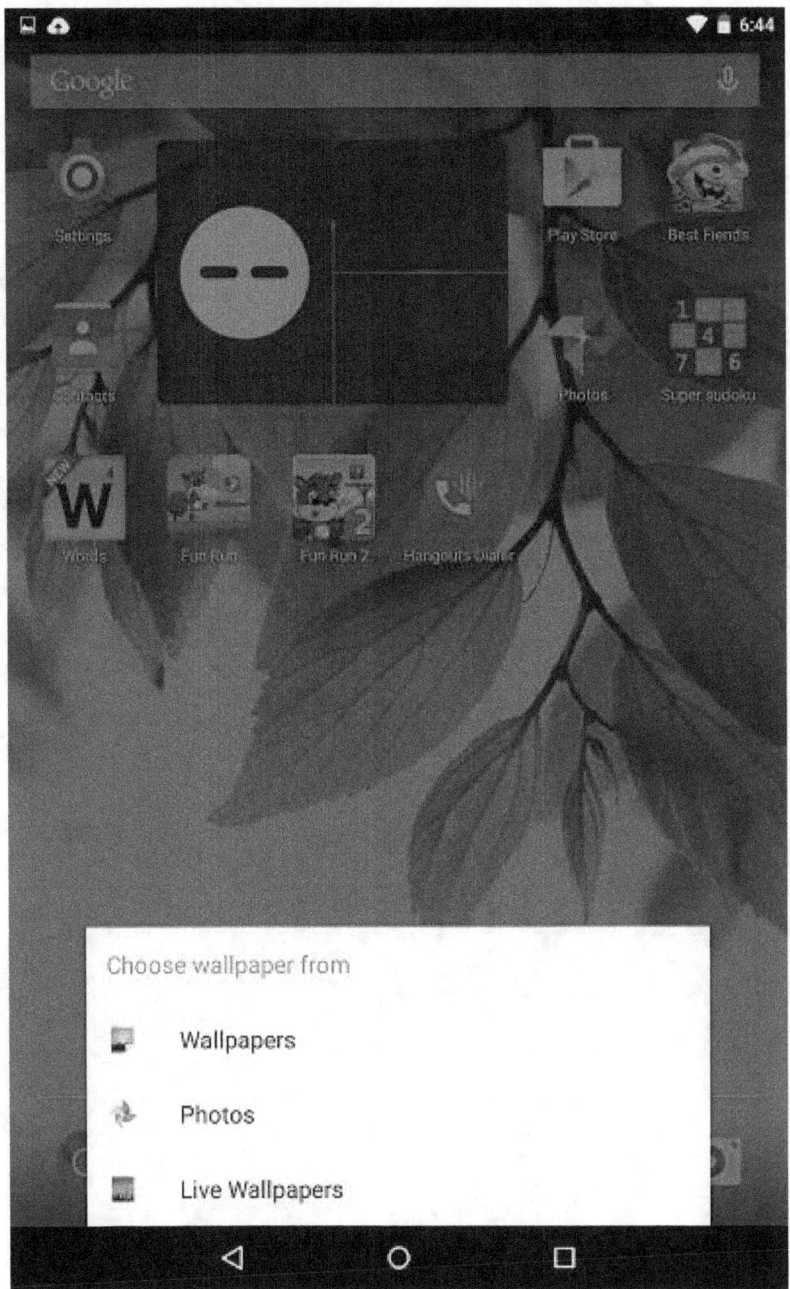

Figure 4: Home Screen Menu

4. Setting the Amount of Time Before the Device Locks Itself

The Sleep Timer determines the amount of time that passes before the screen goes black and the device is automatically locked. To set the Sleep Timer:

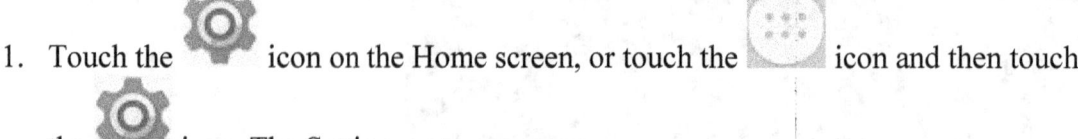

1. Touch the ⚙ icon on the Home screen, or touch the ⠿ icon and then touch the ⚙ icon. The Settings screen appears.
2. Touch **Display**. The Display Settings screen appears.
3. Touch **Sleep**. The Sleep Timer options appear, as shown in **Figure 5**.
4. Touch an option in the list. The Sleep Timer is set.

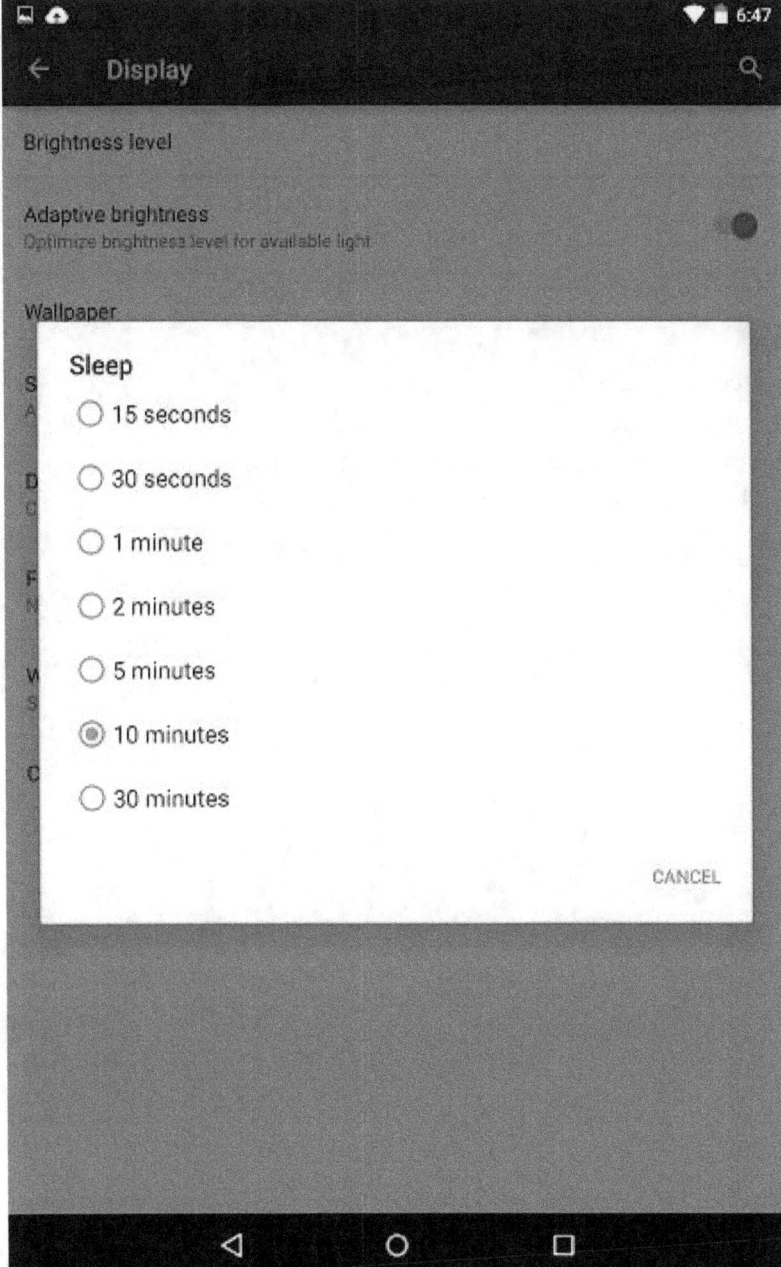

Figure 5: Sleep Timer Options

5. Adjusting the Font Size

If you have trouble seeing text in menus and applications, try increasing the font size. To adjust the font size on the device:

1. Touch the 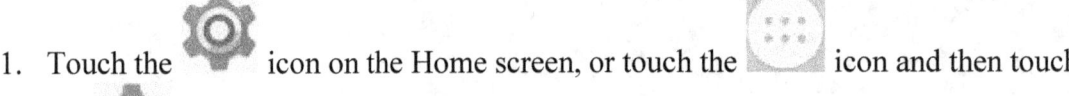 icon on the Home screen, or touch the icon and then touch the icon. The Settings screen appears.
2. Touch **Display**. The Display Settings screen appears.
3. Touch **Font size**. A list of available font sizes appears, as shown in **Figure 6**.
4. Touch one of the options in the list. The font size is adjusted.

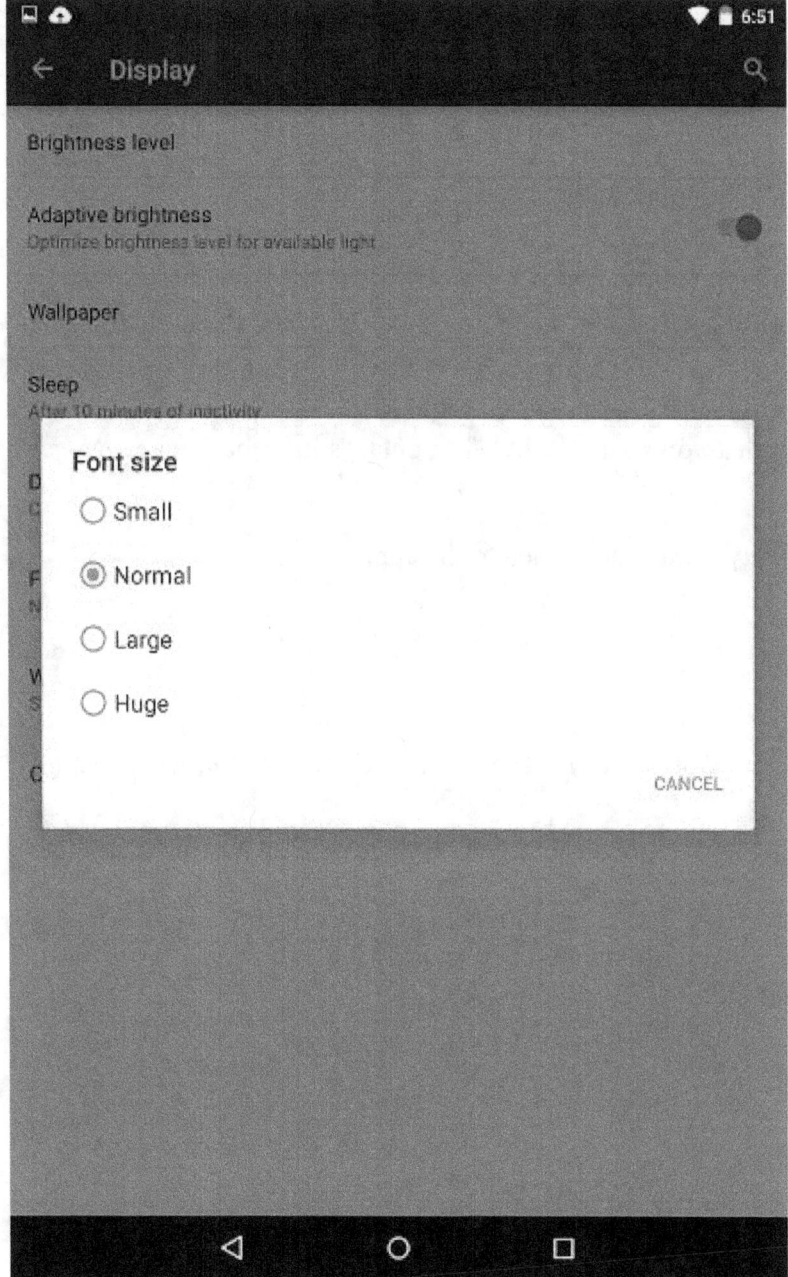

Figure 6: List of Available Font Sizes

6. Customizing Notification Priorities

You can customize notifications on Lollipop devices to help you avoid unnecessary interruptions when you are busy. First, set your 'Priority' contacts, for whom notifications will show when in Priority mode. To add the 'Priority' status to a contact:

- Touch the [icon] icon on the Home screen, or touch the [icon] icon and then touch the [icon] icon. The Phonebook appears, as shown in **Figure 7**.
- Touch the name of the contact that you wish to edit. The contact's information appears, as shown in Figure 8.
- Touch the [icon] icon. The Priority status is assigned to the contact.

To customize notifications:

1. Press the **Volume Up** or **Volume Down** button. The Volume Controls window appears, as shown in **Figure 9**.
2. Touch **Priority**. Priority mode is turned on, and only notifications for Priority contacts are allowed.
3. Touch **For one hour** to set a specific amount of time to learn Priority mode turned on. By default, Priority mode is enabled until you manually disable it (Indefinitely).

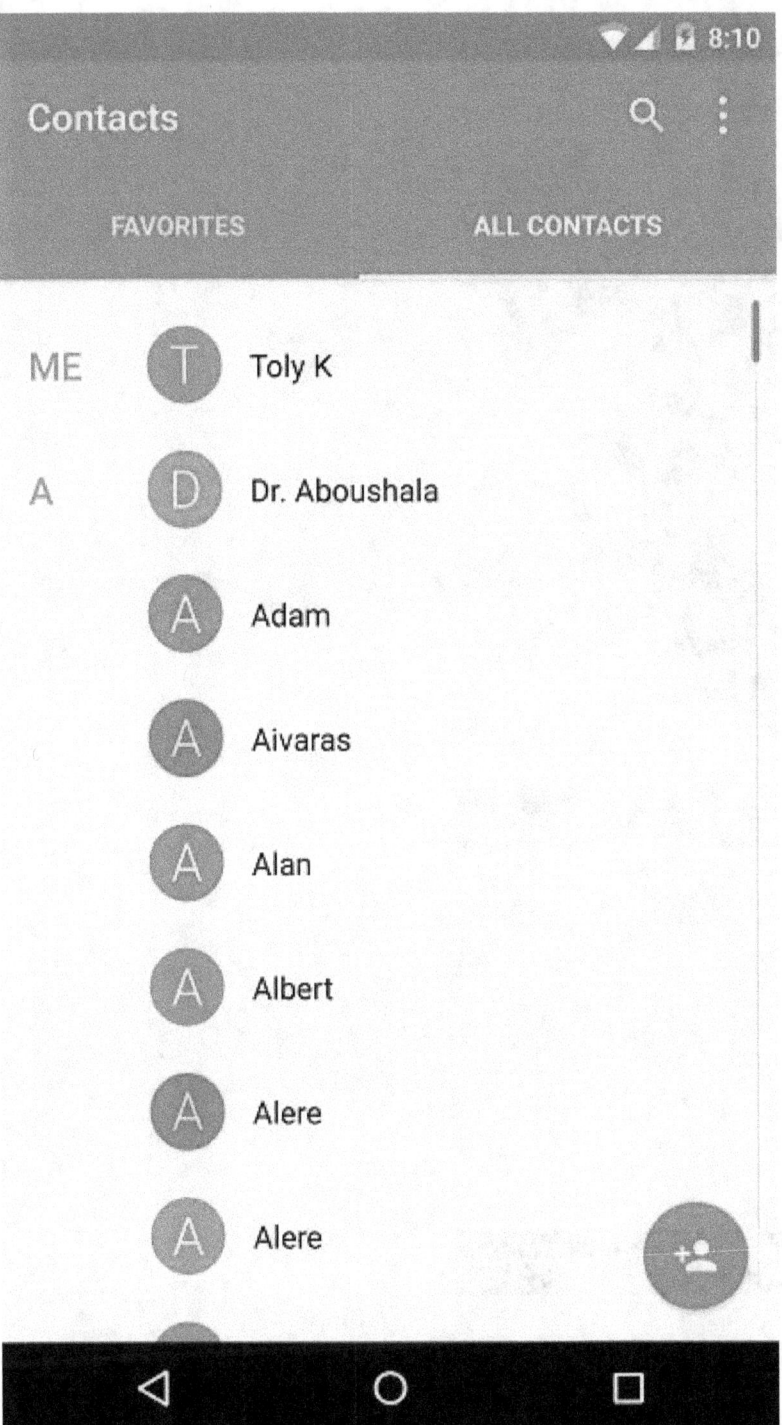

Figure 7: Phonebook

Figure 8: Contact Information

Figure 9: Volume Controls Window

Adjusting Security Settings

Table of Contents

1. Locking the Screen with a Slider

Prevent the device from waking up accidentally by setting up a Slider Lock. Note that a Slider Lock does not prevent unauthorized users from accessing your device. Refer to one of the next four sections to learn how to prevent unauthorized users from accessing your device. To set up a Slider Lock:

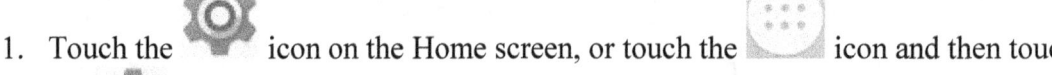

1. Touch the ⚙ icon on the Home screen, or touch the ⋮⋮⋮ icon and then touch the ⚙ icon. The Settings screen appears, as shown in **Figure 1**.
2. Touch **Security**. The Security Settings screen appears, as shown in **Figure 2**.
3. Touch **Screen lock**. The Screen Lock Settings screen appears, as shown in **Figure 3**. If a screen lock has already been set up, you will need to enter the corresponding passcode or pattern before proceeding.
4. Touch **Swipe**. The device will be locked using a basic slider. To unlock it, touch the screen anywhere and slide your finger up. The device is unlocked.

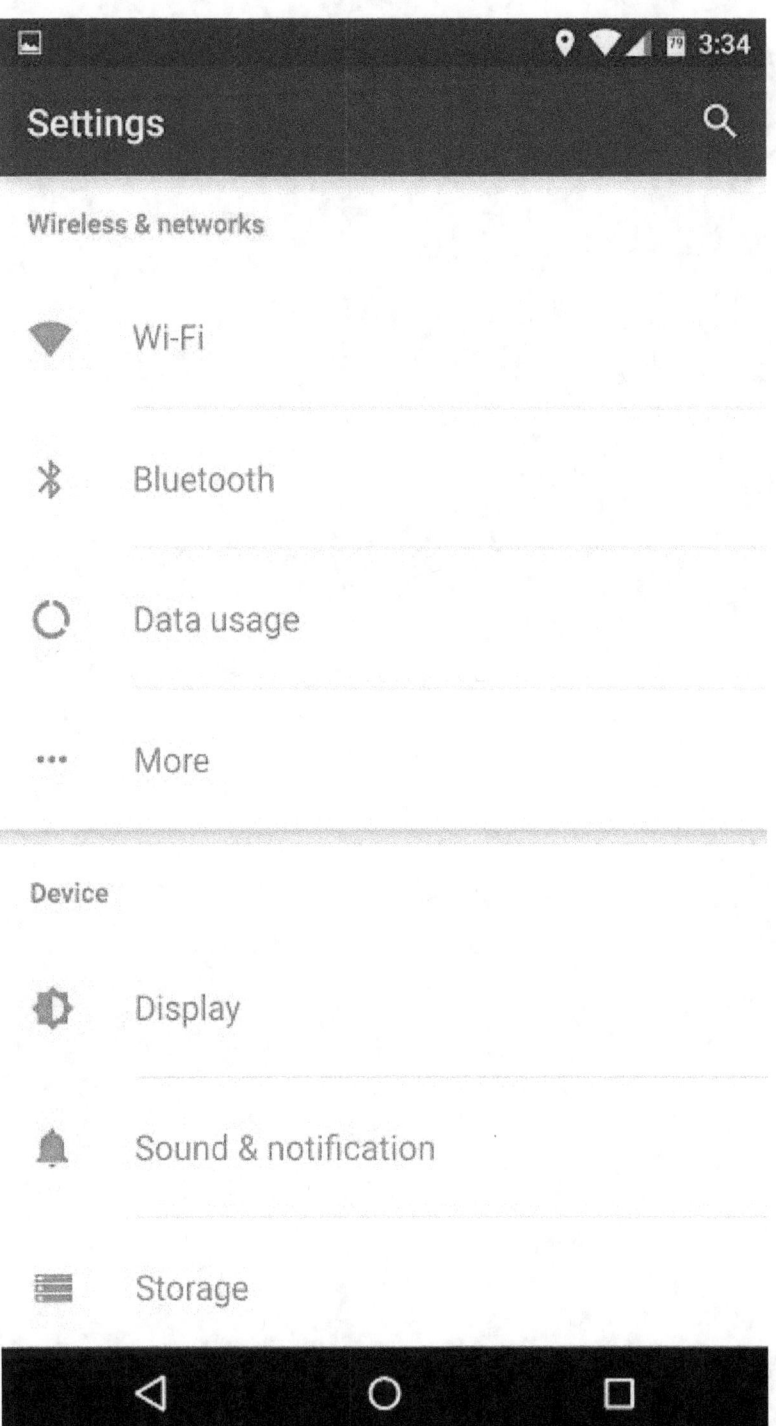

Figure 1: Settings Screen

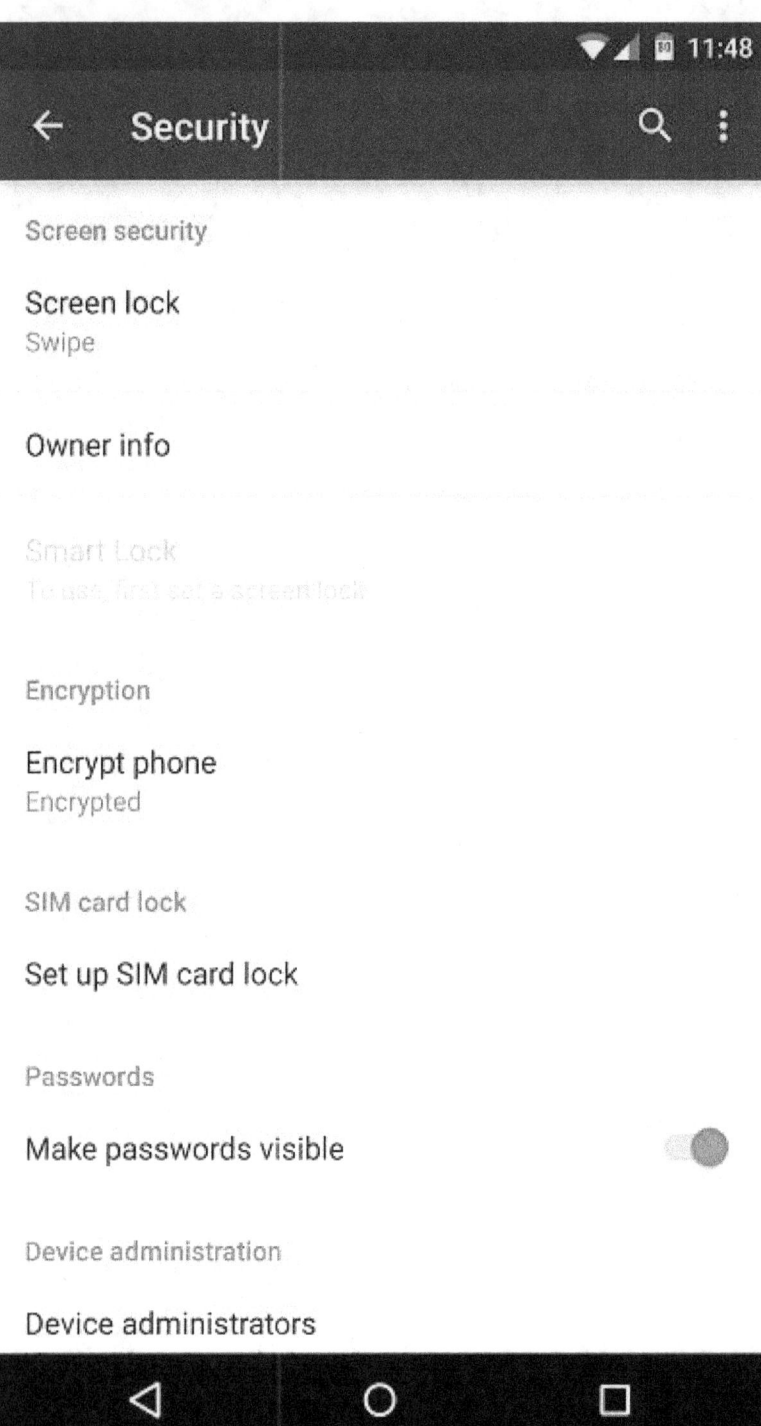

Figure 2: Security Settings Screen

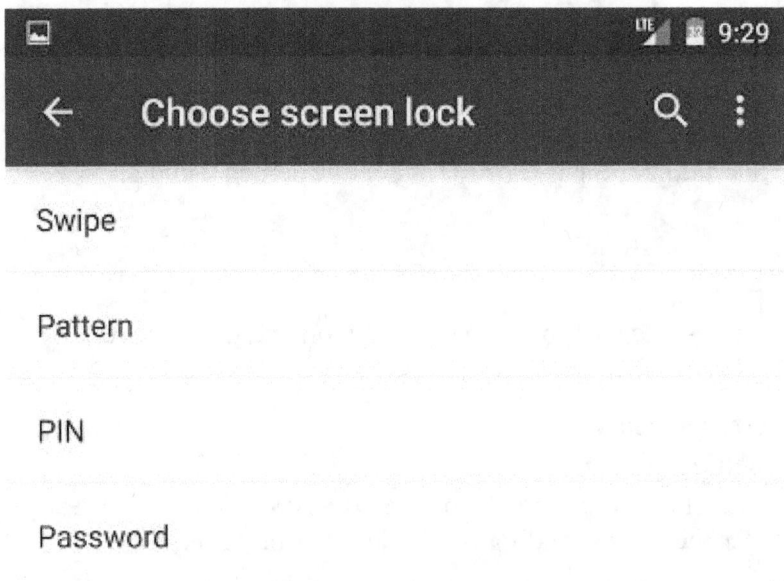

Figure 3: Screen Lock Settings Screen

2. Locking the Screen with an Alphanumeric Password

In order to prevent unauthorized users from accessing your device, you may wish to lock the device using an alphanumeric (letters and numbers) password. To lock the screen using an alphanumeric password:

1. Touch the icon on the Home screen, or touch the icon and then touch the  icon. The Settings screen appears.
2. Touch **Security**. The Security Settings screen appears.
3. Touch **Screen lock**. The Screen Lock Settings screen appears. If a screen lock has already been set up, you will need to enter the corresponding passcode, PIN, or pattern before proceeding.
4. Touch **Password**. The Encryption screen appears.
5. Touch **Require password to start device** to turn on a feature that will not allow anyone to turn on your phone without entering your password. This feature helps to protect sensitive data. Touch No thanks to turn off this feature. Then, touch **Continue**. The Choose Your Password screen appears, as shown in **Figure 4**.
6. Enter the desired password. The password must contain at least one letter, and must be at least four and no more than 16 characters in length. Touch **Continue**. The Password Confirmation screen appears.
7. Enter the same password again. Touch **OK**. The Notification Settings screen appears.
8. Touch one of the following options to configure notification behavior while the device is locked with a password:
    - **Show all notification content** - Displays all notifications while the device is locked.
    - **Hide sensitive notification content** - Displays only the name of the application that sent the notification, such as Messenger or Gmail, but does not display the contents of the notification.
    - **Don't show notifications at all** - Hides all notifications while the device is locked.
9. Touch **Done**. The Password lock is set. The password will now be required to unlock the screen.

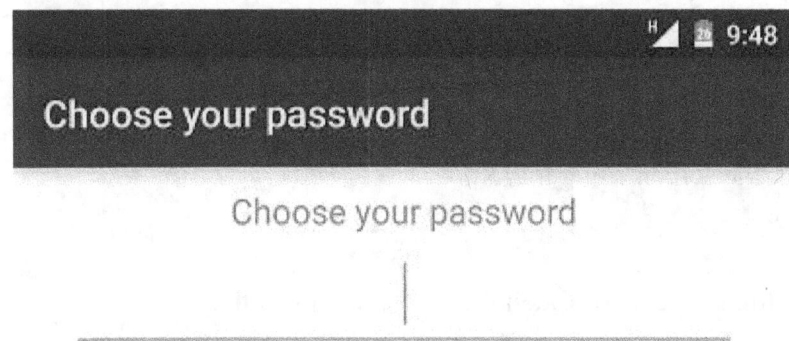

Figure 4: Choose Your Password Screen

3. Locking the Screen with a Personal Identification Number (PIN)

In order to prevent unauthorized users from accessing your device, you may wish to lock the device using a numerical PIN. To lock the screen using a PIN:

1. Touch the  icon on the Home screen, or touch the  icon and then touch the  icon. The Settings screen appears.
2. Touch **Security**. The Security Settings screen appears.
3. Touch **Screen lock**. The Screen Lock Settings screen appears. If a screen lock has already been set up, you will need to enter the corresponding passcode, PIN, or pattern before proceeding.
4. Touch **PIN**. The Encryption screen appears.
5. Touch **Require PIN** to start device to turn on a feature that will not allow anyone to turn on your phone without entering your PIN. This feature helps to protect sensitive data. Touch **No thanks** to turn off this feature. Then, touch **Continue**. The Choose Your PIN screen appears, as shown in **Figure 5**.
6. Enter the desired PIN, which must be at least 4 and no more than 16 digits in length. Touch **Continue**. The PIN Confirmation screen appears.
7. Enter the same PIN again. Touch **OK**. The Notification Settings screen appears.
8. Touch one of the following options to configure notification behavior while the device is locked with a PIN:
    - **Show all notification content** - Displays all notifications while the device is locked.
    - **Hide sensitive notification content** - Displays only the name of the application that sent the notification, such as Messenger or Gmail, but does not display the contents of the notification.
    - **Don't show notifications at all** - Hides all notifications while the device is locked.
9. Touch **Done**. The PIN lock is set. The PIN will now be required to unlock the screen.

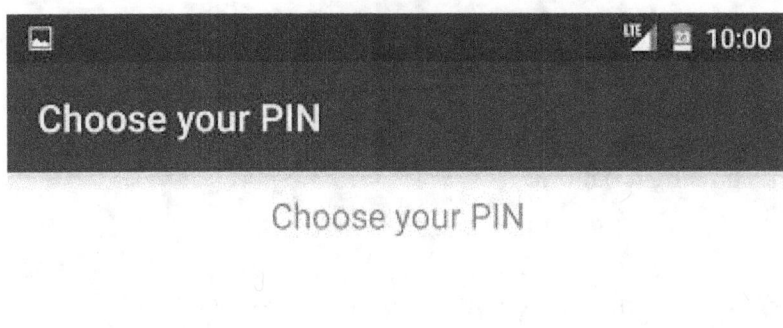

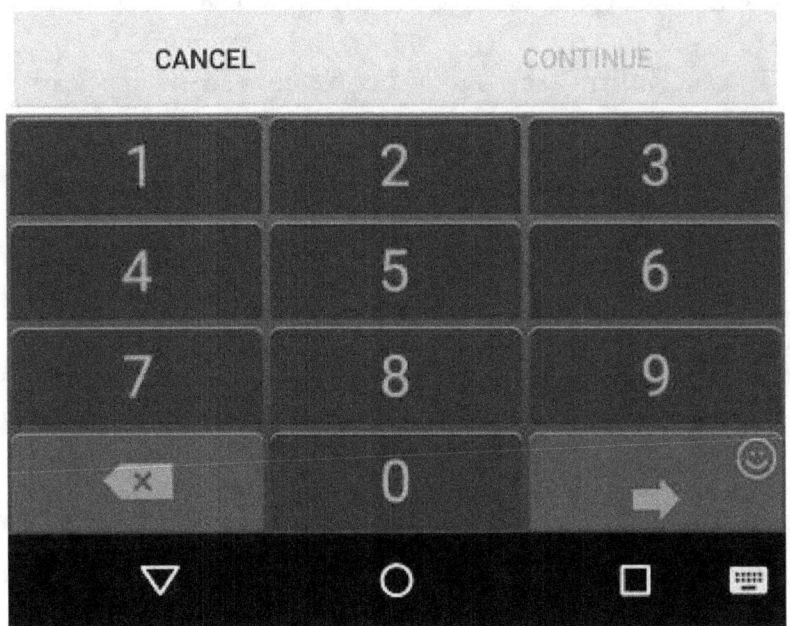

Figure 5: PIN Selection Screen

4. Locking the Screen with a Pattern

In order to prevent unauthorized users from accessing your device, you may wish to lock the device using a pattern. To lock the screen using a pattern:

1. Touch the icon on the Home screen, or touch the icon and then touch the  icon. The Settings screen appears.
2. Touch **Security**. The Security Settings screen appears.
3. Touch **Screen lock**. The Screen Lock Settings screen appears. If a screen lock has already been set up, you will need to enter the corresponding passcode, PIN, or pattern before proceeding.
4. Touch **Pattern**. The Encryption screen appears.
5. Touch **Require pattern** to start device to turn on a feature that will not allow anyone to turn on your phone without entering your pattern. This feature helps to protect sensitive data. Touch **No thanks** to turn off this feature. Then, touch **Continue**. The Choose Your Pattern screen appears, as shown in **Figure 6**.
6. Draw the desired pattern. You must connect at least four dots, and no more than one line can pass through a dot in a pattern. Touch **Continue**. The Pattern Confirmation screen appears.
7. Draw the same pattern again. Touch **Confirm**. The Notification Settings screen appears.
8. Touch one of the following options to configure notification behavior while the device is locked with a pattern:
    - **Show all notification content** - Displays all notifications while the device is locked.
    - **Hide sensitive notification content** - Displays only the name of the application that sent the notification, such as Messenger or Gmail, but does not display the contents of the notification.
    - **Don't show notifications at all** - Hides all notifications while the device is locked.
9. Touch **Done**. The pattern lock is set. The pattern will now be required to unlock the screen.

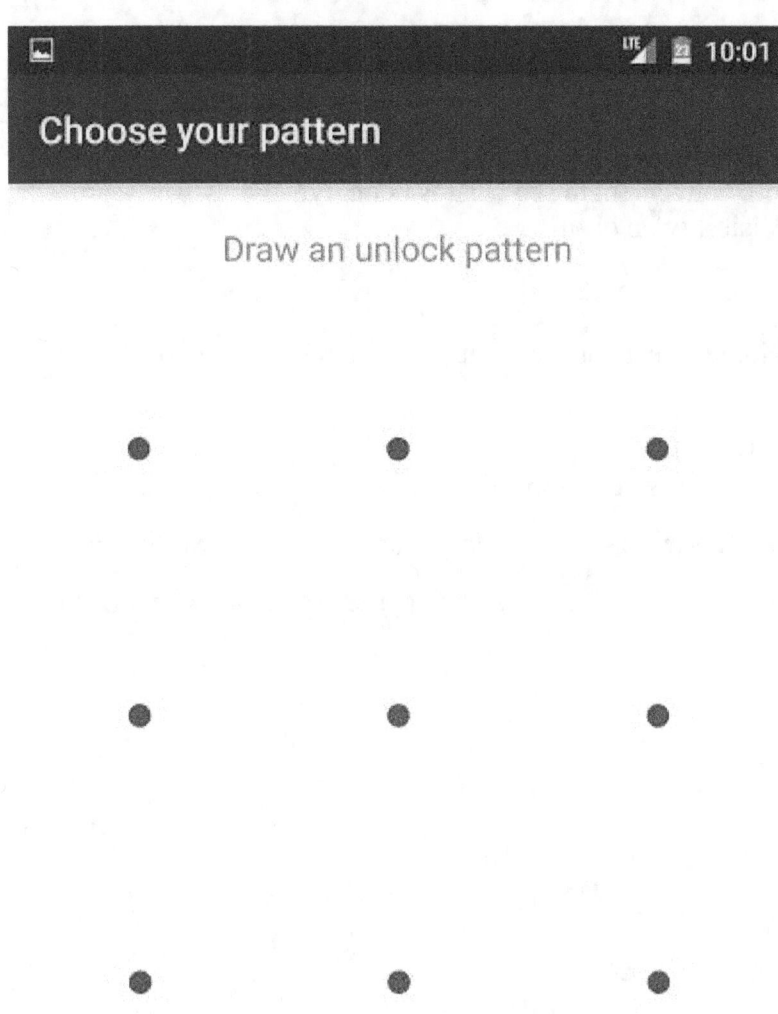

Figure 6: Pattern Selection Screen

5. Turning Password Visibility On or Off

When entering passwords on the device, they can be hidden in case there is somebody else looking at the screen. Otherwise, it may be more convenient to see what is being typed. Passwords are visible by default. To turn Password Visibility on or off:

1. Touch the ⚙ icon on the Home screen, or touch the ⠿ icon and then touch the ⚙ icon. The Settings screen appears.
2. Touch **Security**. The Security Settings screen appears.
3. Touch **Make passwords visible**. The ◯ switch appears and passwords will be visible.
4. Touch **Make passwords visible again**. The ◯ switch appears and passwords will be hidden.

Adjusting Language and Input Settings

Table of Contents

1. Selecting a Language

The device can display menus and applications that come pre-installed on the device, such as Gmail, in any one of 41 languages. To select a language:

1. Touch the ⚙ icon on the Home screen, or touch the ⦂⦂⦂ icon and then touch the ⚙ icon. The Settings screen appears, as shown in **Figure 1**.
2. Touch **Language & input**. The Language & Input Settings screen appears, as shown in **Figure 2**.
3. Touch **Language**. A list of available languages appears, as shown in **Figure 3**.
4. Touch a language in the list. The language is set and will be used in all menus on the device.

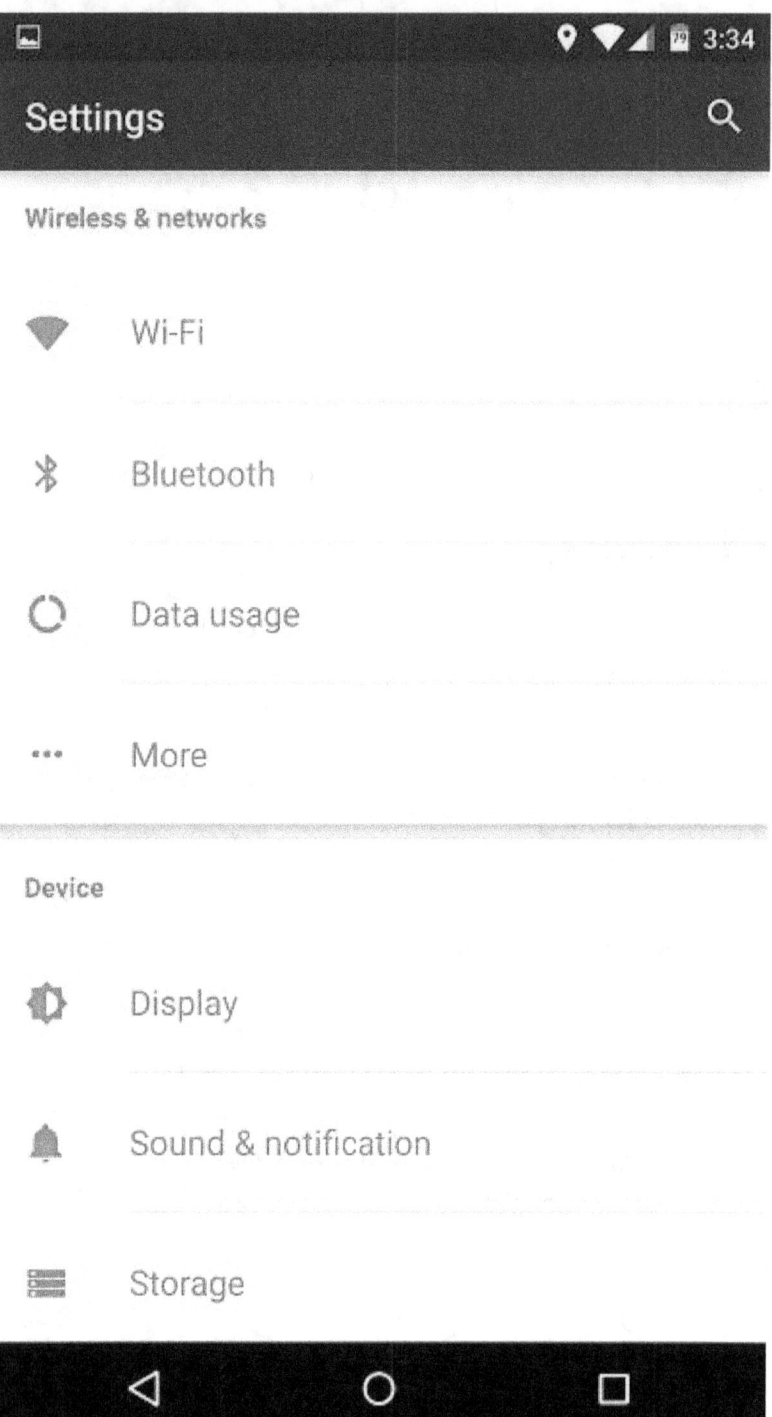

Figure 1: Settings Screen

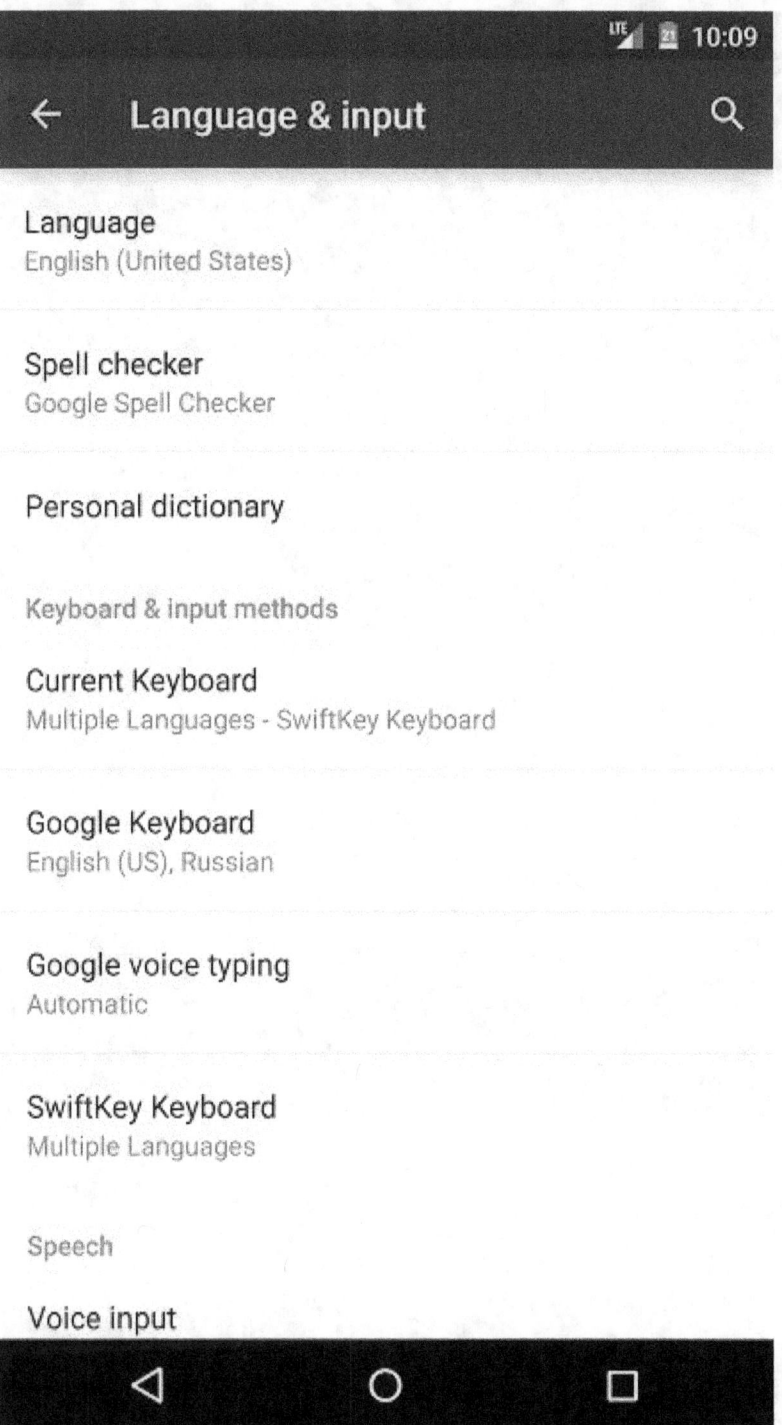

Figure 2: Language & Input Settings Screen

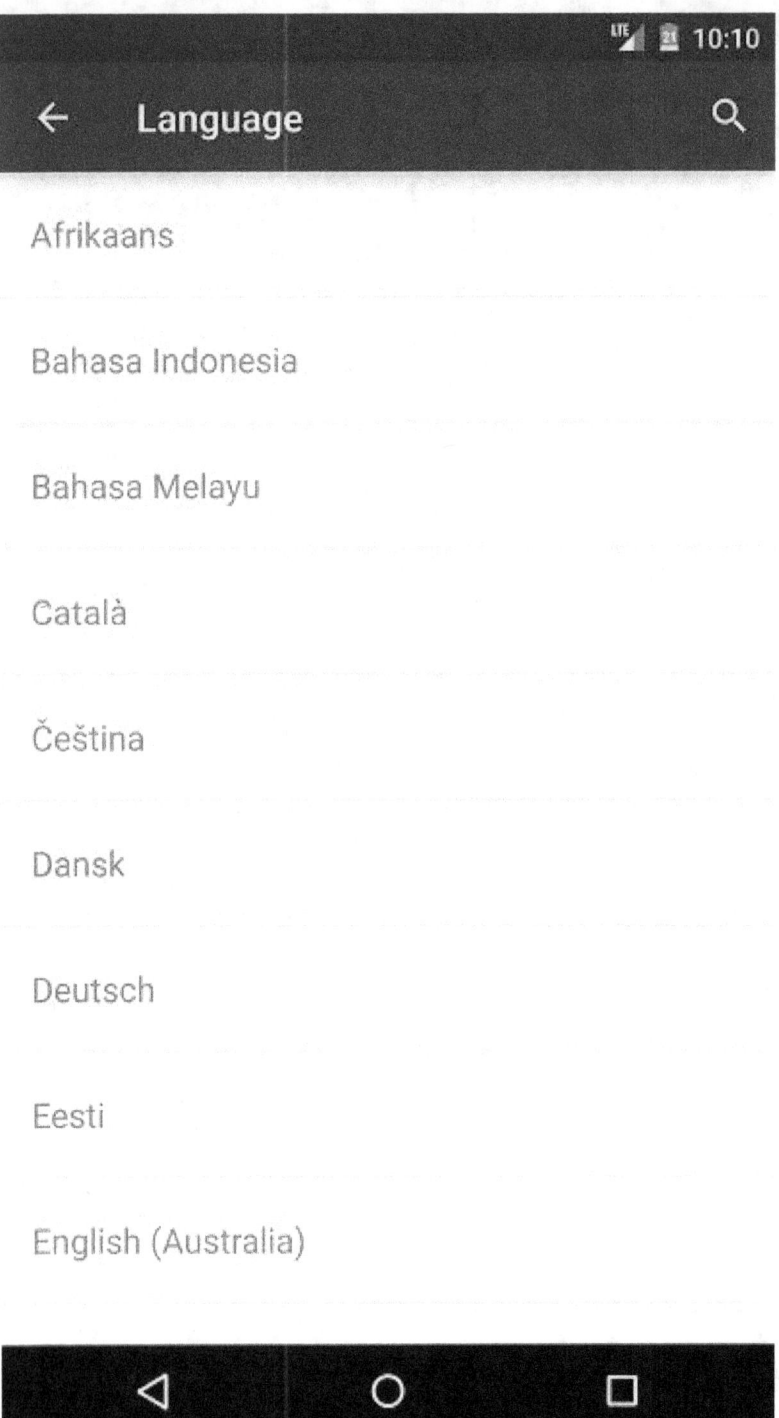

Figure 3: List of Available Languages

2. Turning Spell Checking On or Off

The device can check the spelling of words that you type. By default, the Spell Checker is turned on. To turn Spell Checking on or off:

1. Touch the icon on the Home screen, or touch the icon and then touch the icon. The Settings screen appears.
2. Touch **Language & input**. The Language & Input Settings screen appears.
3. Touch **Spell checker**. The Spell Checker screen appears, as shown in **Figure 4**.
4. Touch **On**. The switch appears and the Spell Checker is turned off.
5. Touch **Off**. The switch appears and the Spell Checker is turned on.

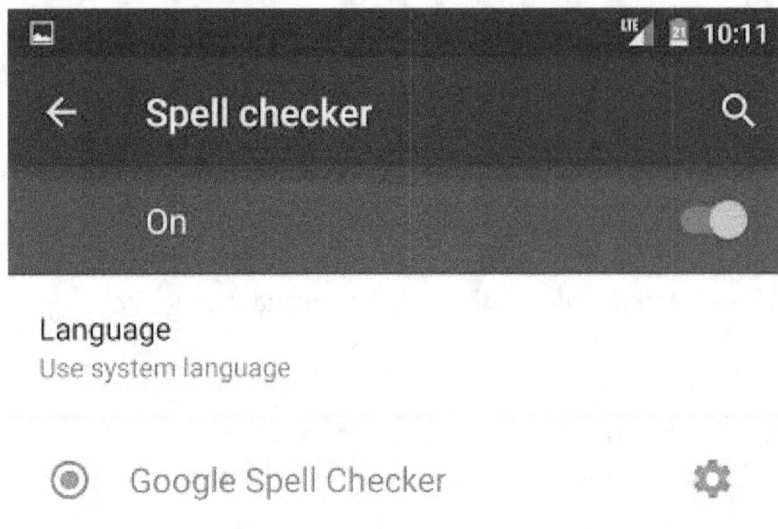

Language
Use system language

Google Spell Checker

Figure 4: Spell Checker Screen

3. Adding Words and Phrases to the Personal Dictionary

The device can store words in a Personal Dictionary to suggest them while you're typing in the future. You can also add shortcuts to phrases, such as "brb" for "be right back." To add an entry to the user dictionary:

1. Touch the 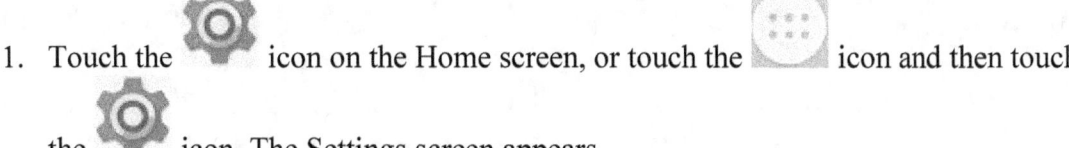 icon on the Home screen, or touch the icon and then touch the icon. The Settings screen appears.
2. Touch **Language & input**. The Language & Input Settings screen appears.
3. Touch **Personal dictionary**. If you have more than one language configured, touch the language for which you would like to add a personal word or phrase. The Personal Dictionary appears, as shown in **Figure 5**.
4. Touch the icon at the top of the screen. The Add to Dictionary screen appears, as shown in **Figure 6**.
5. Enter a word or phrase, and then touch Optional shortcut. The 'Shortcut' field is selected.
6. Enter an optional shortcut, which can be a series of letters or numbers that will be substituted with the entire word or phrase that you entered in the previous step. The shortcut is entered.
7. Touch the button. The word or phrase and the shortcut, if any, are added to the Personal Dictionary.

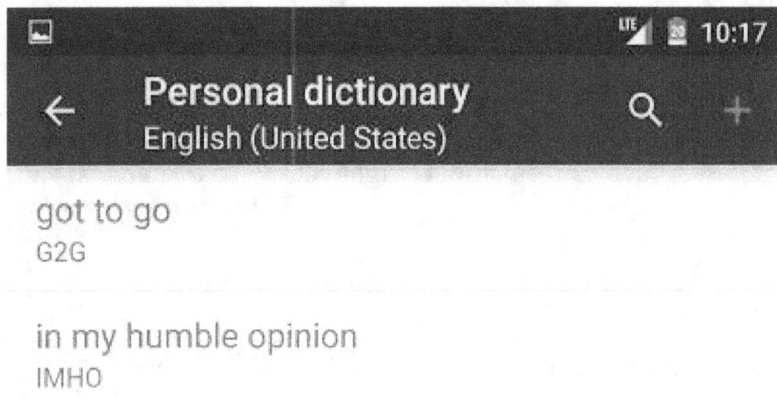

Figure 5: Personal Dictionary

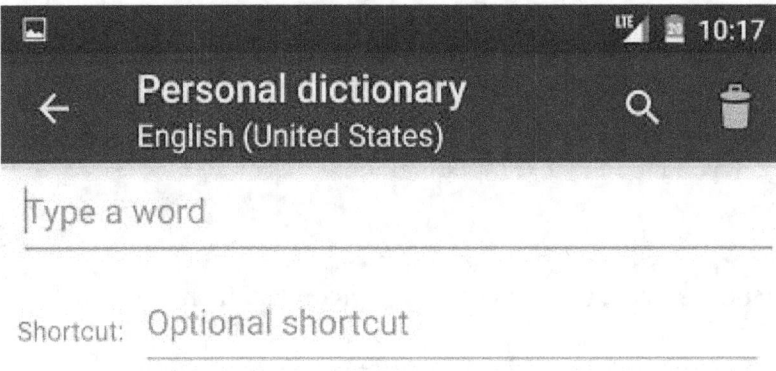

Figure 6: Add to Dictionary Screen

4. Changing the Input Method

The method that you use to input text can be changed. By default, the Android keyboard and Google voice typing are both selected. To change the text input method:

1. Touch the 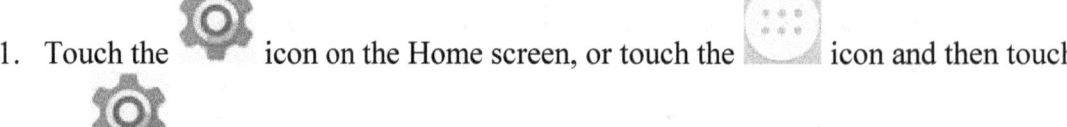 icon on the Home screen, or touch the icon and then touch the icon. The Settings screen appears.
2. Touch **Language & input**. The Language & Input Settings screen appears.
3. Touch **Current Keyboard**. The Keyboard Selection window appears, as shown in **Figure 7**. If you have installed a third-party keyboard, such as SwiftKey, it will appear in this list.
4. Touch an input method in the list. The new input method is selected.

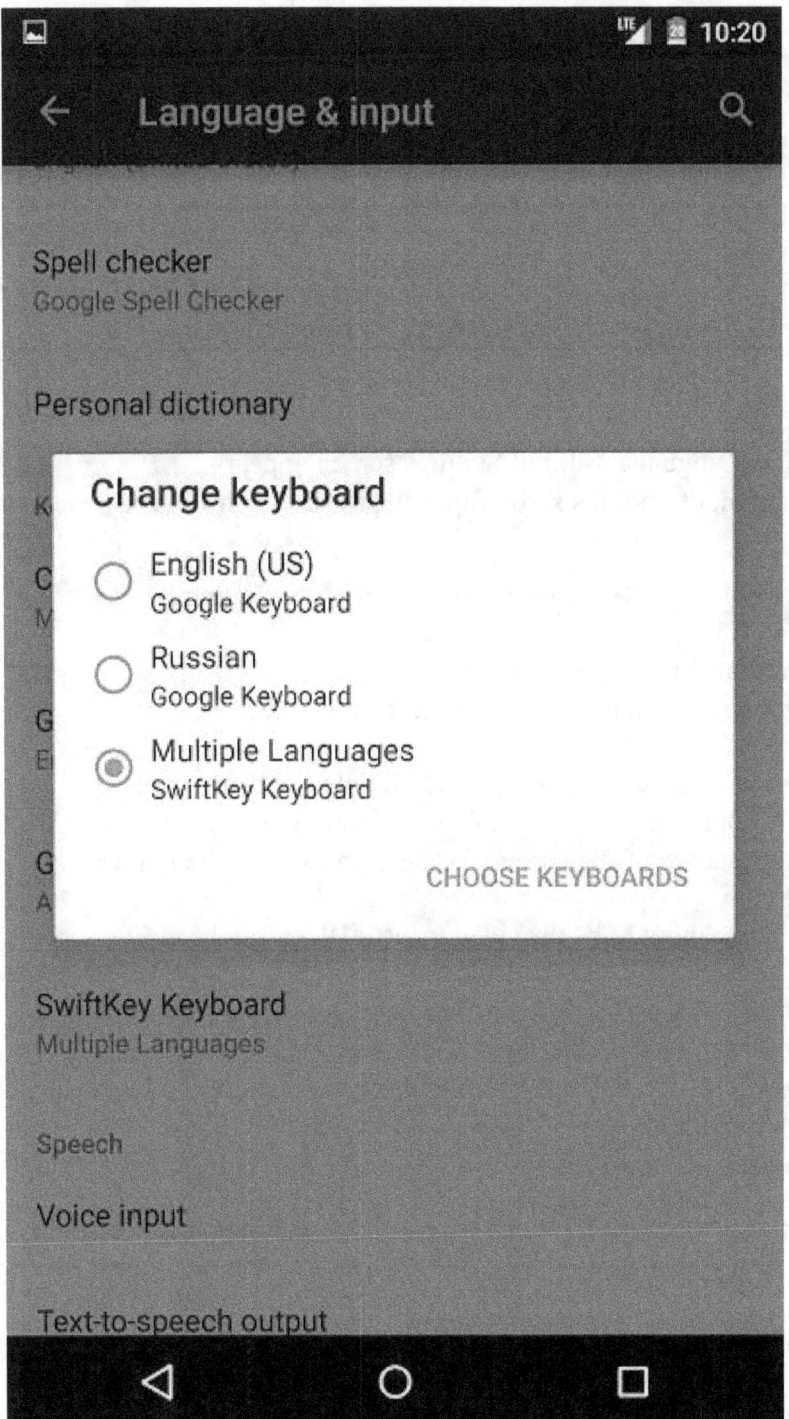

Figure 7: Keyboard Selection Window

5. Customizing Voice Search Settings

The Voice Recognition feature on the device can be customized to improve accuracy and filter voice results. To customize Voice Recognition settings:

1. Touch the ⚙ icon on the Home screen, or touch the ⊞ icon and then touch the ⚙ icon. The Settings screen appears.
2. Touch **Language & input**. The Language & Input Settings screen appears.
3. Touch **Voice Input**. The Voice Input Settings screen appears, as shown in **Figure 8**.
4. Touch the ⚙ icon next to 'Enhanced Google services'. The Voice Settings screen appears, as shown in **Figure 9**.
5. Touch one of the following options to edit the setting:
    *   **Languages -** Sets the languages that are recognized by the voice recognition software.
    *   **"OK Google" Detection** - Allows you to say **OK Google** to launch the Voice when using the Google application, or at all times, depending on your settings. Touch **Always on** after touching "OK Google" Detection to leave the feature on at all times.
    *   **Hands free** - Allows voice input to be provided using a Bluetooth headset or a wired headset.
    *   **Speech output** - Determines whether Speech Output is always enabled or is only turned on when using a hands-free device with the device.
    *   **Offline speech recognition** - Downloads additional speech recognition languages to be used offline; touch **All** at the top of the screen to view all options.
    *   **Block offensive words** - Hides offensive words when showing voice results, even if they are recognized. A ✓ mark appears to signify that the option is turned on.

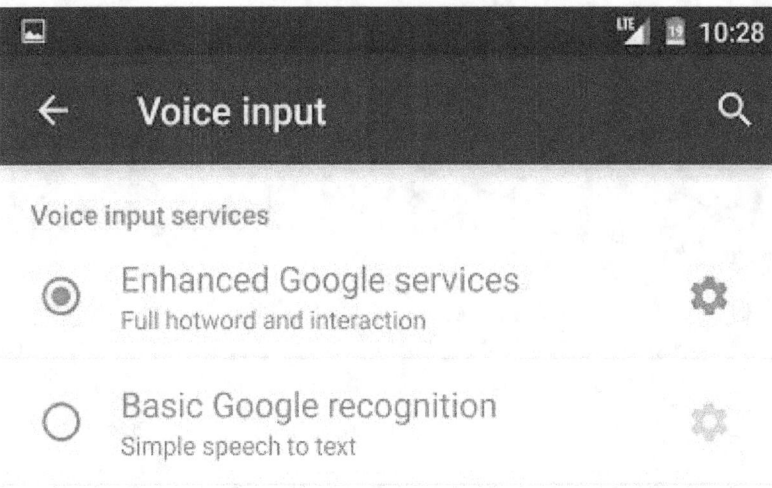

Figure 8: Voice Input Settings Screen

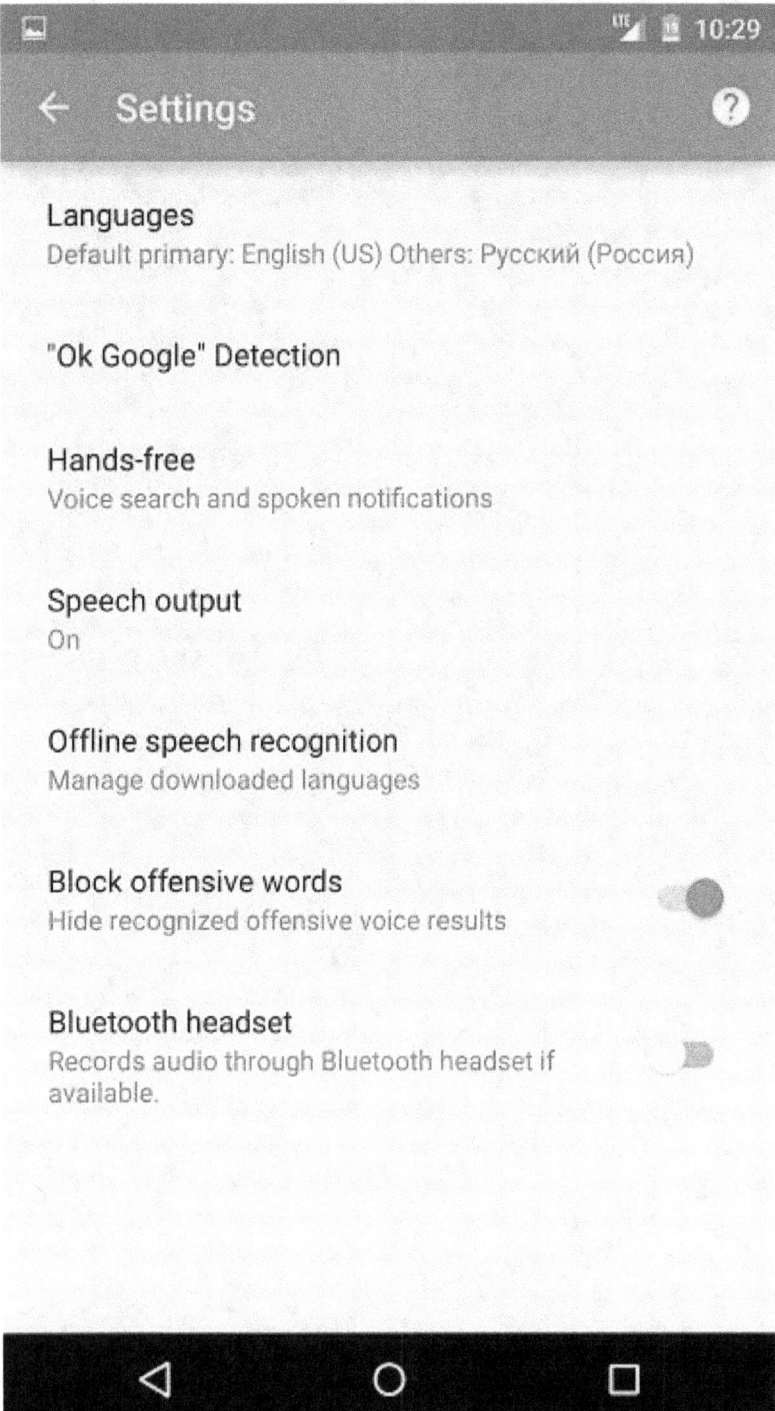

Figure 9: Voice Settings Screen

6. Changing the Text-to-Speech Speaking Rate

Some applications on the device can use the Text-to-Speech feature, which reads the text on the screen aloud. To change the speech rate of the Text-to-Speech feature:

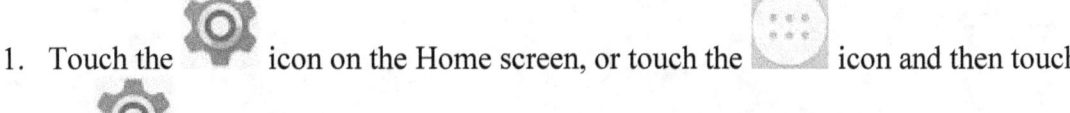

1. Touch the 🔧 icon on the Home screen, or touch the ⚙ icon and then touch the 🔧 icon. The Settings screen appears.
2. Touch **Language & input**. The Language & Input Settings screen appears.
3. Touch **Text-to-speech output**. The Text-to-Speech Settings screen appears, as shown in **Figure 10**.
4. Touch **Speech rate**. A list of speech rates appears, as shown in **Figure 11**. You can also touch **Listen to an example** to get an idea of how the text-to-speech output will sound.
5. Touch one of the nine speeds, ranging from 'Very slow' to 'Fastest'. The rate at which the speaker pronounces the words is adjusted.

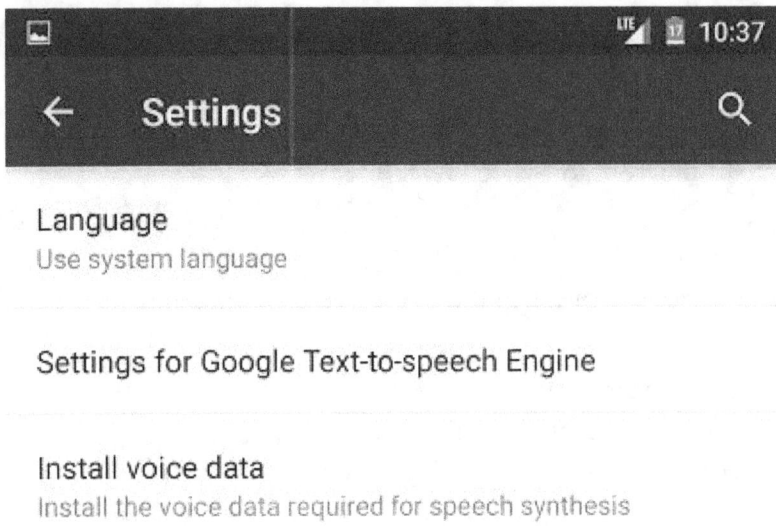

Figure 10: Text-to-Speech Settings Screen

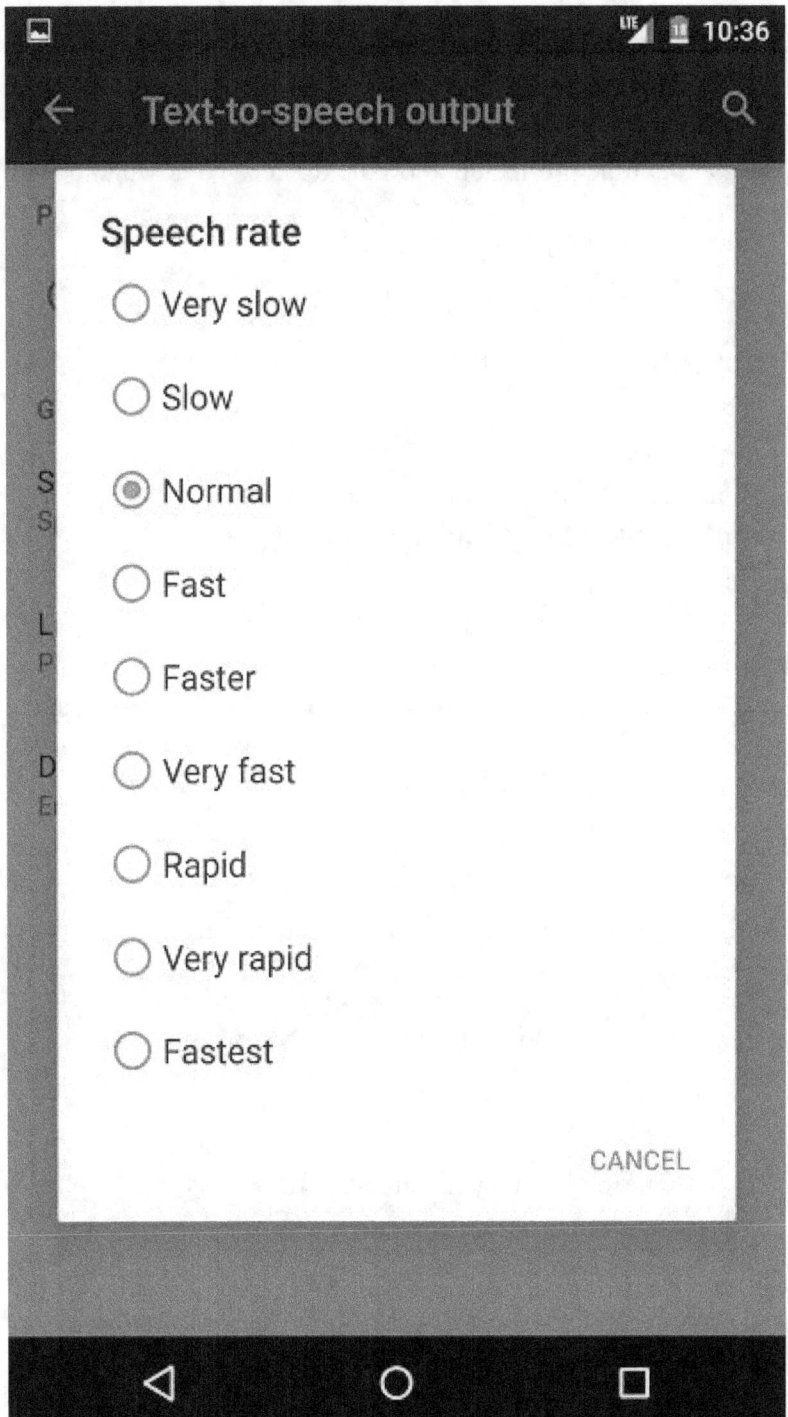

Figure 11: List of Speech Rates

7. Downloading Additional Text-to-Speech Languages

The Text-to-Speech feature can pronounce phrases in any of five languages, including English. However, languages other than English do not come pre-installed on the device. To download additional Text-to-Speech languages:

1. Touch the 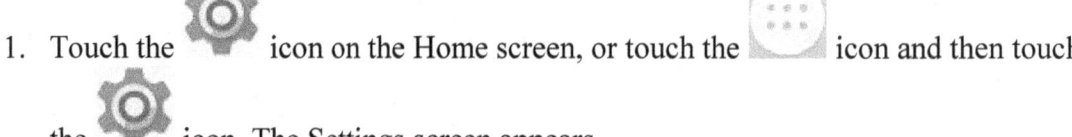 icon on the Home screen, or touch the icon and then touch the icon. The Settings screen appears.
2. Touch **Language & input**. The Language & Input Settings screen appears.
3. Touch **Text-to-speech output**. The Text-to-Speech Settings screen appears.
4. Touch the icon next to 'Google Text-to-speech Engine'. The Text-to-Speech Settings screen appears, as shown in **Figure 12**.
5. Touch **Install voice data**. A list of voice data that is available for download appears, as shown in **Figure 13**.
6. Touch the language that you want to download. The list of available voices for the language appears.
7. Touch the button next to the language that you wish to download. The corresponding Text-to-Speech language is downloaded. The button appears next to the language once it has been installed.
8. Touch the button. The Text-to-Speech language is uninstalled.

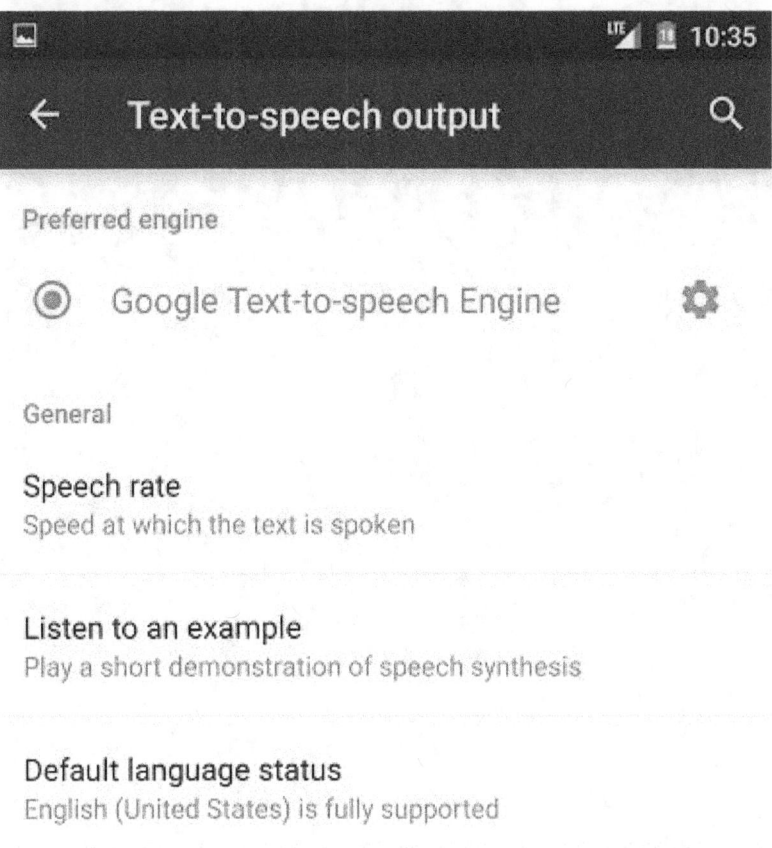

Figure 12: Text-to-Speech Settings Screen

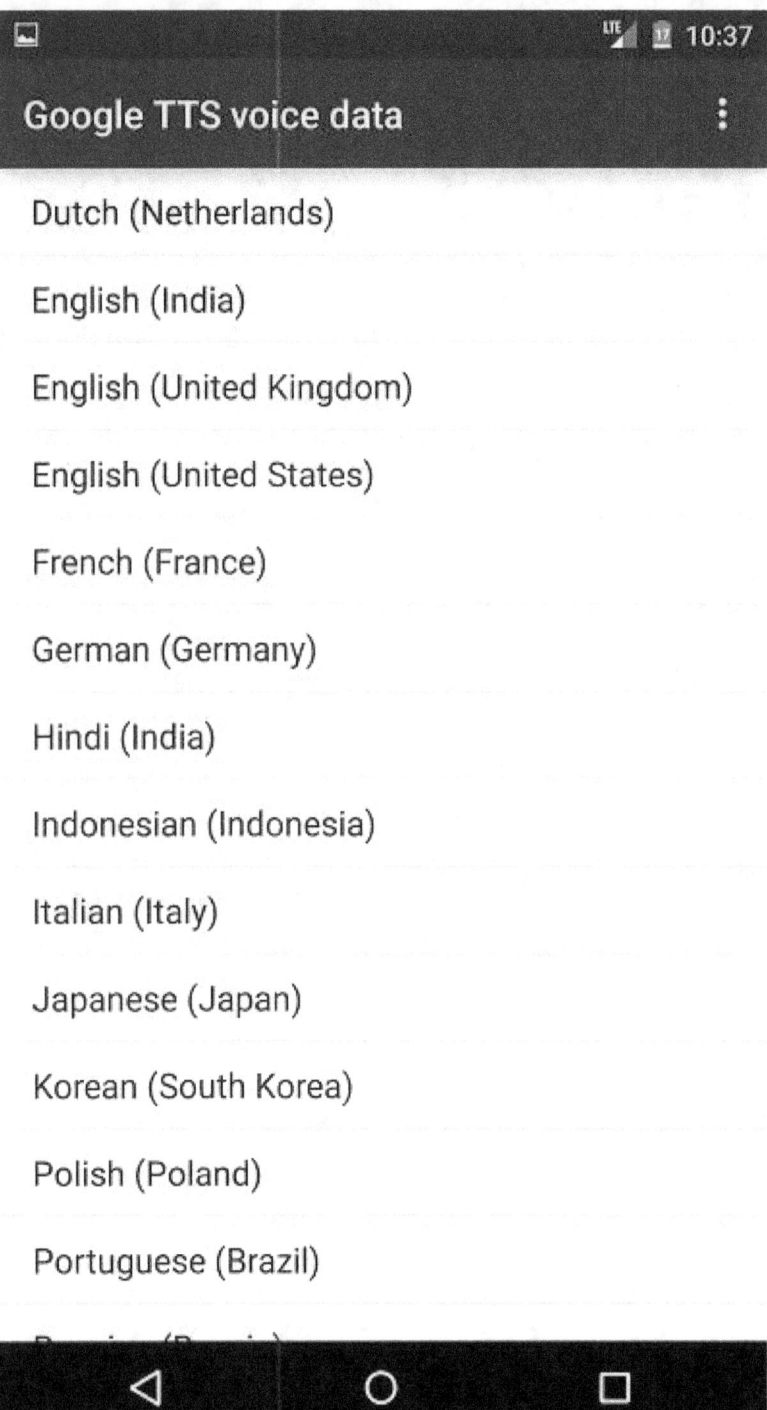

Figure 13: List of Voice Data Available for Download

Tips and Tricks

Table of Contents

1. Maximizing Battery Life

There are several things that you can do to increase the battery life of the device:

- Lock the device whenever it is not in use. To lock the device, press the **Power/Sleep** button once.
- Keep the Sleep Timer set to a small amount of time before it dims and turns off the screen when the device is idle. Refer to *"Setting the Amount of Time Before the Device Locks Itself"* on page 273 to learn how to change the Sleep Timer.
- Turn down the brightness or turn on Automatic Brightness. Refer to *"Adjusting the Brightness"* on page 266 to learn how to change Brightness settings.
- Turn off Wi-Fi and Bluetooth when you are not using them. Refer to *"Connecting to a Wi-Fi Network"* on page 247 to learn how to turn Wi-Fi off. Refer to *"Using Bluetooth"* on page 251 to learn how to turn off Bluetooth.
- Do not use the camera, if possible. The camera uses a lot of battery power.
- Close applications that are running in the background. Refer to *"Viewing Recently Opened Applications"* on page 116 to learn how.

2. Checking the Amount of Available Memory

To check the amount of available memory at any time, touch the icon on the Home screen, or touch the icon and then touch the icon. The Settings screen appears. Touch Storage. The available memory appears under 'Available'.

3. Freeing Up Memory

There are two actions that can free up memory on the device: uninstalling applications and removing temporary internet files stored by the Chrome browser. Refer to *"Quickly Uninstalling Applications"* on page 313 to learn how to uninstall an application. Refer to *"Clearing the Data that is Used to Speed Up Browsing"* on page 241 to learn how to delete temporary internet files stored by Chrome.

4. Quickly Uninstalling Applications

Getting rid of applications you no longer use will reduce clutter and free up memory. While applications may be uninstalled from Settings, this is a rather long process. To quickly uninstall an application:

1. Touch the icon at the bottom of the Home screen. The Applications screen appears.
2. Touch and hold an application icon. The Home screen appears and 'Uninstall' appears at the top of the screen.
3. Drag the application icon over the word 'Uninstall'. A confirmation dialog appears.
4. Touch **OK**. The application is uninstalled.

5. Viewing the Desktop Version of a Website

By default, the Chrome browser displays mobile versions of websites. You can also view the desktop version of a website, if it is available. To view the desktop version of a website:

1. Touch the ![icon] icon on the Home screen, or touch the ![icon] icon and then touch the ![icon] icon. The Chrome browser opens.

2. Navigate to a website. Refer to *"Navigating to a Website"* on page 211 to learn how.

3. Touch the ![icon] icon in the upper right-hand corner of the screen. The Chrome menu appears.

4. Touch **Request desktop site**. The desktop version of the website that you are currently visiting will appear when you re-enter the URL of the current site. Some websites do not have a desktop version that is available on your mobile device.

6. Accessing the Settings Screen Quickly

Instead of navigating through the list of applications to find the ![icon] icon, you can access the Settings screen by touching the status bar at the top of the screen with two fingers, and sliding your fingers down. Then, touch the ![icon] icon. The Settings screen appears.

7. Clearing the Data Stored by a Single Website

If you do not wish to delete all data stored by every website that you have visited, you can instead delete the data stored by a single website. Refer to *"Clearing the Data that is Used to Speed Up Browsing"* on page 241 to learn how to delete all website data. To clear the data stored by an individual website:

1. Touch the ![icon] icon on the Home screen, or touch the ![icon] icon and then touch the ![icon] icon. The Chrome browser opens.

2. Touch the ![icon] icon in the upper right-hand corner of the browser. The Chrome menu appears.

3. Touch **Settings**. The Chrome Settings screen appears.

4. Touch **Privacy**. The Privacy Settings screen appears.

5. Touch the ![icon] icon. The Browsing Data menu appears.

6. Touch **Clear browsing data**. A confirmation dialog appears.

7. Touch **Clear**, or touch each option in the menu to select it, and then touch **Clear**. The data stored by the selected website is deleted.

8. Taking Away a Website's Access to Your Location

Some websites will be able to access your location, if you allow them to do so. To take away a website's access to your location:

1. Touch the 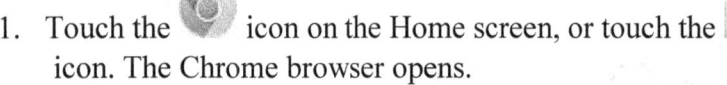 icon on the Home screen, or touch the 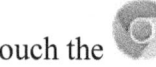 icon and then touch the icon. The Chrome browser opens.

2. Touch the icon in the upper right-hand corner of the browser. The Chrome menu appears.

3. Touch **Settings**. The Chrome Settings screen appears.

4. Touch **Site settings**. The Site Settings screen appears.

5. Touch **Location**. A list of previously visited websites appears. The websites that have access to your location have the icon next to them.

6. Touch a website that can access your location. The Website Settings screen appears.

7. Touch **Location access**. The Location Access menu appears.

8. Touch **Ask first**. Repeat steps 6 and 7 for all websites with access to your location.

9. Clearing One or All Notifications

You may clear all notifications at once in the Notification center. To do so, touch the status bar in the upper left-hand corner of the screen (if you touch the upper right, the Quick Settings window will appear) and drag down. The Notifications center appears. Touch the icon. All notifications are cleared. You may also clear a single notification by touching it and sliding your finger to the left or right.

10. Using Voice Search

Google Now is a handy search assistant introduced in Android 4.1 Jelly Bean, which responds to voice commands. To activate Google Now, touch and hold the ⬤ key and slide your finger up to **Google**. Google Now opens. Touch the 🎤 icon to activate the Voice Search. Alternatively, you may say "OK Google" if Hotword Detection is turned on. Refer to *"Customizing Voice Search Settings"* on page 303 to learn how to turn it on. You can say one of the phrases below followed by your query when using Google Now:

- Map of
- Directions to
- Navigate to
- Go to
- Send email
- Note to self
- Set alarm
- Listen to

11. Turning Google Now On or Off

You may turn off Google Now altogether. To turn Google Now on or off:

1. Touch and hold the ⬤ key and slide your finger up to **Google**. Google Now opens.
2. Touch the left-hand side of the screen, and slide your finger to the right. The Google Now menu appears.
3. Touch **Settings**. The Google Now Settings screen appears.
4. Touch **Now cards**. The Now Cards screen appears.
5. Touch **Show cards**. A confirmation dialog appears.
6. Touch **TURN OFF**. Google Now is turned off.
7. Touch **Show cards** again to turn Google Now back on.

Note: You need a data network connection (AT&T, Verizon, T-Mobile, etc.) to turn on Google Now.

12. Adding a Navigation Shortcut to the Home Screen

Instead of opening the Maps application every time that you wish to navigate to an address that you often visit, add a Navigation shortcut to the Home screen. To add a Navigation shortcut:

1. Touch an empty space on a Home screen. The Home screen menu appears.
2. Touch **Widgets**. A list of available widgets appears.
3. Scroll to the right and touch and hold the ▨ icon. The Home screen appears.
4. Drag the shortcut to an empty space on the Home screen. The Navigation shortcut is added to the Home screen and the Create Widget screen appears.
5. Enter the address and a Shortcut name (both required), and touch **Save**. The Navigation shortcut is set up. Touch the navigation shortcut at any time to navigate to the selected address.

13. Capturing a Screenshot

To capture what is on the screen and save it as a photo, press and hold the **Volume Down** and **Power/Sleep** buttons simultaneously. Keep holding the buttons until your screen momentarily flashes a white color. The screenshot is stored in the 'Screenshot' album in the Gallery.

14. Searching the System Settings

If you are having trouble finding a particular setting, try searching the system settings. To search the settings:

1. Touch the ▨ icon on the Settings screen. The Search field appears at the top of the screen.
2. Start typing the search keywords. Matching results appear as you type.
3. Touch a result in the list to navigate to the corresponding settings screen.

Troubleshooting

Table of Contents

1. Device does not turn on

Try one of the following:

- Recharge the battery using the included wall charger. If the battery power is extremely low, the screen will not turn on for several minutes. Do NOT use the USB port on your computer to charge the device; it may not properly charge the device.
- Replace the battery. If you purchased the device a long time ago and have charged and discharged the battery approximately 300-400 times, you may need to replace the battery. Contact the manufacturer of your device if you are unable to remove the battery. Some Lollipop devices do not have a removable battery cover.
- Press and hold the **Power/Sleep** button for 30 seconds. The device should reset and turn on.

2. Device is not responding

If the device is frozen or is not responding, try one or more of the following. These steps solve most problems on the device:

- **Restart the device** - If the device freezes while running an application, hold down the **Volume Up** button and the **Power/Sleep** button. The device restarts.
- **Remove Media** - Some downloaded applications or music may freeze up the device. Try deleting some of the media after restarting the device. Refer to *"Uninstalling an Application"* on page 110 or *"Quickly Uninstalling Applications"* on page 313 to learn how to delete an application.

  - Reset the device - If the above suggestions do not help, you may also reset and erase all data at once by doing the following (if you are able to access the Settings screen):

Warning: Any erased data is not recoverable.

1. Touch the 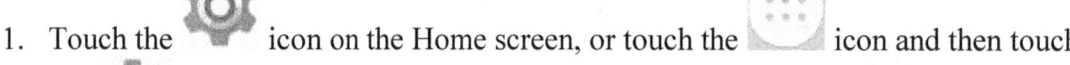 icon on the Home screen, or touch the ⬚ icon and then touch the 💠 icon. The Settings screen appears.
2. Touch **Backup & reset**. The Backup & Reset screen appears.
3. Touch **Factory data reset**. The Factory Reset screen appears.
4. Touch **Reset device** ('Reset phone' on a smartphone) at the bottom of the screen. A confirmation screen appears.
5. Touch **Erase Everything**. The device is reset and all data is erased.

3. Can't surf the web

Make sure that Wi-Fi is turned on and the device is connected to a network. Refer to *"Connecting to a Wi-Fi Network"* on page 247 to learn how to connect to a network.

4. Screen or keyboard does not rotate

If the screen does not rotate or the full horizontal keyboard is not appearing when rotating the device, it may be one of the following issues:

- The application does not support the horizontal view.
- The device is lying flat when rotating. Hold the device upright for the view to change in applications that support it.
- You are viewing one of the Home screens. By default, the screen will not rotate when you are viewing a Home screen.

5. Application does not download or install correctly

Sometimes applications may not download or install correctly. If this happens, try uninstalling and re-installing the application. Refer to *"Uninstalling an Application"* on page 110 and *"Purchasing Applications"* on page 105 to learn how.

6. Touchscreen does not respond as expected

If the touchscreen does not perform the desired functions or does not work at all, try the following:

- Remove the screen protector, if you use one.
- Make sure that your hands are clean and dry, and that the touchscreen is clean. Oily fingers can make the screen dirty and unresponsive.
- Restart the device.
- Make sure that the touchscreen does not come in contact with anything but skin. Scratches on the screen are permanent and may cause the device to malfunction.

7. Device is hot to the touch

When running some applications for extended periods of time, the device may become hot. This is normal and will not harm the device in any way.

8. Computer does not recognize the device

If your computer does not recognize the device, try one of the following:

- Only use the provided USB cable to connect the device to your computer.
- Connect the device directly to the computer, since some USB hubs will not work.
- Make sure that the correct drivers are installed on your computer, if any are needed. If using a Mac, make sure that you have installed the Android File Transfer application. Download this application at **www.android.com/filetransfer**. Without this application, the device will not be recognized by your Mac.

9. Device does not detect a Bluetooth device

If the device does not detect a Bluetooth device, try one of the following:

- Move the device closer to the Bluetooth device
- Make sure that Bluetooth is enabled on the device
- Make sure that Bluetooth is enabled on the Bluetooth headset or other device

10. What to do if you could not solve your problem

Contact Google Play Help at **855-836-3987** or check the **Google Play Help Center**.

Index

V	W

Other Books from the Author of the Help Me Series, Charles Hughes

Help Me! Guide to the iPad Air

Help Me! Guide to the iOS 8

Help Me! Guide to the iPhone 5S

Help Me! Guide to the iPhone 6

Help Me! Guide to the iPhone 4

Help Me! Guide to the Nexus 7

Help Me! Guide to the Galaxy S4

Help Me! Guide to the Kindle Fire HD

Help Me! Guide to the HTC One

Help Me! Guide to the iPod Touch

Help Me! Guide to the iPad Mini

Help Me! Guide to the Kindle Touch

Help Me! Guide to the Samsung Galaxy Note

Help Me! Guide to the Kindle Fire HD 6

Help Me! Guide to the Kindle Fire TV

Help Me! Guide to the Nexus 5

Help Me! Guide to the Samsung Galaxy Note 3

Help Me! Guide to the Android Lollipop

Author: Charles Hughes

This book is also available in electronic format from Amazon.com